Donald Davidson's Triangulation Argument

According to many commentators, Davidson's earlier work on philosophy of action and truth-theoretic semantics is the basis for his reputation, and his later forays into broader metaphysical and epistemological issues, and eventually into what became known as the triangulation argument, are much less successful. This book by two of his former students aims to change that perception. In Part One, Verheggen begins by providing an explanation and defense of the triangulation argument, then explores its implications for questions concerning semantic normativity and reductionism, the social character of language and thought, and skepticism about the external world. In Part Two, Myers considers what the argument can tell us about reasons for action, and whether it can overcome skeptical worries based on claims about the nature of motivation, the sources of normativity and the demands of morality. The book reveals Davidson's later writings to be full of innovative and important ideas that deserve much more attention than they are currently receiving.

Robert H. Myers is Professor of Philosophy at York University, Canada.

Claudine Verheggen is Associate Professor of Philosophy at York University, Canada.

Routledge Studies in Twentieth-Century Philosophy

For a full list of titles in this series, please visit www.routledge.com

30 **Russell vs. Meinong**
   The Legacy of "On Denoting"
   Edited by Nicholas Griffin and Dale Jacquette

31 **Philosophy and the Vision of Language**
   Paul M. Livingston

32 **The Analytic Turn**
   Analysis in Early Analytic Philosophy and Phenomenology
   Edited by Michael Beaney

33 **The Existentialism of Jean-Paul Sartre**
   Jonathan Webber

34 **Heidegger and the Romantics**
   The Literary Invention of Meaning
   Pol Vandevelde

35 **Wittgenstein and Heidegger**
   Pathways and Provocations
   Edited by David Egan, Stephen Reynolds, and Aaron James Wendland

36 **The Textual Genesis of Wittgenstein's *Philosophical Investigations***
   Edited by Nuno Venturinha

37 **The Early Wittgenstein on Metaphysics, Natural Science, Language and Value**
   Chon Tejedor

38 **Walter Benjamin's Concept of the Image**
   Alison Ross

39 **Donald Davidson's Triangulation Argument**
   A Philosophical Inquiry
   Robert H. Myers and Claudine Verheggen

Donald Davidson's Triangulation Argument
A Philosophical Inquiry

Robert H. Myers and
Claudine Verheggen

LONDON AND NEW YORK

First published 2016 by Routledge

2 Park Square, Milton Park, Abingdon, Oxfordshire OX14 4RN
711 Third Avenue, New York, NY 10017

Routledge is an imprint of the Taylor & Francis Group, an informa business

First issued in paperback 2018

Copyright © 2016 Taylor & Francis

The right of Robert H. Myers and Claudine Verheggen to be identified as authors of this work has been asserted by them in accordance with sections 77 and 78 of the Copyright, Designs and Patents Act 1988.

All rights reserved. No part of this book may be reprinted or reproduced or utilised in any form or by any electronic, mechanical, or other means, now known or hereafter invented, including photocopying and recording, or in any information storage or retrieval system, without permission in writing from the publishers.

Notice:
Product or corporate names may be trademarks or registered trademarks, and are used only for identification and explanation without intent to infringe.

Library of Congress Cataloging-in-Publication Data
Names: Myers, Robert H., author.
Title: Donald Davidson's triangulation argument : a philosophical inquiry / by Robert H. Myers and Claudine Verheggen.
Description: 1 [edition]. | New York : Routledge, 2016. | Series: Routledge Studies in Twentieth-Century Philosophy ; 39 | Includes bibliographical references and index.
Identifiers: LCCN 2016005443 | ISBN 9780415710275 (alk. paper)
Subjects: LCSH: Davidson, Donald, 1917–2003.
Classification: LCC B945.D384 M94 2016 | DDC 191—dc23
LC record available at http://lccn.loc.gov/2016005443

ISBN: 978-0-415-71027-5 (hbk)
ISBN: 978-1-138-34673-4 (pbk)

Typeset in Sabon
by Apex CoVantage, LLC

For our nieces

Contents

Acknowledgements — ix

Introduction — 1

PART I
Language, Thought and Knowledge

1 Davidson's Triangulation Argument — 11

2 From Triangulation to Semantic Normativity — 41

3 From Triangulation to Semantic Externalism — 65

4 From Triangulation to Global Anti-Skepticism — 95

PART II
Desires, Reasons and Morality

5 Triangulation and Normative Skepticism — 119

6 Pro-Attitudes and Normative Beliefs — 139

7 Normative Properties and Explanation — 158

8 Normative Realism and Morality — 179

Bibliography — 199
Index — 209

Acknowledgements

It would not be much of an exaggeration to say that we have been working on the themes of this book ever since we met as beginning PhD students at Berkeley. That was a long time ago, so the list of people we could thank has grown long as well—much too long for us to try to reconstruct here. With apologies to all the others, therefore, we shall mention just the special few who most helped us to get clear about Davidson's philosophy and its bearing on current debates.

The most special of the few—without whom not!—is of course Donald Davidson himself. He supervised Verheggen's dissertation, served on Myers's committee, and was a terrific mentor to both. We also learned a great deal about many of the topics discussed in these pages from Barry Stroud, who served on both committees, and Samuel Scheffler, who supervised Myers's dissertation.

After Berkeley came New York. Thinking back to those years, we would especially like to thank Kathrin Glüer, Noa Latham, Kirk Ludwig, Liam Murphy, Peter Pagin, Karsten Stueber, Åsa Wikforss, and Steven Yalowitz. Sue Larson and Mary Mothersill, now, sadly, both deceased, were great colleagues and interlocutors during that period.

More recently, since moving to Toronto, we have benefitted from discussions with Kristin Andrews, Jacob Beck, David Checkland, Olaf Ellefson, Bogdan Florea Alexandru, Michael Giudice, Jagdish Hattiangadi, Louis-Philippe Hodgson, Brian Huss, Imola Ilyes, Henry Jackman, Muhammad Ali Khalidi, Alex Leferman, Ernie Lepore, Alice MacLachlan, Shyam Ranganathan, David Rocheleau-Houle, Stéphane Savoie, Samuel Steadman, Olivia Sultanescu and Ben Winokur. Special thanks are owed to Louis-Philippe Hodgson, Muhammad Ali Khalidi, and Olivia Sultanescu for helpful comments on the manuscript, and to the many graduate students at York who have made our recent seminars on these topics so productive.

We have tackled many of the issues discussed here in previously published work, and on a few occasions draw very directly on those efforts.

Acknowledgements

We would therefore like to express our thanks to the editors and publishers concerned for permission to use material from the following sources:

1. In Chapter 1, from Claudine Verheggen, "Triangulation", in Ernie Lepore and Kirk Ludwig, eds., *A Companion to Donald Davidson*. Wiley Blackwell 2013.
2. In Chapter 2, from Claudine Verheggen, "Towards a New Kind of Semantic Normativity", *International Journal of Philosophical Studies*, 23–3: 410–24. July 2015.
3. In Chapter 2, from Claudine Verheggen, "Semantic Normativity and Naturalism", *Logique et Analyse*, 216: 552–67. October 2011.
4. In Chapter 3, from Claudine Verheggen, "How Social Must Language Be?", *Journal for the Theory of Social Behavior*, 36–2: 203–19. June 2006.
5. In Chapter 4, from Claudine Verheggen, "Triangulation and Philosophical Skepticism", in Maria Cristina Amoretti and Gerhard Preyer, eds., *Triangulation: From an Epistemological Point of View*. Frankfurt: Ontos Verlag, 2011.
6. In Chapter 5, from Robert Myers, "Finding Value in Davidson", *Canadian Journal of Philosophy*, 34–1: 107–36. March 2004.
7. In chapters 5 and 6, from Robert Myers, "Interpretation and Value", in Ernie Lepore and Kirk Ludwig, eds., *A Companion to Donald Davidson*. Wiley Blackwell 2013.
8. In chapters 6 and 7, from Robert Myers, "Desires and Normative Truths: A Holist's Response to the Sceptics", *Mind*, 121–482: 375–406. April 2012.

Introduction

Donald Davidson is widely acknowledged to be one of the greatest philosophers of the twentieth century. According to most commentators, however, his earlier work on philosophy of action and truth-theoretic semantics is the real basis for this reputation, and his later forays into broader metaphysical and epistemological issues, and eventually into what became known as his triangulation argument, are much less successful. We believe that this perception is badly mistaken and hope in this book to correct it.

In Part One, Claudine Verheggen begins by providing an explanation and defense of the triangulation argument, then explores its implications for questions concerning semantic normativity and reductionism, the social character of language and thought, and skepticism about the external world. In Part Two, Robert Myers considers what the argument can tell us about reasons for action, and whether it can overcome skeptical worries based on claims about the nature of motivation, the sources of normativity, and the demands of morality.

These inquiries reveal Davidson's later writings to be full of innovative and important ideas that deserve much more attention than they are currently receiving. Meaning could be essentially social without being strictly communitarian or conventional, and intrinsically normative without generating categorical imperatives. Reasons for action could be real properties of situations or outcomes, and primary qualities rather than secondary ones. And skepticism, both regarding the external world and regarding reasons for action, could prove to be not just impossible to entertain but flatly mistaken.

These are evidently very large claims. So what exactly is the argument? For now, it is perhaps best introduced by way of its conclusion. The triangulation argument purports to show that *only someone who has interacted linguistically with another person and the world they share, i.e., only someone who has actually triangulated, could have a language and thoughts*. (The hint of circularity here is not inadvertent and will be much discussed in Part One.) So it concerns the most basic questions in the philosophy of language: What makes it possible for someone to have a language and thoughts, and what makes it the case that a person's words and thoughts have the meanings and contents they have?

Because it requires speakers and thinkers to have interpreted others and to have been interpreted themselves, and not merely to be interpretable, many commentators hold that the triangulation argument marks a significant break in Davidson's thought from his earlier preoccupation with radical interpretation (the interpretation from scratch of an alien speaker's thoughts and utterances). As we argue throughout this book, however, nothing could be further from the truth. Not only is the triangulation argument perfectly compatible with the arguments concerning radical interpretation; it also provides them critical support. But even this understates their connections, for *radical interpretation is an instance of triangulation*. The triangulation argument thus brings to the fore considerations that were already implicit in the earlier arguments concerning radical interpretation.

(If anecdotal evidence is also admissible, we can attest that not once during his seminars at Berkeley in the late 1980s and early 1990s, when he was first discussing his ideas about triangulation, did Davidson suggest that he previously believed only the interpretability of a person's utterances and thoughts is essential to her being a speaker and thinker but that he subsequently realized it is her actually having interpreted others and having been interpreted herself that is required. One can only wonder how this misunderstanding has come to dominate the literature. Had there been such a profound change in his thinking about such a central topic, surely he could have been expected to make note of it and to defend it!)

This continuity in Davidson's thought has important ramifications that many of his commentators miss, with disastrous results for all concerned. For one thing, it explains why Davidson was careful always to treat the possibility of radical interpretation as an illuminating (because especially clear and unobstructed) window on the nature of meaning and content, but never as the full story about them. For another thing, it explains why Davidson always regarded the principle of charity, not as just one potential interpretative principle among any number of other possible candidates, but as a constitutive principle capturing something essential to meaning and content themselves. For a third, it explains why Davidson's famous (or infamous) omniscient interpreter argument was merely superfluous and not actually wrong.

But the importance of Davidson's triangulation argument extends far beyond the various ways in which it underwrites such earlier claims. Most importantly, by highlighting the respects in which meanings and contents are determined, in part, by the choices of interacting agents, it shows reductive accounts of these notions to be impossible. As we might say, loosely paraphrasing Barry Stroud (2000), meaning and content can be understood only from within. This is another theme that will recur throughout the book. As Verheggen emphasizes throughout Part One, in part against Stroud, Davidson's non-reductionism is particularly noteworthy because it is not quietist. It clearly demonstrates that constructive theorizing about meaning and content remains possible even though reductive explanations of them do not.

Resistance to this possibility may actually be the principal reason why the triangulation argument has not met with greater acceptance. Philosophers do have a tendency to assume that explanations will inevitably be reductive and that non-reductionism will inevitably be quietist, leaving no space at all for a position like Davidson's. If there is one lesson to take from this book, it is that such assumptions are entirely without merit. Non-reductive explanations will no doubt have several important limitations. In particular, one would expect them to provide only necessary conditions for the phenomena under scrutiny, and not sufficient conditions. As we shall see, however, some conditions on language and thought can be necessary without being even remotely trivial.

Part One starts with a presentation and defense of the triangulation argument, which, Verheggen argues, has been almost systematically misunderstood and, consequently, often simply dismissed. What most commentators have failed to recognize is the intimate connection between the two points they see the triangulation argument as attempting to make. The first is that triangulation is needed to fix the meanings of one's words and the contents of one's thoughts. The second is that triangulation is needed to have the concept of objectivity, i.e., "the idea of the difference between how something seems and how it is" (Davidson 1995a, 4). Verheggen argues that these two tasks can be accomplished only in tandem: Meanings and contents can be fixed only by someone who has the concept of objectivity, which one can have only if one has triangulated with others. So understood, the triangulation argument becomes much harder to resist. If successful, it also vindicates one of Davidson's most controversial claims, according to which only someone who has the concept of objectivity could have a language and thoughts. Furthermore, the triangulation argument reinforces the claim that no reductionist account of meaning and content is possible. That is, the question of what one means by one's utterances and what thoughts one has can be answered only within a semantic context, by saying that one *means* or *thinks* such and such or so and so. And the question of what makes possession of language and thoughts possible cannot be answered without appealing to semantic notions. Thus, sufficient conditions for words meaning what they do and thoughts having the content they have, and sufficient conditions for being a speaker and thinker, cannot be provided in a non-circular way. But this does not entail that interesting necessary conditions cannot be given. One such condition has already been mentioned: The determination of meaning and content requires possession of the concept of objectivity. Others are developed in subsequent chapters.

Thus, in Chapter 2, Verheggen argues that it follows from the triangulation argument, specifically, from the way it establishes semantic non-reductionism, that meaning is essentially normative in two distinct ways. (Contra the received view, it is not because meaning is normative that it cannot be reductively naturalized, but because it cannot be reductively naturalized that it is normative.) First, meaning is normative in that, unless one has had normative attitudes towards one's own and others' uses of words, that is, unless one has distinguished, on some occasions at least, between the correct and incorrect applications that one and others make of words, one cannot have a language and thoughts. Davidson himself did not make explicit that meaning is normative in this sense, but it is in fact closely related to his claim that one must have the concept of objectivity in order to have a language and thoughts. For one has this concept only if one has been able to display it through triangulation, which is to say that one has this concept only if one has made judgments of correctness and incorrectness towards one's own and others' uses of words. The second sense in which meaning is normative was never discussed by Davidson himself. And it is indeed a sense that has been hotly debated only in the past decade. Verheggen argues that it follows from the first sense in which meaning is essentially normative. According to this second sense, meaning is normative in that statements about the meaning of one's words have normative implications about how one should use them. These implications have been said to be either categorical, independent of one's goals in using words, or hypothetical, dependent on those goals. Verheggen maintains that only hypothetical implications follow from these statements, but, contra the anti-normativists, she argues that these implications are essential to meaning. There is a third sense in which some have thought meaning to be normative, which Davidson consistently rejected, according to which meaning is essentially conventional. This rejection is reinforced by the triangulation argument and discussed in the third chapter.

Verheggen's goal in the third chapter is to articulate and defend the particular brand of semantic externalism advocated by Davidson from the beginning and further supported by the triangulation argument. Davidson argues both for a version of physical or perceptual externalism, according to which, broadly speaking, the meanings of words and the contents of thoughts are determined, at least in part, by the physical features of the world surrounding thinkers and speakers, and for a version of social externalism, according to which, broadly speaking, meanings and contents are determined, at least in part, by thinkers' and speakers' relations to others. What, to begin with, is highly distinctive about Davidson's semantic externalism is that he believes perceptual externalism can be secured only through social externalism. In addition, his social externalism is distinctive in being interpersonal rather than communitarian—to have a language and thoughts one must have been understood by others, but one does not have to mean the same things by the same words. Moreover, his perceptual externalism is distinctive in being both historical—the meanings of words and the contents of thoughts are determined, in part, by the history of speakers' and thinkers' causal interactions with their environment—and holistic—no words have their meaning and no thoughts have their content determined in isolation from others. It is in this chapter in particular that Verheggen establishes the continuity of Davidson's thought, for semantic externalism can be seen to be an outcome already of reflection about radical interpretation, once it is recognized that reflecting on radical interpretation yields an understanding, not only of how meanings and contents could be attributed, but also of how they necessarily are constituted. Contra many commentators, Verheggen argues that Davidson's semantic externalism has always been historical and holistic, in addition to having always been non-reductionist and non-conventionalist. The major improvement introduced by the triangulation argument is that it vindicates Davidson's long-standing assumption that meaning and content are essentially public. This vindication allows him to use his theory of content to argue against global or Cartesian skepticism in a non-question-begging way. Skepticism about the external world is the topic of the fourth chapter.

There, Verheggen argues that Davidson has addressed the skeptic by showing that the skeptic's hypothesis that one could have all the beliefs one has about the world around one even if they were all false is mistaken. She argues that it follows from Davidson's theory of content that, in his famous words, "belief is in its nature veridical" (Davidson 1983, 146), and not just that, in Stroud's words, "belief-attribution is in its nature (largely) truth-ascribing" (Stroud 1999, 146). Moreover, she argues, it follows from the theory that beliefs are known to be generally true. Thus, since many of our beliefs about the external world are true and we know that they are true, we do have knowledge of the external world. The only option for the skeptic who accepts Davidson's theory is to maintain that we do not know what beliefs we have, which is to say, the only option for the skeptic is to remain silent. In this chapter, Verheggen again takes issue with the non-reductionist who claims that non-reductionism entails quietism. She argues that it is precisely because it does not that Davidson is in a position to make the strong claims against the skeptic that he is making.

While Part Two builds squarely on Part One, it takes the discussion in a different direction, focusing less on the general merits of the triangulation argument, and its general implications, and more on a particularly vexing question about its scope. When Davidson originally advanced the argument, he did not address it to normative thought and talk, i.e., to thought and talk regarding reasons. But was this really to suggest that the argument does not apply to them as well?

Subsequent papers eventually made it clear that this was not Davidson's intention, and that he believed the meanings and contents of people's normative talk and thought are also fixed through their triangulations with one another and the world they share. And he was perfectly happy to embrace the implications of this belief—that the world people share must have normative properties on which they can triangulate, and that people can know that their beliefs about these properties are largely correct.

Very much as before, however, these large and ambitious metaphysical and epistemological claims might seem to be at odds with some of Davidson's own best early work, this time, with his influential arguments for a causal theory of action. For causal theories of action are typically associated with non-cognitivist accounts of normative judgment, accounts to the effect that normative judgments are nothing more than expressions of desires, and thus lack contents of the sort that might be constituted through triangulation.

The central concern of Chapter 6, therefore, is to establish that Davidson's causal theory commits him to no such account of normative judgment. The crucial point here is to distinguish Humean theories of motivation from Humean theories of desire. As Myers demonstrates, Davidson clearly endorses the Humean claim that motivations are partly constituted by desires and never by beliefs alone, not even by normative beliefs (despite his tendency occasionally to count normative judgments as pro-attitudes). But he does not accept the Humean view of what desires are, and this makes all the difference for his account of normative judgment. The key to understanding Davidson on this point is to consider what a holistic account of desire might amount to.

What emerges in Chapter 6 is that Davidson holds a view of desire not unlike Thomas Scanlon's "judgment-sensitive" view (Scanlon 1998, Chapter 1). People's desires as a whole aim to get normative matters right, so they are typically sensitive to their normative beliefs. And because normative judgments do not merely express desires, they have contents that might be determined via triangulation after all. Here again, therefore, a better appreciation of the continuity of Davidson's thought, this time concerning the explanation of action, leads both to a richer understanding of his earlier work and to a more positive outlook on the triangulation argument. However, the fact that the argument entails a commitment to normative realism might still seem problematic in several ways.

One set of problems concerns the very idea that reasons for action might exist as real properties in the world. How would Davidson reply, for example, to Christine Korsgaard's charge (1996, Chapter 1) that realists cannot make good sense of normative authority? Or to John Mackie's charge (1976a, Chapter 1) that there are no properties of the queer sort normative properties would have to be? Or to Gilbert Harman's charge (1977, Chapter 1) that normative properties never have any role to play in reasonable explanations of people's motivations? Davidson addressed such questions towards the end of his life, but never fully, and at best with only mixed results. However, as Myers demonstrates in Chapter 7, he did have, in his anomalous monism, the resources to do better.

The account that ultimately emerges is noteworthy for the fact that it gives normative properties an explanatory role to play, but without either modeling them on secondary qualities or in other ways jeopardizing their normative authority. This is reminiscent of the manner in which Davidson's views about meaning and content are neither reductionist nor simply quietist, and it gives his version of normative realism an advantage over those recently advanced by David Enoch (2011) and Thomas Scanlon (2014), according to whom normative properties are "just too different" (Enoch 2011, 4) to play any role at all in explanations of people's motivations—and as a result, one fears, also "just too different" for people ever to have knowledge of what they are.

Another set of problems for normative realism stems from some familiar convictions about the content and the authority of morality. It might be thought that normative properties, especially if they are modeled on primary qualities, must ultimately be the same for everyone, and thus that Davidson's version of normative realism must lead inexorably to consequentialist conclusions about morality. While some might welcome this result, others clearly would not. Davidson did make it clear that he would not either; but he never got around to explaining either how consequentialism could be avoided or with what it should be replaced. Myers thus closes the book on a more speculative note by considering what Davidson could have said on this score.

Here again, Scanlon promises to be both an important ally and a useful foil. He promises to be an ally because Davidson could certainly have endorsed his groundbreaking idea that people's first-order reasons frequently put them at loggerheads, thereby revealing them also to have important second-order reasons to interact with one another on terms of mutual respect. However, whereas Scanlon does not see realism as committing us to the existence of agent-neutral reasons, Davidson does; and this fact, as Myers argues, would seem to put Davidson in a position to offer a much better account both of the content and of the authority of moral reasons than Scanlon himself has so far managed to provide.

As should by now be clear, this is a book, as we might put it, both about and from Davidson. We believe that both his earlier and his later writings have been badly misunderstood on a number of important points, so we spend a considerable amount of time and effort, especially in Part One, attempting to set the record straight. But we also believe that Davidson did not always take full advantage of arguments that he had at his disposal, so we are not shy, especially in Part Two, about presuming to develop his arguments in ways that are new. He may not always have endorsed the conclusions we reach, but he most certainly would have approved of the efforts.

One final note: Recognizing that not all readers will be equally interested in both parts of this book, we have taken pains to ensure that each stands on its own. Thus Part One does not issue any promissory notes that it leaves Part Two to fulfill, and Part Two begins with an account of the lessons it is drawing from Part One. This makes for some overlap between Part One and the initial chapter (Chapter 5) of Part Two, but it also means that readers primarily interested in ethics could start with Part Two, turning to Part One only as they become persuaded, as we hope they will be, that the triangulation argument could have ramifications that would be of great significance for them.

Part One
Language, Thought and Knowledge
Claudine Verheggen

1 Davidson's Triangulation Argument

1. Introductory Remarks

As has often been remarked, there is no such thing as "the" triangulation argument explicitly laid out in Davidson's writings. The closest he comes to laying out an explicit argument is in "The Second Person" (Davidson 1992), the first paper in which he develops and defends the idea of triangulation,[1] which I shall refer to in what follows as the initial article. But the argument in the initial article is at some points difficult to interpret, and subsequent discussions only add to the complexity. Most commentators and critics have concluded that there are actually (at least) two triangulation arguments to be unearthed in Davidson's writings—one for the conclusion that triangulation is required to fix the meanings (i.e., propositional contents, on which more soon) of one's thoughts and utterances, the other for the conclusion that triangulation is needed to have the concept of objectivity, which, for Davidson, is also needed to have a language and thoughts (in addition, that is, to the obvious requirement that meanings be fixed). As we shall see, separating the arguments in such a way has made it much easier to reject them. However, though I grant that Davidson's writings sometimes support this interpretation, I think that they are better understood, both exegetically and philosophically, as supporting a different kind of reading, according to which there is only one complex, multifaceted argument for the general conclusion that triangulation is needed for the possession of language and thoughts. This conclusion is reached by keeping the two requirements tightly connected, and thus by arguing that the meanings of one's thoughts and utterances can be fixed only if one has the concept of objectivity, possession of which requires triangulation.[2] Here is a passage in which Davidson makes the connection pretty apparent:

> A grasp of the concept of truth . . . depends on the norm that can be provided only by interpersonal communication; and of course . . . the possession of any propositional attitude . . . depends on a grasp of the concept of objective truth.
>
> (Davidson 1994, 124)

Thus, according to my reading, the elements of what are often taken to be two arguments for two different conclusions are meshed in a single, integrated argument. As a result, the triangulation argument becomes much harder to resist, or so I hope to demonstrate in this chapter.

I shall start with a few clarifying remarks about what Davidson means, first, by "concept of objectivity" and, second, by "propositional content".

Davidson refers to the concept of objectivity interchangeably as the concept of objective truth or, sometimes, as above, just truth, or the concept of belief, or the concept of error, or the belief-truth contrast.[3] To have the concept of objectivity is to have the "awareness, no matter how inarticulately held, of the fact that what is thought [or said] may be true or false" (Davidson 1995a, 4). It is to be aware of "the distinction between what is believed or seems to be the case and what is objectively so" (Davidson 2001c, 294), that is, what is so independently of anyone thinking or speaking about it, between "what is asked or demanded and what is answered or done" (Davidson 1998, 86).[4] So Davidson's argument, as I read it, will be that the meanings of one's thoughts and utterances can be fixed only if one has this sort of awareness of the contrast between belief and truth, and that one needs to have triangulated with others in order to have this sort of awareness.

I glossed the 'meanings' of thoughts and utterances above as their 'propositional contents', and I will use mostly 'meanings' to talk even of the contents of thoughts as a constant reminder that it is propositional thoughts that I am discussing—that is, thoughts with propositional content. Propositional content is not something whose nature Davidson ever made terribly explicit even though he acknowledged that different philosophers may have different conceptions of propositional thought (Davidson 2003, 698). But it is crucial for what follows to distinguish Davidson's notion of propositional content from other notions of content, some of which have become much in vogue in the past few years, but all of which were largely neglected by Davidson. These are, to cite the dominant ones, the notions of non-conceptual content, intentional content, conceptual content, perceptual content, representational content and, perhaps the most recent, intuitional content. I will not even try to explain what these are, especially since very few philosophers agree on any one understanding of them.[5] But I will try to say what Davidson understands by propositional content.

Note first that Davidson would use the notion interchangeably with that of conceptual or intentional content. However, though everyone may agree that all propositional content is conceptual and intentional, not everyone agrees that all conceptual or intentional content is propositional.[6] Propositional content belongs, in the first instance, to propositional attitudes and thoughts. Davidson is indeed happy to say that propositions make up their content, just as they make up the meaning of sentences, provided, however, that no ontological commitment is implied by this (Davidson 1988b, 45). There is, for Davidson, a pretty strict parallel between the contents of propositional attitudes and thoughts and the meanings of sentences (Davidson 1989a, 57). The former are composed of concepts that contribute to their content, just as the latter are composed of terms whose meanings contribute to the meaning of the sentences in which they occur. Again, though, no ontological commitment concerning concepts or meanings follows from this. These have no existence apart from the communicative acts out of which they are abstracted.[7] I think that, for Davidson, three features characterize propositional attitudes and thoughts and hence propositional content. (From now on, I will often drop 'propositional' in 'propositional thought' and 'propositional content'.)

First, content of this kind is both attributed and constituted holistically. According to Davidson, all thoughts require beliefs, for the content of a thought is identified by its location in a pattern of beliefs, just as the meaning of a sentence is given by a pattern of sentences held true, i.e., believed (Davidson 1975, 162). Davidson uses 'identify' and 'give' here seemingly interchangeably because, I think, he means to be describing both the way content is attributed to someone's thoughts and how it is constituted (fixed, determined) in someone's thoughts. Thus, to use one of Davidson's examples, one cannot attribute to another a thought about cats unless one can attribute to her some general beliefs about cats, such as the belief that cats can scratch or climb trees, some particular beliefs about cats, such as the belief that the cat seen running a moment ago is still in the neighborhood, and some logical beliefs, such as the belief that either the cat seen running a moment ago is still in the neighborhood or it is not (Davidson 1982, 99). No fixed list of beliefs of the kinds just described is necessary, but numerous beliefs of these kinds must be attributed before any thought about cats can be attributed. As Davidson summarizes it, "the system of such beliefs identifies a thought by locating it in a logical and epistemic space" (Davidson 1975, 157). And, to repeat, what holds of content attribution also holds of content constitution.[8]

The second feature that characterizes propositional attitudes and thoughts is that they can be expressed or reported using sentences that have truth-conditions and are thus true or false. According to Davidson, the core of meaning and content is truth-conditional. He never gave up the claim that reflecting on the construction of Tarski-style theories of truth, that is, theories from which we could derive the truth-conditions of a speaker's utterances, is the key to understanding the philosophical nature of meaning. He did wonder "to what extent such theories can be made adequate to natural languages", but never doubted that "they are adequate to powerful parts of natural languages". It is not that he thought that "speakers and interpreters actually formulate such theories", but rather he maintained that, "if we can describe how they *could* formulate them, we will gain an important insight into the nature of the intentional (including, of course, meaning)" (Davidson 1993a, 83–4). Thus we might say that the meaning of words, and what concepts they express, is, in the first instance, a matter of how they contribute to the truth-conditions of the sentences in which they occur, or of the beliefs these sentences express.

Now, for the sentences giving the truth-conditions of a speaker's utterances to be truly meaning-giving, one must be careful how these truth-conditions are expressed. For instance, " 'Hesperus is identical with Phosphorus' is true iff Hesperus is identical with Hesperus" would not be meaning-giving, for presumably the meaning of 'Hesperus' is different from that of 'Phosphorus', as revealed by the fact that someone may fail to believe that Hesperus is identical with Phosphorus. The axiom that eventually tells us how a name contributes to the truth-conditions of the sentences in which it occurs is extensional, in the sense that it picks out an entity in the world which, in my example, could be named either Hesperus or Phosphorus. However, if we want to make sense of someone's saying that he just found out that Hesperus is identical with Phosphorus, we will make sure that the axiom for 'Hesperus' says that this word designates Hesperus, and not Phosphorus.[9] This is to say that, for Davidson, meaning and content are, as might be expected, intensional, even though they may be fixed, at least in part, by items in the environment of speakers and thinkers or, as Davidson puts it, even though they "supervene on the observable and non-intentional" (Davidson 1993a, 84).[10] This is of a piece with the third feature characterizing propositional attitudes and thoughts.

This is that sentences attributing propositional attitudes and thoughts are semantically opaque.[11] We cannot substitute co-referring expressions in these attributions without running the risk of changing their truth-value. Thus, though it is true that I think my cat is out, it may not be true that I think the most aggressive cat in the neighborhood is out, even though my cat is the most aggressive cat in the neighborhood. This third feature emphasizes the idea I expressed in the previous paragraph, which is that there is more to meaning and content, even of basic utterances and thoughts, than mere connections between items in the world and the words and concepts that refer to them. That is, we cannot fully account for meaning and content in extensional terms. As Davidson came to say repeatedly, the intensional cannot be reduced to the extensional,[12] even though he never thought that meaning and content could be explained in terms of intensions conceived of as abstract entities.

In short, then, propositional content is holistic, truth-conditional and irreducibly intensional. My intention so far has not been to defend these claims. Though I believe they have considerable intuitive appeal, they should for now be accepted at face value as characterizing the notion of content that Davidson is interested in and which the triangulation argument is concerned with. They will in any case become clearer and, I hope, be vindicated later, starting with my exposition of the triangulation argument in the next section of this chapter.[13] I shall proceed with this exposition from a historical point of view, so to speak, tracing the argument back to the article in which it was first developed and following it through the main ensuing articles, for not all the ingredients were present in the initial piece. The second part of the chapter will be devoted to a discussion of the core objections that have been made to various facets of the argument. These are: first, that triangulation is not needed to fix the meanings of one's thoughts and utterances; second, that triangulation is not needed to have the concept of objectivity; and, third, that one need not have the concept of objectivity in order to be a thinker and speaker. I shall end by addressing a more formal objection that has been made repeatedly to the argument, viz., that the account it gives of what makes thought and language possible is circular.

2. The Triangulation Argument

> [Triangulation consists of] the mutual and simultaneous responses of two or more creatures to common distal stimuli and to one another's responses.
>
> (Davidson 2001a, xv)

This quotation suggests that triangulation is a rather vague affair, which may take different, more precise, forms in different contexts. This may explain in part why so many commentators have taken there to be different triangulation arguments, perhaps meant to establish different conclusions. The first thing to note is indeed that there are two kinds of triangulation that Davidson has in mind, one pre-conceptual and the other fully linguistic, between which he unfortunately does not always sharply distinguish. The first kind, which he often calls "primitive",[14] "does not require intensional attitudes" (Davidson 2001c, 292). "It is the result of a threefold interaction, an interaction which is twofold from the point of view of each of the two agents: each is interacting simultaneously with the world and the other agent" (Davidson 1999a, 128).[15] It is the kind of triangulation in which non-linguistic creatures can engage, as in Davidson's example of two lionesses trying to catch a gazelle and coordinating their behavior by watching each other and the gazelle and reacting to each other's reactions (Davidson 2001b, 7). The second kind of triangulation involves full-blown linguistic interaction. It is the kind of situation in which the learner of a first language eventually finds herself, once she has the concept of objectivity. It is also the kind of situation in which the radical interpreter—in effect the learner of a second or additional language *in situ*—finds herself.[16] We may add that it is the kind of situation in which we sometimes find ourselves, whenever ostension is needed to determine the cause, and hence the meaning, of a speaker's utterance. Both kinds of triangulation are supposed to be necessary for someone to be a thinker and speaker, but only the second kind is sufficient—indeed, one might say redundantly so; we shall come back to this in Section 3. For now, let us ask why the first kind is necessary to begin with. What first prompted Davidson's idea of triangulation?

2.1 Primitive Triangulation

The triangulation argument is premised on Davidson's perceptual externalism, the view "that the contents of our thoughts and sayings are partly determined by the history of causal interactions with the environment" (Davidson 1991a, 200).[17] Thus, take the thought, 'there's a cow'. "What determines the content of such basic thoughts (and what we mean by the words we use to express them) is what typically caused similar thoughts" (Davidson 1991a, 201). The question is, though, what are the typical (or "normal" or "usual" (Davidson 2001b, 4)) causes of our basic thoughts and sayings? Davidson claims that if we were to observe a person who had never interacted with another and the world they share—call this person a solitaire—we could not answer this question. And, crucially, neither could she, for the problem here is not that we could not verify what the causes of her thoughts and utterances are, but that such causes could not be uniquely determined (Davidson 1992, 119).[18] Just as the stimulus causing the dog to salivate could be said to be the ringing of the bell or the vibration of the air close to its ears, and just as the stimulus causing the child to mouth 'table' could be said to be a table in its vicinity or the pattern of stimulations at its surface (Davidson 1992, 118), so the stimulus causing the solitaire to produce a sound apparently in response to her environment could be said to be "anything from the stimulation of [her] nerve endings to the original big bang" (Davidson 2001b, 4).[19] And of course, in the absence of any determinate answer to the question of what caused someone's thoughts or utterances, given perceptual externalism, there could be no answer to the question what she is thinking or saying, indeed, no reason to believe that she is thinking or saying anything. According to Davidson, matters change dramatically if the solitaire interacts with another person. They change dramatically if, specifically, the (no longer) solitaire interacts with an interlocutor as well as with objects or events in her environment with which her interlocutor is also interacting. Then it becomes possible to start answering the question what the causes of her utterances are. For any such utterance, the cause is what can be found at the intersection of the two lines that may be drawn from each participant in the interaction, what is common to each respondent, "the nearest mutual cause of the joint reaction" (Davidson 1999d, 84).[20] Exactly what, however, is the difference between the solitaire, who after all does interact with her environment, and the triangulator, such that we (and the triangulator, too, eventually) can say what it is she is reacting to and thus what it is she is thinking and talking about?

Davidson states that it is when three similarity patterns are present that we can locate the relevant cause of the child's uttering 'table': the child's finding tables similar, our finding tables similar, and our finding the child's responses in the presence of tables similar. He stresses, though, that the kind of triangulation just described, while necessary, is "not sufficient to establish that a creature has a concept of a particular object or kind of object"

(Davidson 1992, 119). Still we may ask, at this stage, why the solitaire could not find, say, blackberries similar and her responses in the presence of blackberries similar. Indeed, Davidson also states that what prompts our saying that the dog is responding to the bell, or that the child is responding to tables, is our finding it natural so to classify their responses (Davidson 1992, 118).[21] But then, again, why could the solitaire not find it natural to say (if she were to consider her own utterances) that she is responding to blackberries? The only potentially significant difference between the solitaire and the triangulator is that, whereas for the latter there can be a *common* cause of her and her interlocutor's responses, since two persons may be reacting simultaneously to one common object when they interact with each other; for the former there can be only *similar* causes of the responses she gives at different times, since the solitaire cannot interact with herself in the relevant sense, that is, while reacting to a common cause. But this difference fades on reflection, for scenarios can be found either that suggest that there can be no common cause even of triangulators' responses, or that suggest that there is more than one common cause of their responses, or that suggest that single common causes of the solitaire's responses can also be found.

To begin with, it may be argued that, even though two triangulators may be said in one sense to be reacting to a common cause, say, the table, they may also be said in another sense never to be reacting to the same cause, since they *per force* have different perspectives on what they are reacting to and so are reacting to different things, say, different angles on the table. If so, why not say that triangulators too, just as the solitaire, are reacting to similar causes but not to common causes? What may be replied here is that we are conceiving of the objects and events they are reacting to in too fine-grained a way and further that, even though triangulators may have slightly different perspectives on what they are reacting to, there is a perfectly good sense in which it is the same common object or event to which they are reacting. But then the worry, and this is the second scenario, is that, as a result of our less fine-grained conception, we may have introduced the possibility that there are several common causes to which triangulators are reacting. Why say, e.g., that they are reacting to the table rather than to the set of the table and the chairs around it? Unless we answer this question, we are in a predicament similar to that which motivated triangulation in the first place. Even if we are in a position to choose distal causes over proximal ones, these distal causes are still indeterminate. (I shall come back to this, as we shall soon see that this is a kind of ambiguity that Davidson himself is aware of and that is the real problem with perceptual externalism.)[22] As for the third scenario, it may be argued that we could imagine situations in which a solitaire could be said literally to be reacting to a common cause, e.g., when she is perceiving a stick that simultaneously feels straight and looks bent. In short, so far it is not clear why triangulation is needed, or even how it helps, to fix the causes, and hence the meanings, of one's thoughts and utterances. All the aspects we have so far considered of the predicament the solitaire is in can be seen to affect the triangulator as well. And many of the ways the triangulator may have to fix the causes, and hence the meanings, of her responses seem to be available to the solitaire as well. Should we therefore conclude that the triangulation argument fails, at least as a demonstration that triangulation is needed to fix the meanings of one's thoughts and utterances?

We should not, for there is much more to the triangulation argument than what has been discussed so far. Let us, to begin with, return to the problem left over even for triangulators, viz., that of isolating one and only one common cause of their responses. This is a problem that, though he did not mention it in the initial article, Davidson eventually made explicit. He writes:

> [For a solitaire] the cause is doubly indeterminate: with respect to width, and with respect to distance. The first ambiguity concerns how much of the total cause of a belief [or utterance] is relevant to content ... The second problem has to do with the ambiguity of the relevant stimulus, whether it is proximal (at the skin, say) or distal.
> (Davidson 1999a, 129–30)

We saw above that it is far from obvious that triangulation is needed to solve the second problem. More importantly, we saw that triangulation, at least of the primitive kind discussed so far, does not help to solve the first problem. This problem is made perhaps more perspicuous if we remind ourselves of Wittgenstein's discussion of ostensive definition and thus of the idea that mere association of utterances with items in the world is not enough to endow these utterances with meaning. And this is so no matter how repeated these associations may be and no matter how many people may participate in them. The problem always remains of specifying which aspect of the item designated—which aspect of the cause—is the relevant one in the determination of meaning. Is it, say, the surface of the table, its color, its shape, the table itself, the table and its surroundings ... ?[23] Davidson briefly addresses this (first) problem immediately after introducing it by saying that the relevant part of the total cause is "the part or aspect of the total cause that typically causes relevantly similar responses. What makes the responses relevantly similar in turn is the fact that others find those responses similar; once more it is the social sharing that makes the objectivity of content available" (Davidson 1999a, 130).[24] But sheer social sharing does not tell us in what respect shared responses are similar. Moreover, we are not told why a solitaire could not also find her responses similar, thereby putting herself in a position to fix their relevant causes.

The brief answer just adumbrated by Davidson is, as we shall soon see, slightly misleading, however, and needs to be unpacked. Not surprisingly, Davidson is aware of the problem left over when we appeal to social sharing. He writes: "This difficulty [of saying what is being meant] remains no matter how many people follow the same course of action" (Davidson 2001b, 8). This suggests that primitive triangulation is not supposed to provide the whole answer to the question of how the meanings of one's thoughts and utterances are fixed. Though it may be seen as making room for there being determinate causes of one's thoughts and utterances, these causes are not yet fixed in such a way that those reacting to them can be said to be thinkers and speakers. As I have indicated above, I believe that Davidson's claim that primitive triangulation is necessary to distinguish distal from proximal causes is mistaken. The crucial point, however, is that Davidson did not take primitive triangulation to be also sufficient for possession of language and thoughts.[25] What is of utmost importance here, and something on which I take Davidson to concur, is that reflecting on primitive triangulation affords us a diagnosis of the extent of the problem facing the externalist view, according to which the meanings of one's thoughts and utterances are in part determined by what typically cause them. What the discussion of primitive triangulation brings to the fore is that the causes of one's responses to one's environment are ambiguous not just for the solitaire but for the triangulator as well. No matter how similar shared responses may seem, they may be responses to different aspects of what cause them, and so they remain ambiguous.[26] This is a good place to see how a similar kind of problem plagues internalist theories of meaning, and so how Davidson's assumption of perceptual externalism can be vindicated.[27]

It might be argued that the problem for the solitaire as well as that left over, so far, for the triangulator is a problem only for those who wish to defend perceptual externalism. If we were to abandon that goal and turn internalist instead, the problem would disappear. Instead of appealing to external causes, we could appeal to features of the mind that are independent of the world surrounding it, such as mental pictures or abstract entities grasped by the mind. It would seem, then, that even a solitaire could have a language and thoughts. I am afraid this is an illusion, however. Or, to put it more carefully, I am afraid the internalist has no advantage over the externalist here. For, as Wittgenstein has argued more forcefully than anyone, the internalist solitaire, if I may call her that, is in the exact same kind of predicament as the externalist solitaire. Any mental item that we may think of can be thought of in various ways, and its providing a term with a specific meaning will depend on what the solitaire takes the item to be. But until she has a language or thoughts, the solitaire is in no position to take anything as anything. The predicament for the internalist solitaire is really a version of the aspect problem. To take one of Wittgenstein's examples, a mental sample of green could be taken as a sample of all that is greenish, or as a sample of pure green, or as a sample of the particular shape it has, assuming it has a shape at all, or as a sample of everything that has a shape for that matter, or even as a sample of any combination thereof (Wittgenstein 1958, §73). And what meaning it would provide the term associated with it would depend on how it is taken. Making the sample mental does not solve the problem we have when the sample is physical. Mental items, considered in and of themselves,[28] are no better off than the external objects and events causing our thoughts and utterances, at least as long as these are considered in and of themselves.[29]

Now, to return to the main stream of the argument, the urgent question before us is, what does disambiguate the causes of one's responses to one's environment and thus put one in a position to think and speak? To answer this question, I turn to the second type, which is in effect the second stage of triangulation, discussion of which may be construed as the second step of the triangulation argument, providing the solution to the problem uncovered in the first step.

2.2 Linguistic Triangulation

The crude answer is that, since no non-intensional magic trick will do to fix the causes, and hence the meanings, of one's thoughts and utterances, only those producing the thoughts and utterances could achieve this feat. And they could achieve it only by having the concept of objectivity and triangulating *linguistically* with others.

As I suggested above, Davidson does not think that for the meanings of one's thoughts and utterances to be fixed, it is enough that room be made, via primitive triangulation, for there being determinate causes. Already when he first introduced the triangulation argument, he stressed that one must also be in a position to recognize these causes as such, that is, as the specific aspects of one's environment that cause one's thoughts or utterances. Thus, it is not enough that one interact with another; the interaction must also be one that "matters to the creatures involved". For them to get the idea "that they are reacting to one thing rather than another", they must take "cognitive advantage of the three-way relation", and thus must "react to the interaction" (Davidson 1992, 120).[30] But this, in effect, is to say that they must also have the concept of objectivity, for to recognize causes as such is to recognize that some of the items causing their responses are the same as others and that some are not, and it is to recognize that these causes occur independently of one's thinking or talking about them. To recognize causes as such is to recognize that one's words and concepts may be applied to them correctly or incorrectly. Let us leave aside, for a moment, the fact that this looks tantamount to saying that to have a language and thoughts one must in effect have a language and thoughts, and focus first on the concept of objectivity. It might immediately be protested that the concept of objectivity is something that the solitaire could be in a position to have; indeed, it might be protested that this is something a non-linguistic creature could be in a position to have.[31] Davidson's view, however, is that "unless the creatures can communicate, unless they can engage in the exchange of propositional contents, there is no way they can take cognitive advantage of their ability to triangulate their shared world" (Davidson 2001b, 13). This claim, for one thing, reinforces the suspicion of circularity just broached. For another, it makes it clear that, according to Davidson, neither non-linguistic creatures nor solitaires could have thoughts since possession of these requires possession of the concept of objectivity, which in turn requires linguistic triangulation. The charge of circularity will be addressed in the last section. At this stage, what I wish to do first is to take stock and emphasize an aspect of the structure of the triangulation argument that has been missed by many commentators and that is central to it. Then I will examine Davidson's reasons for maintaining that possession of the concept of objectivity requires a social setting.

As mentioned at the outset of this chapter, many commentators maintain that there are two triangulation arguments that should be considered and assessed separately. One is the argument for what makes it possible for meanings to be fixed; the other is the argument for what makes it possible to have the concept of objectivity.[32] Some do recognize (and complain) that Davidson often runs the arguments together or that he does not sharply distinguish between the questions they are meant to address. But it should be clear by now that this is how Davidson intended it to be. Triangulation is not supposed to answer, first, the question of how meanings can be fixed and then, only afterwards, the question of how one may possess the concept of objectivity. Rather, triangulation accomplishes both tasks at once, for possession of the concept of objectivity is required for the determination of meanings. Only those who possess the concept are in a position to disambiguate the causes of their utterances in that only they can solve the aspect problem. This is not to say, though, that people first acquire the concept and then fix the meanings of their words. Rather, both achievements are concurrent. Perhaps the best way to express the idea here is to say that only of someone who is in a position to have the concept of objectivity can we say that her utterances are meaningful because only of such a person can we say that the meanings of her utterances have been fixed.

In fairness to his commentators, Davidson's contention that having the concept of objectivity is needed to have beliefs and hence language predates the fully developed triangulation argument.[33] And the reasons he often states for this contention are not obviously connected to the triangulation argument. These reasons are simple: to conceptualize is to classify, and to classify is to be aware of the possibility of misclassification. As Davidson writes, "being able to discriminate cats is not the same thing as having the concept of a cat. You have the concept of a cat only if you can make sense of the idea of misapplying the concept, of believing or judging that something is a cat which is not a cat" (Davidson 1999a, 124).[34] It may even be said that in the initial article the connection between fixing meanings and having the concept of objectivity is not made explicit, leaving the impression that the two tasks are to some extent independent. But the idea which, as I indicated above, I think was already present in the initial article became more and more obvious subsequently. This is that, to put it slightly differently from above, if thoughts and utterances are to be meaningful, the concepts and words they involve must be subject to conditions of correct application. And, if thinkers and speakers are to determine these conditions, they must be aware of the distinction between correct and incorrect applications of their words and concepts (which is not to say they must know how to draw it in any particular case, however), and thus of the fact that what they apply them to is independent of what they take it to be, which is tantamount to saying that they must be aware of the concept of objectivity.[35] Now, why does Davidson think that possession of the concept of objectivity requires a social setting?

He writes: "by yourself you can't tell the difference between the situations seeming the same and being the same" (Davidson 1994, 124).[36] Whenever he makes this point, Davidson mentions Wittgenstein to back him up, but he never himself defends it in any detail. Why exactly, then, could the solitaire not be in a position to have the concept of objectivity? Recall the predicament she is in: no matter how regular her responses to the environment may be, they may still be responses of different kinds; they may be responses to different aspects of the environment. Thus she must be the one to tell, objectively, at least for some of the causes of her responses, which causes are the same as which, which of her responses are correct. But how is she supposed to draw such an objective line between what seems to her to be the same cause, or the correct response, and what is in fact the same cause, or the correct response? Well, it may be replied, she might have the following kind of experience: As a result of regularly finding blackberries in some particular bush, she one day experiences frustration upon not finding any in that bush. And it may be argued that experiences of this kind put her in a position to have the concept of objectivity since by hypothesis she realizes that her belief about what is in the bush is false and thus that there is a distinction between what she believes to be the case and what is the case.[37] Now, strictly speaking, by assuming that the solitaire has beliefs, this scenario begs the question against Davidson, if he is right to say that only those who have the concept of objectivity can have beliefs with determinate contents. Thus what we have to imagine here is some experiences of the solitaire putting her in a position to possess both. But then what we have to imagine is the solitaire being able to notice that her present and her former "thoughts" do not match and to decide objectively which way to go. This in turn entails the question, what reason is there to think that she is having a thought about the same bush? Perhaps she is "thinking" that she passed the fruity bush, or that she took the wrong turn, or whatever. The point is that, whatever she is "thinking", be it that it is the same bush or that it is not, will be correct, according to her. She does not have to draw one conclusion rather than another. However she draws the line between correct and incorrect responses that will be right to her. There is no way she can do this objectively. But the situation changes dramatically if the solitaire starts triangulating. Thus Davidson continues the above-quoted passage:

> If you and I each correlate the other's responses with the occurrence of a shared stimulus, however, an entirely new element is introduced. Once

the correlation is established it provides each of us with a ground for distinguishing the cases in which it fails.
(Davidson 1994, 124)

There is space for the concept of error, which appears when there is a divergence in normally similar reactions.
(Davidson 2001b, 12)[38]

Note, though, that there being space for the concept of error is not yet sufficient for someone to be in a position to have the concept of error. After all, one may again imagine a scenario where space for the concept of error could also be made by the solitaire. What changes dramatically for the triangulator is that she is interacting and so can settle with another person, rather than just with herself, the ways in which perspectives on a given event or state of affairs may diverge. As long as the responses of triangulators do not diverge, they presumably cannot yet objectively distinguish between what seem to them to be the same, or the correct, responses and what are the same, or the correct, responses to their environment. But if their responses diverge, the distinction is "forced" upon them, as Davidson once put it (Davidson 1975, 170). It is forced upon them because they have no choice but to negotiate, so to speak, the resolution of the divergence. Thus, suppose that they have been picking blackberries in a particular bush and one day they come across a bush that is empty of blackberries. One of them insists that it is the same bush now empty of blackberries; the other maintains that it is a different bush because they took a wrong turn. How they settle the dispute cannot be dependent on one or the other interlocutor but must be the result of genuine communication between them. Indeed, we might say that whereas the solitaire "communicates" with herself regardless of how she settles the matter under dispute, interpersonal communication could not succeed if it were left to one or the other interlocutor to decide which way to go. Communication requires them to agree, or at least to agree to disagree. And, even in order to disagree, they have to agree on how their utterances are to be understood by each other, something that can only be settled, ultimately, on the basis of regular connections between their utterances and their environment. It is important to note also that, for the divergence of responses to put someone in a position to have the concept of objectivity, the matter must be settled linguistically. Someone who interacts with a non-linguistic creature would be no better off than the solitaire, having the only say on the matter and thus no say at all.[39]

Such is my unpacking of Davidson's claim that only linguistic triangulators can be in a position to draw objective lines between what seems to them to be the same and what is in fact the same, and thus only linguistic triangulators can be in a position to have the concept of objectivity. If Davidson's triangulation argument is unobjectionable, the conclusion we have reached is that only in a social setting could one have a language and thoughts, and there could not be thought without language. But is the argument unobjectionable?

Before addressing this question, let me return briefly to the three features which, according to Davidson, characterize propositional content, or meaning, as I have preferred to call it, viz., its being truth-conditional, holistic and irreducibly intensional. And let me ask to what extent the triangulation argument confirms that meaning has these features. It clearly confirms that meaning is, in the first instance, truth-conditional, as speakers need to triangulate on objects and events in the world around them in order to fix the meaning of their thoughts and utterances.[40] So, what determines the meaning of basic utterances, such as 'there is a cow', is what makes these utterances true. It also confirms that meaning is holistic. For the kind of disagreement and negotiation that triangulation involves ensures that any expression whose meaning is fixed by triangulation will have been used in many different contexts. Thus, if a triangulator observes that there are no blackberries left in the bush where she and her interlocutor expected to find some, and her interlocutor insists that they took a wrong turn and so it is not the same bush that they are currently talking about, they will have to agree on what they mean by 'bush', 'blackberries', etc. And this is something they can come to do only by considering how they would use the words in other contexts of utterance, which pretty obviously entails that the meaning of these words cannot be fixed independently of the meaning of other words they employ. As for the intensionality of meaning, the triangulation argument confirms that meaning cannot be characterized in terms of extensionally described relations—more on this in the next chapter.

3. Objections to the Triangulation Argument

To begin with, commentators have objected to some of the steps of the argument, specifically, to the claim that triangulation is needed to fix the meanings of thoughts and utterances, to the claim that triangulation is needed to have the concept of objectivity, and to the claim that possession of the concept of objectivity is needed to have a language and thoughts. More generally, they have objected to the triangulation argument on the grounds that it gives a circular account of what makes language and thought possible. I examine each objection in turn.

3.1 Fixing Meanings Does Not Require Triangulation

I already have, in the course of my presentation of primitive triangulation, discussed objections that may be made to the claim that this kind of triangulation is necessary to fix meanings. We saw that the solitaire and the primitive triangulator are in the same position when the question arises of how the causes, and hence the meanings, of their thoughts and utterances could be fixed. In either case it seems that, to express it in Davidson's terms, room could be made for there being distal causes of their responses, but the relevant aspects of these causes could not be fixed. These objections are worth discussing further, as some commentators not only have insisted that isolated non-linguistic animals react to distal causes, that is, to middle-sized objects and events in the world surrounding them, rather than to proximal causes. Thus Jason Bridges has insisted that the presumption that they do so "is essential to our ordinary understanding of animal life" (Bridges 2006, 307). This, as we have seen, is a claim that I am happy to accept. It simply is not the case that the cat is chasing the big bang or the stimulation of its nerve endings; the cat is chasing the dog. But some have made a much more radical claim. Thus Tyler Burge has declared that "the triangulation problem . . . is no longer a serious problem" (Burge 2003a, 687). "It has long been solved in perceptual psychology" (Burge 2010, 275). Burge has recently further developed his account of perceptual content, which is externalist (what he calls anti-individualist[41]) and, he maintains, in tune with the findings of perceptual psychology, indeed, in tune with common sense, according to which the behavior of a whole range of non-linguistic animals is best explained by attributing to them representational states as of features of the environment with which they interact. Burge makes clear that the kind of content he is focusing on is non-conceptual and non-propositional; so it may be wondered why he also thinks of himself as addressing Davidson's triangulation argument, or at least what kind of triangulation problem he thinks has been solved. And it may at first be surmised that Burge thinks that it is the distance problem that has been solved, a problem which, even according to Davidson, can to some extent be addressed without appeal to propositional content—primitive triangulation, recall, "does not require intensional attitudes" (Davidson 2001c, 292). I have conceded that the presence of triangulation is not needed to justify our saying that non-linguistic beings respond to distal causes, and so, to that extent, that triangulation is not needed to solve the distance problem. But this leaves us with the other, more pressing problem, the aspect problem, the solution to which, I have argued, does require triangulation. It is here that Burge deserves some attention, for he seems to think that even the aspect problem is solved in perceptual psychology,[42] and he does think that perceptual representational content grounds propositional content, suggesting that triangulation is not needed for the latter to be present—[43] this may indeed be why he thinks he is addressing Davidson even though he is not focusing on propositional content.

Burge claims that animals, both human and non-human, already triangulate on distal objects and events via their visual apparatus. And this provides, indeed fixes, the minimal kinds of contents that they entertain (Burge 2003a, 687). He further writes:

> Davidson underestimates the dependence of psychology on biological sciences. Primitive perceptual categories are closely connected to attributes that are relevant to explaining animals' basic biological needs

and activities. Given that animals can discriminate these attributes, and given that animals have perceptual subsystems that differentiate, in exercises of perceptual constancies, between proximal registration and environmental attributes, there is a rich, natural framework for attributing perceptual and other representational kinds to non-linguistic beings (Burge 2010, 276). ("Perceptual constancies ... are capacities to represent environmental attributes, or environmental particulars, as the same, despite radically different proximal stimulations.")

(Burge 2010, 114)

This suggests that, for Burge, the causes of one's responses to the environment are not ambiguous for any being that may be said to interact with it. For instance, a cat may represent a piece of fish as an edible body (Burge 2010, 258), or it may represent a dog as a moving body (Burge 2010, 24). The main point of interest here is that the cat is said not just to be reacting to distal causes but also to be representing distal causes. And presumably, if it is genuinely representing them, it is representing them under some aspect or another—I take it that this is what makes it possible to distinguish among different representations; indeed, the idea of representing a cause, distal or proximal for that matter, under no aspect makes no sense. (This confirms my reading of Burge as focusing on the aspect problem of giving an account of representational content.) But then the urgent question for us is, does Burge provide an explanation of how the aspects of the causes of non-linguistic animals' representations are fixed? Even if, as Burge claims, it is true that animals, both human and non-human, already triangulate on distal objects and events via their visual apparatus, the question remains, what determines the specific aspect of the object or event on which they triangulate? After all, the perceptual focus of the cat chasing the dog might be the four-legged animal, or the furry animal, or the cute animal, for that matter.

Burge says that the methodology of perceptual science easily dismisses "candidates for perceptual objects" such as stimulations and sense-data (given the nature of perceptual constancies), but also "philosophical contrivances" such as "abstractions and temporal stages" because they "do not ground relevant biological explanations" (Burge 2010, 324). As noted above, biological explanations of animal activity are what guide our attributions of perceptual states, and such explanations "refer to macro-particulars and macro-attributes that are of some ecological importance to the animal's functions" (Burge 2010, 323). In other words, the aspects under which we deem non-linguistic animals to represent their environment are dictated by the explanatory demands of science and common sense. As I see it, there are two problems with this line of argument, if it is to serve as a solution to the aspect problem.

First, why should we think that isolated non-linguistic animals succeed in capturing and thus representing specific aspects of their environment as such, that is, as the same as others or not, in responding to them correctly or not, given that, as I have argued, solitary human beings seem to fail? If Burge is right, where have I gone wrong? What, to begin with, needs to be stressed here is that, as indicated in the above paragraph, it is we who project onto the animals the concepts we have and which we think are best suited to explain their behavior. We fix the content of their representations, if any, from our, scientific or otherwise, third-person point of view. Of course, in doing so, we describe non-linguistic animals the way we describe each other. Thus, we will not say, as I have already acknowledged, that the cat "thinks" its sensory stimulation disappeared, nor will we say that it "thinks" a temporal stage of a dog disappeared. Rather, we use descriptions that are intelligible to us. However, as Davidson put it, repeatedly, "When it is conceptualization that is to be explained, it begs the question to project our classifications on to nature" (Davidson 2001d, 135). As he continues elsewhere, triangulation introduces a crucial difference: "the difference between an external commentator slipping in his categories to make sense of an isolated creature, and a participant observing another participant doing his or its thing" (Davidson 2001b, 8). Triangulation yields an account of how contents are constituted in the first place and not just how scientists and others project their independently established contents onto other creatures. Burge's focus, as I said, is not conceptualization but non-conceptual representation; but I think that, insofar as representation is to be aspectual, it invites the same kind of worry. Burge seems to think that in order to address the worry it is enough to point out that recasting scientific explanations in terms of proximal causes—say, photons or surface stimulations—"would be complicated in ways that undermine the viability of alternative explanations" (Burge 2010, 272). But here is the second problem with Burge's "solution" to the triangulation problem.

As should be obvious by now, the crucial question is not, what reason do we have to think that non-linguistic animals react to distal rather than proximal causes, but what reason do we have to think that non-linguistic animals isolate one rather than another aspect of the distal cause they are reacting to? Even if we grant that our describing the cat chasing the dog as reacting to the dog, rather than to its retinal surface stimuli, affords a better explanation of the cat's behavior, the fact of the matter is that we could also describe the cat as reacting to its worst enemy, or to something that deeply aggravates it, or, in short, to something that causes it to feel in a certain way. Likewise, the cat jumping onto the kitchen counter may be described as its reacting to the fish lying there. But it could also be described as its reacting to something edible, or to its preferred food or, in short, to something that causes it to feel in a certain way.[44] This is to say that there is room for doubt that the animal is reacting to something that it takes to be objectively out there. That is, this suggests that the animal has no conception of anything existing independently of itself, which Burge is happy to accept (while insisting that the animal's representations are objective). However, more importantly, this suggests, not only that the animal has no concept of any kind, but also that it does not represent what it is reacting to in any way insofar as its reaction can be described in several ways that are extensionally equivalent. There is no principled way for us, let alone the animal, to choose among those descriptions. Or, if we do choose one of the possible descriptions, there is no reason to think that it captures the animal's representation.

Burge may insist that the choice among these descriptions is based, as quoted above, on the ecological importance of what is described to the animal's functions. This may allow us to distinguish between, say, representations of something edible and representations of something moving. But then there is the question whether the animal is representing objective features of its environment or simply, as John Campbell has forcefully argued against Burge, affordances of such features—that is, what the environment "offers the animal, what it provides or furnishes, either for good or ill" (Campbell 2011, 272). As Campbell remarks, "the opportunities and threats are really there in the world, but they are defined in relation to the needs of [the animal]." If so, as he continues, "the ongoing problem is to understand how [representing a species-independent reality, that is, as I understand this, representing a reality independently of how it affects the species] is achieved" (Campbell 2011, 284). Now, even if these states of animals are representational, and so even if they are in some sense contentful, I do believe that representational content is importantly different from propositional content. It is not just that the representations under consideration are representations of animals' environment in so far as this affects them in certain ways. The representational contents involved are also much less fine-grained than propositional contents. We may indeed substitute descriptions of these representations without risk of changing the truth-values of the sentences in which they occur. Perhaps we could say that, insofar as these representational contents are intensional, they are so in a way different from propositional contents. Of course we do not usually bother to substitute descriptions of animal behavior. But those we settle on are ours; the representational contents they invoke are, to repeat, ultimately fixed by us, from a third-person perspective, and not, as in the case of linguistic beings, by the beings themselves, albeit by interacting with one another.[45] What I further believe is that, even if those states of animals are representational and thus in some sense contentful, there is no indication of how they could develop into propositional states, into thoughts about, say, furry animals or four-legged animals—that is, into thoughts that are both fine-grained and fully objective. The central triangulation problem, i.e., the aspect problem, has in effect not been solved.[46] And thus, in the end, even if one grants Burge that his notion of representational content genuinely qualifies as a notion of content, this does not affect the conclusion of the triangulation argument, according to which fully intensional, propositional content rests on beings interacting linguistically with one another and the world they share.

If my reading of the triangulation argument is right, the reason linguistic triangulation is needed to fix the meanings of one's thoughts and utterances is that this fixing can be done only by those who possess the concept of objectivity. But the claim that possessing the concept of objectivity requires triangulation has also been called into question.[47] This is the next objection I examine.

3.2 Possessing the Concept of Objectivity Does Not Require Triangulation

This objection has been made by numerous commentators.[48] Either they maintain that the claim that possession of the concept of objectivity requires triangulation is "sheer empirical speculation" (Pagin 2001, 207; Glüer 2006, 1017), or they tell us a story about how someone needs no other person's help in order to have the concept of objectivity. Thus Martin Montminy writes:

> There are at least three ways in which . . . [a solitary creature] can come to understand that one of its beliefs is wrong. First . . . [it] can compare its current reaction to a past one . . . A second method . . . is to try to see if her current reaction satisfies a generalization it has so far admitted . . . Thirdly, the solitary creature can compare its actual reaction to one it would have if it observed the same situation from a different perspective.
> (Montminy 2003, 38–9)

The problem with all the ways that Montminy envisages for being in a position to have the concept of objectivity is that they assume that the solitary creature already has beliefs and so already is a thinker. But Davidson's argument, as I have construed it, is that a creature who does not have the concept of objectivity could not have thoughts because their meanings could be fixed only by someone who has the concept of objectivity. That is, possession of the concept and of thoughts, and of course of language, comes at once.

Ernest Lepore and Kirk Ludwig give this story about what may put someone in a position to have the concept of objectivity:

> Accustomed to the persistence of solid objects, one glances at a table and comes to believe there is a book lying there. Looking up moments later, one sees nothing there where one had thought there was a book. One may achieve a smaller adjustment of one's theory of the world by supposing that one was mistaken the first time around, rather than supposing solid objects go out of existence without explanation.
> (Lepore and Ludwig 2005, 402)[49]

It is rather hard to see just what has been explained here. The question is not how someone can apply the concept of objectivity without communicating with another. If she has it and thus has beliefs, there is no reason to think she could not do that. But Davidson's question has been how someone who has never communicated with another could have both beliefs and the concept of objectivity. Lepore and Ludwig observe that "it could not be a request for a story about how a creature with beliefs could acquire the concept of error by engaging in certain sorts of activities" (Lepore and Ludwig 2005, 401). I think they are right in maintaining not only that, for Davidson, beliefs and the concept of objectivity come together, but also that Davidson is not trying to spell out the process through which they are acquired. As he writes: "Triangulation does not pretend to explain, explicate, or describe [the] process [through which] the learner, taking advantage of the space created by triangulation, becomes aware of the possibility of error" (Davidson 2001c, 294). He is trying, however, to discover what puts someone in a position to have beliefs and the concept of objectivity. Specifically, he is trying to articulate what he sees as the conceptual relations between the two achievements and between them and linguistic triangulation. And, whereas he sees linguistic triangulation as shedding light on our understanding of what makes having beliefs and the concept of objectivity possible, he finds that no such light is being shed, either if we consider a solitaire interacting with herself and her environment, or if we consider creatures engaging merely in primitive triangulation. This leads to the first complaint I mentioned against the claim that possession of the concept of objectivity requires triangulation, viz., that it is sheer empirical speculation.

In response, Davidson has happily admitted that his remarks about triangulation are speculation. But he has also indicated why he does not think that they are sheer speculation. Thus he writes:

> There cannot be said to be proof of this claim [that aspects of our interactions with others and the world are partly constitutive of what we mean and think]. Its plausibility depends on a conviction which can seem either empirical or a priori; a conviction that this is a fact about what sort of creatures we are. Empirical if you think it just happens to be true of us that this is how we come to be able to speak and think about the world; a priori if you think, as I tend to, that this is part of what we mean when we talk of thinking and speaking. After all, the notions of speaking and thinking are ours.
>
> (Davidson 2001c, 294)

These comments might however strike us as rather indecisive. Are the claims being made empirical or a priori? For all we have seen so far, we may expect Davidson to be claiming the latter, as he himself suggests. He is after all telling us a conceptual story about the relations among the concepts of error, thought, speech and linguistic triangulation, articulating how making sense of the possibility of the one is related to making sense of the possibility of the others. As he also writes, "the concepts of truth, error, belief, and propositional content are so closely related to conceptualization and to one another that an insight into conditions for attributing any of them to a creature will lead directly to conditions for attributing the others" (Davidson 2006, 1065). But this claim, too, could be taken to be either empirical or a priori, depending on whether the focus is on what makes it possible to attribute those concepts to others, that is, what the evidence must be like, or on what makes it possible for a creature to have those concepts, that is, what constitutes having any one of them. His claims, Davidson says, can be considered as a priori if they have to do with what we mean by 'thinking' and 'speaking'. Thinking and speaking, for Davidson, require not only having concepts, and words that express them, with determinate meanings, but also the ability to distinguish between correct and incorrect applications of those concepts and words, and this ability having been exercised on at least some occasions. This ability, for Davidson, is an essential part of what it takes to make sense of the idea of someone having and expressing concepts to begin with. As he constantly reminds us, it is what enables us to distinguish between mere discrimination and actual conceptualization. Furthermore, as I have argued on his behalf, the presence and exercise of this ability is also necessary for there being determinate meanings.

As we shall see in the next section, I think it is crucial to consider Davidson's claims about triangulation as a priori. But we may also understand why Davidson might have played loose with them and left it to us to decide whether they are empirical or a priori, for there is much that counts in their favor even on the empirical side. It would indeed be hard to come up with empirical evidence that thought, speech and linguistic triangulation are not interdependent. For one thing, every known speaker has come to have a language by interacting with others and the world they share. (Of course, experiments on solitary beings are ruled out.)[50] For another thing, as we have seen, the kind of intensionality attached to propositional thought precludes us from attributing thoughts to non-linguistic beings. As Davidson writes, "the intensionality we make so much of in the attribution of thoughts is very hard to make much of when speech is not present" (Davidson 1975, 163). Thus Davidson's suggestion that it just happens to be true of us that interacting linguistically with others is how we come to be able to speak and think about the world is to a large extent supported empirically. It has been contended, however, that this is not true of Davidson's claim that possession of the concept of objectivity is needed to be a thinker and speaker, for empirical evidence against this claim has allegedly been found. This is the next objection I examine.

3.3 Possession of a Language and Thoughts Does Not Require Possession of the Concept of Objectivity

The main empirical evidence that has been used to support this claim involves autistic people. There are some high-functioning autistic people who, we are told, are perfectly good speakers of a language even though they lack the concept of objectivity.[51] Though they can engage in dialogue with other people, they cannot attribute to them beliefs and other propositional attitudes, which seems to be required in order to engage in linguistic triangulation. The evidence provided for this claim is two-fold. First, autistic speakers fail false-belief tests, which are designed to test their ability to attribute false beliefs to others.[52] Second, actual cases of autistic speakers not capable of attributing beliefs to others have reportedly been found. However, it is not that easy empirically to determine which speaker may or may not have the concept of belief or objectivity. How to interpret tests that are supposed to demonstrate who may or may not have it is highly controversial. Passing a false-belief test may demonstrate possession of the concept.[53] But failing the test definitely does not demonstrate lack of the concept. Furthermore, that autistic speakers cannot attribute beliefs to others is at best underdetermined by the evidence. What some philosophers have considered the best example of an autistic speaker who lacks this ability has been shown, successfully to my mind, to support the opposite claim.[54] Indeed, it has been argued that, rather than being a counter-example to higher-order theories of thought, of which Davidson's theory is an instance, autistic speakers can be taken to support such theories.[55] But let us, for a moment, reflect on the reasons why some are willing to deem someone a genuine speaker of a language, even though she lacks the concept of objectivity.

Presumably, they have some preconception of what it is to speak meaningfully and how this is to be distinguished from mere parroting. Thus, genuine speakers will presumably be able to communicate on a number of topics concerning the environment they share with their interlocutors, to understand statements they make, answer questions they ask, etc. But some speakers, the objectors urge, are able to do all of this even though they do not seem to have the concept of objectivity. This is where I, with Davidson, balk. I wish to suggest that, if they do all of the above, they do have the concept, "albeit inarticulately held", as Davidson said. That they succeed in communicating in relatively complex ways is evidence that they have the concept.[56] Alternatively, I might deny that those who give no evidence whatsoever of possessing the concept actually communicate with others, or at least that they communicate in the way we do. Following Davidson, I would not know, for one thing, how to distinguish between the genuine speaker and the automaton unless I could invoke the concept. Indeed, since I would have no explanation of how the meanings of the person's thoughts and utterances were fixed, I would have no reason to believe that they are genuinely hers rather than meanings I have imposed on her thoughts and utterances. In other words, I see a strong empirical connection between what counts as evidence for the possession of language and thoughts and evidence for the possession of the concept of objectivity. If there is strong reason to believe that someone is communicating with others, this gives us strong reason to believe that she has the concept of objectivity. And if there is strong reason to doubt that someone lacks the concept of objectivity, this gives us strong reason to doubt that she has a language and thoughts. The answer to the question what kind of empirical data are relevant, and how to interpret them, is indeed dictated by our reflections on what it takes to have a language and thoughts or, as Davidson put it, on what we mean when we say that someone is a speaker and a thinker. I do not think that Davidson's opponents are different in this respect. It is just that they leave it mysterious what accounts for meaning and communication if, as they claim, there can be genuine speakers and thinkers who do not have the concept of objectivity.[57]

Davidson never addressed the empirical worries broached by his opponents. We can now see that there may be a reason for this. Very likely, the "evidence" provided by autistic speakers would not budge him and he would insist that the burden of proof, or at least of convincing argument since there can be no proof, is on his opponents, who, to repeat, have to show two things. First, they have to show how to distinguish between genuine speaking and parroting, or between conceptualizing and discriminating, or, as Davidson sometimes put it, between following a rule and merely having a disposition (Davidson 2001b, 9), without invoking the concept of objectivity. Second, they have to show how the meanings of thoughts and utterances of those who lack the concept can still be fixed.[58] This, as I have mentioned several times, is not a demand that is usually acknowledged by Davidson's opponents, especially not by those who make the objection under consideration. But, as I have argued, it is a central part of Davidson's triangulation argument. Indeed, I believe that the need for the connection between meaning determination and possession of the concept of objectivity is part and parcel of what makes the account of language and thought unavoidably circular. This is the topic of the next and last objection I examine.

3.4 The Account of What Makes Language and Thought Possible Is Circular

I have at several points already alluded to the circularity of the account. The crudest way to expose it is this. Primitive triangulation, though it may make room for there being determinate causes, and hence determinate meanings, of one's thoughts and utterances, and thus though it may be, as Davidson insists, necessary for thought itself to emerge, is nonetheless not sufficient. What must be added is linguistic triangulation. To say this, Davidson acknowledges, is "not very helpful [for] it assumes what was to be explained. Of course if there is language, there is thought [and of course if there is language there is language!] . . . Nevertheless, it is useful to recognize the somewhat surprising fact that the social element that is essential to language is essential to thought itself" (Davidson 2001b, 13).[59] Now the circle seems to be shrinking when we next acknowledge that the social element that is essential to language is linguistic communication. "With the second, final, step we move in a circle, for we grasp the concept of truth only when we can communicate . . . the propositional contents of the shared experience, and this requires language" (Davidson 1997b, 141). The circle seems unavoidable, Davidson further insists, "for a non-circular answer would tell us how to account for intensionality in non-intensional terms" (Davidson 1997b, 139). And this reduction is "not to be expected" (Davidson 2001b, 13).[60] Those who underline the circular aspect of Davidson's account in fact realize that he thinks it is due to the failure of reduction. Still, this does not help, they contend, for there remains the question how the awareness or recognition that one is triangulating could "in any sense be part of the *explanation* of the acquisition of the capacity for thought, given that it presupposes that capacity" (Bridges 2006, 301). In the end, Davidson's whole enterprise of trying to establish the essentially social character of language and thought simply collapses, or so Pagin maintains:

> [I]f the interesting difference between being on one's own and being in a community cannot be stated without presupposing that the community members have the capacities that were considered problematic to begin with, we haven't even been given a reason for disbelieving that isolated individuals can have them, too.
>
> (Pagin 2001, 209)[61]

The question before us is whether, as Bridges puts it, the circle "being vanishingly small, is . . . vicious" (Bridges 2006, 302), or whether, as Dagfinn Føllesdal puts it, "the circle is very large [and so] unobjectionable" (Føllesdal 1999, 726).

To begin with, it must be stressed again that Davidson's goal is "not to explain in detail how the process [i.e., the first entry into thought and language] works . . . but to indicate how the triangular arrangement makes the process possible" (Davidson 2001c, 293). The question is thus whether Davidson has succeeded in doing the latter. Here, I believe that what needs emphasizing is the difference between the solitaire's and the triangulator's positions, a difference which is more interesting than Pagin makes it sound. And the only way to do this is to remind ourselves, once more, of what calls for a non-reductive, and thus circular, account to begin with. It is the appreciation that primitive triangulation leaves the causes, and hence the meanings, of triangulators' responses to their environment indeterminate. Triangulators are no better off than solitaires at that stage—hence the need for would-be thinkers and speakers to have the concept of objectivity and the leap into the intensional realm. It seems to me that the motivation for this need is unobjectionable if the verdict on primitive triangulation is right. Then the question becomes why triangulation is needed to have the concept of objectivity. Just as there might be room for there being determinate causes of her responses for the solitaire, so there might be room for her to become aware of the concept of objectivity. But, as we have seen, this is precisely what Davidson denies. And he does this, as I have tried to show, by articulating a significant difference between the solitaire and the triangulator, which is that only the triangulator is obliged to consider her interlocutor when settling a dispute about diverging responses.[62] One is almost tempted to say, crudely, look, there is a difference between the solitaire and the triangulator: only the latter triangulates!

How large, then, is the circle, in the end?

It is obviously not just the narrow vicious circle that says that there is language and thought only when there is language and thought. It is rather the rich and complex circle that encompasses language, thought (each of which depending on there being fixed meanings), possession of the concept of objectivity and linguistic triangulation. I should say it is an instructive circle, each part of which is such that, if it is absent, the whole circle breaks down. To some, it may in the end be a frustrating story, as non-reductive stories are ultimately bound to be. But it seems to me that the story is compelling and that, within the intensional realm, progress has been made.[63]

4. Conclusion

I see the triangulation argument as a sustained attempt both to strengthen the claim that a reductive account of language and thought is not forthcoming and to develop a constructive theory of the nature of language and thought in light of that conclusion. If intensional concepts cannot be explained in a reductive way, it seems that one promising alternative explanation is in terms of the relations among them. As I see it, this is what the triangulation argument accomplishes. Thus, contrary to what is often maintained, it shows that many philosophically constructive claims can be made about the nature of language and thought even though neither can be explained in non-semantic terms. Semantic non-reductionism is compatible with semantic non-quietism. But semantic non-reductionism, in part because of the argument that leads to it, also has consequences for other aspects of our account of meaning. In particular, it has consequences for the question of whether meaning is essentially normative. This is the topic of the next chapter.

Notes

1. The very idea of triangulation is first introduced in Davidson 1982, 105.
2. Note that the relation between having a language and thoughts and having the concept of objectivity is not temporal but conceptual.
3. See e.g., Davidson 1982, 104–5; 1995a, 10; 1997, 141. I usually will stick with 'concept of objectivity'.
4. See also Davidson 1991a, 202; 1994, 124; 1995a, 7; 2006, 1065.
5. Evans 1982 first introduced the idea of non-conceptual content. See McDowell 2008 for an account of perceptual content that is conceptual, though not propositional but what he calls intuitional. See Burge 2010 for an account of perceptual content that is representational but not conceptual. One might want to add phenomenal content to this list (see, e.g., Kriegel 2002).

6. Indeed, some do not even agree that intentional states are necessarily contentful states (see Hutto and Myin 2013).
7. See Davidson 1977, 220.
8. Thus Davidson's answer to Jerry Fodor and Ernie Lepore's question what "the epistemology of interpretation [has] got to do with the metaphysics of content" (Fodor and Lepore 2007, 687) is: everything! It is the answer, that is, provided that the relationship between the relevant bits of epistemology and metaphysics is understood properly, an understanding which it is the aim of this chapter to supply. Michael Rescorla certainly does not have it when he says that "Intentional phenomena no more depend upon our theorizing about intentionality than physical phenomena depend upon out theorizing about the physical" (Rescorla 2013, 480). Davidson does not think, which would indeed be absurd, that our "theorizing" about the contents of someone's thoughts makes them to be the contents they are. Rather, he thinks that another's interaction with that person has contributed to making it possible for her to have the thoughts she has, that is, with the contents they have. (Note that Davidson never was an "interpretationist" or "interpretivist". As Kathrin Glüer writes, "Metaphysically speaking . . . it is not the radical interpreter that is responsible for meaning. Metaphysically, meaning is determined in a way that makes natural language radically interpretable, but the determination is done by something else" (Glüer 2011, 135).)
9. This was made clear, not by Davidson himself, but by McDowell 1977.
10. This, as we shall see later, is the first hint that meaning and content cannot be analyzed in reductive non-semantic terms—one of the many ways in which we can appreciate the continuity of Davidson's thought. See Davidson 1974a, 154 for an early expression of his non-reductionism.
11. As Davidson writes, "it has long been recognized that semantic opacity distinguishes talk about propositional attitudes from talk of other things" (Davidson 1982, 98).
12. See, e.g., Davidson 2001c, 293; 2003, 697. As we shall see in due time, there is more than this to Davidson's non-reductionism.
13. The rest of this chapter is based on Verheggen 2013. Most of Section 2 is taken almost verbatim from that article. I have tried to clarify matters whenever possible and added a number of footnotes. Section 3 has been considerably expanded.
14. See, e.g., Davidson 1999c, 85; 2001c, 292; 2006, 1066. He sometimes also calls it "basic" (Davidson 1999a, 128) or "simple" (Davidson 2003, 697).
15. See also Davidson 1999a, 128; 1999b, 731.
16. Some quotations are in order here, as they provide evidence for the continuity between Davidson's views on radical interpretation and his views on triangulation. Davidson writes:

> The gearing of verbal (and other) responses to situations, events, and objects through the prompting and perception of others plays a key role both in the acquisition of a first language, or the learning of a second language in the absence of an interpreter or bilingual dictionary . . . Learning a first and learning a second language are, of course, very different enterprises . . . Both, however, depend on similar mechanisms and similar cues (Davidson 1998, 88).
>
> Ostensive learning, whether undertaken by a radical interpreter as a first step into a second language, or undergone by someone acquiring a first language, is an example of triangulation (Davidson 2001d, 144).

See also Davidson 2001c, 294.
17. See also Davidson 1997a, 71. It might be thought that this is quite an assumption to make, but, as we shall see later, considerations invoked in the triangulation argument might be used to vindicate the assumption. I think the argument is also premised on the idea that "it is understanding that gives life to meaning"

(Davidson 1994, 121), which, again, considerations invoked in the triangulation argument might be used to vindicate. As should become clear, however, contra Lepore and Ludwig, Davidson is not presupposing here "the primacy of the third person point of view" (Lepore and Ludwig 2005, 407). Neither, for that matter, is he presupposing the primacy of the second person point of view. Rather, what is being advocated is the interaction between two persons, where neither is primary. Too few commentators have acknowledged this, though see Stoutland 2006, 593, for an exception. Finally, it is interesting to note here that Davidson says he has held perceptual externalism

> for some thirty years . . . insisting that the contents of our earliest and most basic sentences ('Mama', 'Doggie', 'Red', 'Fire', 'Gavagai') must be determined by what it is in the world that causes us to hold them true. It is here, I have long claimed, that the ties between language and the world are established and that central constraints on meaning are fixed; and given the close connections between thought and language, analogous remarks go for the contents of the attitudes" (Davidson 1991a, 200).

Thus, for Davidson, content externalism does not emerge in the early 1980s, as Peter Pagin maintains in 2013, 235. This is yet another indication of the continuity of Davidson's thought. More on externalism in Chapter 3.

18. Thus the charge of verificationism, often raised against Davidson's early writings, is less founded than ever. See, e.g., Williamson 2004, 137, for the charge, and Pagin 2013, 229, for an answer.
19. See also Davidson 1991a, 202; 1991b, 212; 2001d, 142.
20. See also Davidson 2003, 693.
21. See also Davidson 1991a, 202.
22. I first made these objections in Verheggen 1997. Other versions have since been offered. See Lepore and Ludwig 2005, 408–11; Bridges 2006, 307; Ludwig 2011, 87–9.
23. See Wittgenstein 1958, §§28–30 and Verheggen 2006 for a comparison of Wittgenstein's and Davidson's views. Most commentators have missed or ignored the aspect problem. (Note that the only other philosopher I am aware of who has sharply distinguished between the distance problem and (a version of) the aspect problem is Peter Godfrey-Smith—see his 1989, 536.) Interestingly, Glüer mentions the aspect problem in her recent book on Davidson but then fails to address it. See Glüer 2013, 237ff.
24. See also Davidson 1991a, 203.
25. See Davidson 1999a, 128–30, for an explicit formulation of this claim.
26. I first argued for this interpretation in Verheggen 2007. Note that what the discussion of primitive triangulation brings to the fore, in addition to making explicit the problem faced by the perceptual externalist, is that the prospects of explaining meaning in non-intensional terms are rather dim, since non-intensional descriptions of connections between someone's utterances and features of her environment, no matter how regular these connections may seem, are not sufficient to describe the meanings of those utterances.
27. Here is a development in Davidson's thought. He used to motivate perceptual externalism by taking for granted the publicness of language and thoughts. Now, with the triangulation argument, the latter is also being vindicated. Glüer is right about this, but wrong, I think, about the shift from interpretability to actual interpretation being needed for meaning (Glüer 2011, 234). (Note that Glüer does not endorse the triangulation argument.)
28. Of course, if these items are already meaningful, there is no question of our having to take them one way or another; but there is then the question what constituted their meaning what they do in the first place. (Cf. Verheggen 2000.)

29. It might be granted that, if we think of internal determinants of meaning as things with which we associate terms, then the problem under scrutiny is inevitable. But what, it might be asked, if we think of them as dispositions? Dispositions are not the kind of things that we somehow apprehend. I believe, however, that dispositions are subject to a similar kind of problem—I shall argue for this in Chapter 2, where I examine the consequences of the triangulation argument for semantic normativity and reductionism.
30. See also Davidson 2001b, 13.
31. See, e.g., Lepore and Ludwig 2005, 396. More on them later.
32. See Talmage 1997, 143–4; Pagin 2001, 201; Lepore and Ludwig 2005, 408; Bridges 2006, 295; Glüer 2006, 1007; Ludwig 2011, 69; Bernecker 2013, 450. A notable exception is provided by Lasonen and Marvan 2004, 190–1.
33. Indeed, this is how Davidson first makes it clear that possession of a language and thoughts requires actual interpretation and not just interpretability. This is so, he argues, because having beliefs requires having the concept of belief, or "the contrast between truth and error" which "can emerge only in the context of interpretation" (Davidson 1975, 170). Note the early date. Note also that Davidson later points out that "That thought is a social phenomenon is stressed in [that 1975 article]", reinforcing the idea that there has been no change of mind on his part (Davidson 1992, fn 17). It is of course easier for commentators to maintain that Davidson started by claiming that interpretability, rather than actual interpretation, is essential to language possession, if they keep sharply separate the question of how meanings are fixed and the question whether the concept of objectivity is needed to have a language and thoughts.
34. See also Davidson 1995a, 9–10; 2001d, 141; 2003, 698.
35. Cf. Lasonen and Marvan 2004, 190–1.
36. See also Davidson 1991b, 209.
37. Bridges presents a similar kind of scenario in Bridges 2006, 294. This kind of scenario is well worn, as it has been presented numerous times in the debate around the question whether the later Wittgenstein advocates a social or an individualist picture of language and thought. See, for instance, McGinn 1984, 196–7, a scenario I borrow in Verheggen 1997, 366–7.
38. See also Davidson 1999a, 129; 1999d, 84.
39. Cf. Verheggen 1997, 368.
40. Note that the claim is not that, for every word that refers to some external object or event, speakers have to triangulate on the relevant object or event for the word's meaning to be fixed. More on this in Chapter 3.
41. Burge started developing his anti-individualist account of meaning and content in Burge 1979.
42. He himself, like most commentators, does not sharply distinguish between the two kinds of ambiguity that triangulation is meant to resolve. And, like most of them, he fails to connect the two tasks that triangulation is supposed to accomplish.
43. According to Burge, for higher animals and very young children to have beliefs, it is "enough that their perceptual beliefs incorporate perceptual representations into a system of predication and propositional inference" (Burge 2010, 283). (All beliefs have propositional content for Burge—see, e.g., Burge 2010, 277.) Actually, he does not always distinguish between perception and perceptual belief, as here: "Triangulation . . . is not needed to provide a non-arbitrary ground that fixes what perception and perceptual belief represent" (Burge 2010, 275). See also Burge 2003a, 687.
44. Davidson first made this point about the intensionality of the attribution of thoughts a long time ago, acknowledging, however, that this by itself does not "constitute an argument . . . against the attribution of thoughts to dumb creatures" (Davidson 1975, 164).

45. It might almost be said that these representational states of animals are a case of, as Rescorla would put it, intentional phenomena depending upon our theorizing about intentionality (see footnote 8).
46. As Fodor has recently put it, in his usual provocative way, "the sort of account of mental content that Burge offers provides no slightest clue of what the difference in mental content is between frogs who want to eat some flies for dinner and frogs that want to eat some ambient black dots for dinner" (Fodor 2015, 216–7).
47. There are also those who object to the claim that it is *linguistic* triangulation that is needed to fix the meanings of one's thoughts. Thus, Lepore and Ludwig ask "why the *more* that is required in addition to having the same innate similarity responses is *communication*" (Lepore and Ludwig 2005, 409). According to them, thought does not require language. Animals, at least those who engage in primitive triangulation, can think about the features of the world with which they interact. They can "recognize" that they are responding to the same features in similar ways. They can, in effect, have the concept of objectivity. However, Lepore and Ludwig do not explain how this is possible without engaging in linguistic triangulation.
48. In addition to those I discuss below, see Heil 1992, Child 1994, Glock 2003, Bridges 2006, Briscoe 2007 and Ludwig 2011.
49. See also Ludwig 2011, 78.
50. Davidson himself writes: "My version of externalism depends on what I think to be our actual practice" (Davidson 1991a, 199).
51. See Glüer and Pagin 2003; Andrews and Radenovic 2006. The objection that having beliefs does not require having the concept of belief has also been made by Burge 2003a and Glock 2003.
52. See Baron-Cohen, Leslie and Frith 1985.
53. That it demonstrates this has been called into question by Kristin Andrews. See Andrews 2012, Chapter 2.
54. See Andrews and Radenovic 2006, 671–3, as challengers of Davidson, and Bouma 2006, as his defender.
55. See Glüer and Pagin 2003 as challengers of higher-order theories of meaning, and Reboul 2006 as their defender.
56. This does not entail, however, that Swampman was a genuine speaker after all. Recall that Swampman was supposed to be a physical replica of Davidson, created out of a tree while Davidson, standing nearby, was destroyed by lightning. Swampman was supposed to act and talk exactly as Davidson used to. But Swampman, Davidson argued, did not think or mean anything by his utterances, for Swampman had never be in a context that would give his thoughts and utterances any meaning. (See Davidson 1987b, 19.) What should have become clear here is that the thought-experiment is really question-begging. We are to imagine a case where someone is in full possession of a language and thoughts without being given any clue of what might have put him in a position to possess them. It is in effect tantamount to being told to imagine someone who has a language and thoughts, and then asked whether that person has a language and thoughts. No wonder Davidson came repeatedly to disavow the thought-experiment. (See, e.g., Davidson 1999c, 192; Davidson 2006, 1061.)
57. As Anne Reboul complains, it is unclear what alternative account to higher-order theories of meaning and communication is being offered. (See Reboul 2006, 589.)
58. In Verheggen 2007, I suggested, tentatively, that room could be made for someone having a language without having the concept of objectivity in so far as the meanings of her utterances could be fixed by another person with whom she interacts and who has the concept of objectivity. I now think that this suggestion could not be made to work. I believe that, if the speaker herself cannot

       distinguish between correct and incorrect applications of her terms, we cannot really distinguish her from an automaton. It is what she thinks the distinction is, and so what she thinks her terms mean, that determines what they do mean. No one else can do this for her.
59. See also Davidson 1999a, 130.
60. See also Davidson 1999c, 84; 2001c, 293; 2003, 697. Davidson has long argued for this, starting in 1970. But, as I indicated earlier, and as should be clear by now, additional reasons can be found in the triangulation argument. Davidson has also repeatedly argued that the transition from the stage where there is no (as always, propositional) thought to the stage where there is thought cannot be explained. (See Davidson 1999a, 127.) See Brink 2004 and Bar-On and Priselac 2011 for attempts to bridge the gap.
61. See also Yalowitz 1999 and Glüer 2006.
62. Maria Lasonen and Tomas Marvan have argued in a similar vein that "the presence of the second person triggers some change in the first being . . . [which is] brought about when the second person applies these [existing similarity] standards in linguistic training by correcting the learner" (2004, 189). They think this shows that Davidson's account is in fact non-circular. I think, rather, that it again articulates a significant difference between the solitaire and the triangulator. But it is taking place in the intensional realm and so can still be deemed to yield a circular account.
63. For a related discussion, see Sinclair 2005.

2 From Triangulation to Semantic Normativity

1. Introductory Remarks

It is often thought that, if meaning is in some way essentially normative, then it cannot be explained in reductive naturalistic, i.e., non-semantic, terms. After all, the proponents of this thought remind us, one cannot derive an 'ought' from an 'is'. My main purpose in this chapter is to show that things are really the other way around: It is because meaning cannot be reduced to anything non-semantic that it is in some serious sense normative. In fact, as I shall argue, it follows from the triangulation argument that meaning is essentially normative in two distinct ways.

First, it is normative in the sense that, unless one has normative attitudes towards one's own and others' uses of words, that is, unless one distinguishes, on some occasions at least, between the correct and incorrect applications that one and others make of words, one cannot have a language and thoughts. This is a direct consequence of the first part of the triangulation argument, which establishes that meanings and the conditions of correct application that constitute them are not to be discovered in the world ready-made but are at least in part made by interacting speakers and thinkers.

Davidson himself never described this consequence as the claim that meaning is essentially normative. But I think that it should be so described, and that this should be recognized as a new kind of normativity—call it semantic attitudinal normativity. It is in fact closely connected to an idea recently developed by Hannah Ginsborg, according to whom meaning is essentially normative in what she calls a primitive way. She, too, thinks that certain normative attitudes are essential to meaning, but, in her view, these attitudes are not supposed to be semantic. Rather, they are supposed to be part of an explanation of meaning in non-semantic, though still intentional, terms. Thus Ginsborg's account of meaning is quasi-reductive. Addressing it will enable me to further clarify and defend the kind of non-reductionism Davidson is committed to.

The second sense in which meaning is essentially normative is also a consequence of the claim that meanings are in part a human product. In fact, it can be seen as a consequence of the previous way in which I take meaning to be essentially normative. The rough idea is this: If we, language-users, decide what the conditions of correct application of our words are, then it follows that the meanings of our words constrain us to use them in certain ways, on pain of not meaning anything by them. Put slightly differently, to say that meaning is normative in this sense is to say that statements about what we mean by our words[1] have normative implications about how we should use them. These implications might be either categorical, independent of our goals in using words, or hypothetical, dependent on those goals. Let us call this second sense of semantic normativity "meaning engendered normativity"[2]. This construal of semantic normativity is the one that has been most contested and most hotly debated in the past decade. Many philosophers have maintained that categorical implications are unintelligible and hypothetical ones are trivial. I shall argue that, even though only hypothetical normative implications follow from statements about meaning, these implications are far from trivial.

There is another sense in which meaning has been said to be essentially normative, which has been sharply contrasted with the previous one, and which used to be the subject of much dispute. Most generally and crudely put, this is the sense according to which there are norms that precede meaning rather than follow from it, hence the label of "meaning determining normativity".[3] More relevantly for our purposes, this is the sense according to which, for any individual living in a linguistic community, there are social linguistic norms that determine the meanings of that individual's words. That is, this is the sense according to which meaning is essentially conventional. Davidson has always been a fierce non-conventionalist, and this hostility is, I think, reinforced by the triangulation argument. I shall consider this kind of normativity in Chapter 3, where I focus on the specific kind of perceptual and social externalism that follows from the triangulation argument.

There is a sense in which meaning is normative that everyone agrees with, though, because it is trivial, some would rather not use the label 'normative' for it, lest it be confused with the stronger notions of normativity they disapprove of. This is the sense according to which, for expressions to have meaning, they must be subject to conditions of correct application. These conditions describe the semantic relations that obtain between words and features of extra-linguistic reality. For instance, if 'green' means green, then 'green' is applied correctly to all and only green things; if 'Toronto' means Toronto, then 'Toronto' is applied correctly to Toronto and only to Toronto. The problem of providing such conditions is what the first step of the triangulation argument makes evident and what the second step solves.

I shall start by saying a little more about the trivial normativity of meaning, contrasting the sense of 'correctness' that is involved here with others with which it is sometimes confused. Then I shall distinguish the kind of attitudinal normativity I think Davidson is defending, and the kind of non-reductionism associated with it, from Ginsborg's variety. And I shall argue that only full-blown, i.e., semantic, normative attitudes, and only full-blown non-reductionism, what Ginsborg calls austere non-reductionism, can account for the trivial normativity of meaning. In other words, it is only when normative semantic attitudes are present that expressions can be governed by conditions of correct application. And thus it is only if meaning is not reduced to something non-semantic that its trivial normativity can be accounted for, which is to say, that meaning can be accounted for at all! In the last part of the chapter, I shall show that, given how the trivial normativity of meaning is achieved, normative implications about our uses of words follow from statements about what we mean by them, normative implications which are, though hypothetical, intrinsic to meaning. In other words, I shall defend a version of meaning engendered normativity.

2. The Trivial Normativity of Meaning

The trivial normativity of meaning is simply the "familiar fact" (Boghossian 1989, 513) or "platitude" (Wright 1986, 256; Hattiangadi 2006, 222) that for words to have meaning they must have conditions of correct application. Though, for Davidson, these conditions are to be cashed out in truth-theoretical terms, they could also be cashed out in, say, assertion-theoretical terms; thus these conditions could tell us either what in the world words are true of or what they are warranted by. However exactly this condition on meaningfulness is conceived of, meeting it is, as Simon Blackburn puts it, "the fact that distinguishes the production of terms from mere noise, and turns utterance into assertion—into the making of judgment" (Blackburn 1984, 29). More broadly speaking, it is the fact that meaningful utterances have conditions of satisfaction. Hence it is the fact that, for utterances to be meaningful, there must be a distinction between saying something true and saying something false, between obeying an order and disobeying it, fulfilling a wish, answering a question, and failing to do so, etc. In short, it is the fact that, for utterances to be meaningful, their meanings must distinguish between those situations that satisfy the utterances and those that do not. An utterance that is satisfied no matter what is in fact an utterance without meaning (unless of course it is a logical truth). As Blackburn, again, puts it, "it is not seriously open to a philosopher to deny that, in this minimal sense, there is such a thing as correctness and incorrectness" (Blackburn 1984, 29). And so, I should add, it is not seriously open to a philosopher to provide an account of meaning that does not make room for its trivial normativity.

Straightforward though the sense of correctness involved in the trivial normativity of meaning may be, still I want further to distinguish it from other senses of correctness among which some philosophers have not always distinguished carefully enough, and which, contra the trivial sense, could not be simply assumed to be essential to meaning and so to have to be accounted for by an adequate theory of meaning.

First and foremost, the distinction embodied in the trivial normativity of meaning is to be sharply contrasted with the distinction according to which correct applications are applications that are in accord with communal or expert applications and incorrect applications are applications that deviate from communal or expert applications. That there is such a distinction is undeniable; it is the business of lexicographers, among others, to record instances of it. But whether this distinction is also essential to meaning, whether, that is, one could not use words meaningfully unless one spoke like others, is precisely one of the issues dividing philosophers, not only those who defend individualistic theories from those who defend social theories, but also those who advocate social theories that are communitarian from those who advocate social theories that are not. The issue may be put this way: For there to be a distinction (of the trivial sort) between correct and incorrect applications of words, must there be a community of people drawing this distinction in the same way? That is, as we might also put it, for there to be linguistic standards at all, must there be communal standards? Is meaning normative in this sense? As we shall see in more detail in the next chapter, the kind of social view that follows from the triangulation argument makes no appeal to communal standards. This is of a piece with Davidson's anti-conventionalism.

Second, some philosophers, in particular, commentators on Wittgenstein, sometimes talk of the distinction between "correct and incorrect ... continuations in linguistic usage" (Williams 2000, 304).[4] But again such a distinction cannot be simply assumed to be essential to meaning. It cannot be simply assumed that in order to speak meaningfully one must speak as one has spoken before, attaching, that is, the same meanings to the same words. As we shall see also in the next chapter, it follows from the triangulation argument that it is in fact not essential that one do so, at least not for all words at any given time.

Third, some philosophers[5] also talk of the distinction between correctness and incorrectness as that between using a word in accord and using it in conflict with its meaning, where this makes it possible to use a word incorrectly and yet say something true, as when someone uses 'vixen' to mean male cat while applying 'vixen' to a female fox, thereby inadvertently saying something true.[6] I am not sure, though, that this distinction is different from the ones I have mentioned so far—what could it mean to use a word in accord or in conflict with its meaning if this meaning is not to be thought of either as the standard, dictionary meaning of the word or as the meaning that the speaker assigned to the word on previous occasions? And, to repeat, it is far from obvious that attaching to one's words the same meanings as others do, or the same meanings as one did previously, is needed for one to speak meaningfully at all.

Finally, the distinction between correctness and incorrectness may be associated with the distinction between meaning something and thinking that one means something. Davidson thinks that this distinction is essential to meaning, and he accounts for it in terms of one's "intention to be taken to mean what one wants to be taken to mean". This intention, Davidson says, "constitutes a norm against which speakers and others can measure the success of verbal behavior" (Davidson 1994, 120). Thus one may think one means something but be mistaken about this in that one has not succeeded in making oneself understood as intended.[7] As Davidson points out, however, distinguishing between meaning something and merely thinking that one is by appeal to one's intention to be understood in a certain way "assumes the notion of meaning" (Davidson 1994, 120). It does not tell us what it is for an intention to have the content it has and so for an expression to mean what it does to begin with. The distinction that does shed light on meaning is the one embodied in its trivial normativity, and it is the only distinction, I think, that can be assumed pre-theoretically to be essential to meaning.[8] It turns out, however, that it is not a distinction for which it is easy to account.

3. From Trivial Normativity to Semantic Attitudinal Normativity

Wittgenstein was, I believe, the first philosopher to emphasize the trivial normativity of meaning and to argue relentlessly that traditional theories of meaning could not make room for it and therefore failed in their theoretical endeavor. This failure is, as I see it, what is expressed in the famous rule-following paradox, where Wittgenstein concludes that "no course of action could be determined by a rule, because every course of action can be made out to accord with the rule" (Wittgenstein 1958, §201). In terms of meaning, this reads: No application of a linguistic expression could be determined by the meaning of the expression, because every application of an expression can be made out to accord with its meaning. Wittgenstein continues: "The answer was: if everything can be made out to accord with the rule [or the meaning of the expression], then it can also be made out to conflict with it. And so there would be neither accord nor conflict here" (Wittgenstein 1958, §201), which is to say that there would be no rule or meaning after all, for if there is a rule there is such a thing as obeying it or not, just as if there is a meaningful expression, there is such a thing as applying it correctly or not. To talk of a rule that is obeyed no matter what, or of a meaningful expression that is applied correctly no matter what, is paradoxical. Such a rule is not a rule; such an expression is not meaningful. Theories of meaning that lead to this paradox are surely unacceptable. But they are plenty, according to Wittgenstein.

I have no intention of reviewing them here in any detail, but I wish to describe the gist of them and to stress the element that they all share and that is responsible for their failure; for it is the element shared by the individualistic versions of perceptual externalism that Davidson criticizes and which leads him to claim that only linguistically triangulating people can have a language and thoughts. Thus it is also the element that forces non-reductionism upon us.

Throughout the first two hundred sections of *Philosophical Investigations*, Wittgenstein considers several candidates for determinants of meaning and so for what might be appealed to in order to explain what provides expressions with conditions of correct application. He starts with familiar features of the world around us, such as tables, chairs, people and colors. He continues with essences or ideal samples of some of those things, such as the sample of green discussed in the previous chapter. He goes on to examine rules, which he compares to signposts, followed by mental pictures, such as that of a cube, and formulas grasped by the mind, such as the algebraic formula for the continuation of a series. He ends by considering the uses of expressions, where these uses are not to be conceived of as endowed with meaning. On the face of it, there is little that all these candidates have in common. But this should come as no surprise, for the problem they all encounter has nothing to do with the proposed entities per se—it had better not if you think, as Davidson does, that features of the world around us do play a role in the determination of meaning. Rather, the problem stems from our having to consider them in themselves, independently of how we regard them and how we use them in our linguistic practices, as if they could magically impose themselves on our words, thereby endowing them with meaning. The source of the problem is not, strictly speaking, entities of any of these kinds but a certain conception of how they are supposed to provide words with meaning. It is the claim that they could do this independently of how we apprehend or relate to them. But, until we apprehend them in a specific way, by thinking or talking about them, they are semantically inert.

Thus, to focus on a familiar feature of the world around us, say, the color sepia, Wittgenstein suggests that unless one already has a language one cannot establish a connection, e.g., by pointing, between the utterance of the word and the color, for the sheer pointing and utterance leave it indeterminate whether it is the color or, say, the material or the shape, of an object that one is talking about. Of course, if one is allowed to say that it is a color that one is talking about, then the indeterminacy problem disappears. But there is then the question what determines the meaning of that new word, 'color'. And if its meaning, too, is to be explained, at least in part, by means of other words, then there is the question of what determines their meaning.[9] So, there are really two problems here. On the one hand, there might be no principled way to pick out the relevant aspect of the thing one is talking about, in which case one is always free to pick out a feature of the thing that makes any application of the word with which it is connected correct, or incorrect, as the case may be, so that no conditions of correct application have been established. On the other hand, there might be a principled way to pick out the relevant aspect, a way which is presumably linguistic, but then we have a regress problem or the problem of accounting for the meanings of the words used in solving the indeterminacy problem. Thus, at bottom, there is no way that mere connections between words and external things can be what determine the conditions under which words are correctly applied and so what determine their meaning.

It might be protested here that, of course, one single utterance, perhaps accompanied by pointing, will not do to fix the feature of the world a word is connected to and so to fix its meaning. But surely several such acts will succeed in isolating the relevant feature—it will be the feature that all the "things" responded to have in common. What, however, will that be? Any "thing" responded to can have a great variety of features in common with others. Anything that has a shape has a size and has a color, just for starters.[10] Which is one to focus on? It will obviously not do to say it is the same as the feature that one focused on the previous time or the first time around, because no feature was isolated previously, let alone to begin with. It will not do either to say that it is the feature responded to simultaneously, or even repeatedly, by a group of people. The problem is the same as before, which is that it will remain just as ambiguous what that feature is. Needless to say, it will not do either to say that it is the feature one, or even more than one person, has in mind while responding, for to have it in mind requires precisely the ability that is in question here.

As I stated, the same problem affects the other candidates for determinants of meaning that Wittgenstein considers. As we saw before, a sample of green has to be taken as just that in order to determine the conditions of correct application of 'green'. Likewise, the picture of a cube has to be taken as just that in order to determine the conditions of correct application of 'cube'. The same is true of formulas, which, considered in and of themselves, can determine several applications, all of which could be taken to be correct depending on how the formula is interpreted. The same is true of past uses of these formulas, which are also compatible with several "correct" applications, depending on how the uses are construed. More generally, needless to say, the same is true of rules, whose meaning has to be fixed somehow before they can determine which applications are correct or not.[11] And, of course, for any of those candidate determinants of meaning, if an interpretation can be settled on, there is then the question what determines the conditions of correct application of the words used in that settlement. In short, the problem is a very general one, having to do with the kind of account of meaning traditional theorists considered by Wittgenstein wanted to give, according to which what determines the conditions governing the applications of words are extra-linguistic entities we somehow associate with them. But the very idea of meaning resting solely on the association of words with extra-linguistic entities is incoherent because we in fact need a language to be able to do what is alleged to provide us with one in the first place. We need something to do the associating, something that fixes what it is that we are connecting the word with, for any entity that we may think of, if it is not yet endowed with meaning, is open to various interpretations.

Consequently, mere connections of this kind cannot be what ultimately provides our words with conditions of correct application and hence with meaning. And so no reductionist account of meaning is forthcoming.[12]

The above remarks may strike some as utterly familiar and convincing. Not everyone, however, has recognized that the trivial normativity of meaning was the central issue Wittgenstein was addressing when he claimed, as I understand him, that traditional views of meaning are committed to the paradox.[13] More to the point, few, if any, have recognized that the problem Wittgenstein uncovers is similar to that developed by Davidson in the first step of the triangulation argument. Davidson himself did not express it in those terms. But doing so, I think, makes it more perspicuous what the problem is, and what kind of solution is called for. To repeat, the problem of providing conditions of correctness for the application of words is what the first step of the triangulation argument, as I have construed it, makes explicit. Davidson describes it as the problem of fixing the causes of one's utterances, but this amounts to the same claim. The difficulty in saying what the causes of the solitaire's utterances are, what causes are the same as others, is the difficulty in saying which responses to her environment are correct, and which are not. That is, it is the difficulty in saying which responses apply to the causes that fix their meaning to begin with. For the solitaire, or for a group of non-triangulating creatures for that matter, simply giving what appear to be regular responses to their environment does not fix the aspect of the environment they are responding to. There is no such fixing the first time the response is given, and no such fixing thereafter, since there is no way to tell in what respect the cause is the same the ensuing times as it was the first time around (Wittgenstein 1958, §201)— same as what?

As we saw in Chapter 1, Davidson solves the problem with the second step of the triangulation argument, by arguing that only those who have distinguished, at least on some occasions, between what is the case and what seems to them to be the case, and thus only those who have the concept of objectivity are in a position to have fixed the causes, and hence the meanings, of their utterances. To put it in the present terms, if the conditions of correctness that govern the applications of words cannot be fixed by mere connections between productions of sounds or inscriptions and extra-linguistic reality, then the producers of those sounds or inscriptions must have a say as to what conditions of correctness govern their applications. And this in turn requires that they be able to appreciate that there are such conditions. If so, there being trivial normativity, that is, meaningful expressions being subject to conditions of correct application, comes only with the appreciation of there being such conditions, that is, with the recognition, in effect, of the trivial normativity of meaning or with what I am calling semantic attitudinal normativity. It is because people have semantic normative attitudes towards the use of their, and others', words, attitudes they can have only if they have triangulated, that these words have conditions of correct application, and hence are meaningful. Note that the relation between these normative attitudes and expressions being meaningful is to be understood, not in the temporal sense that, once the attitudes are present, meaning can be, but in the conceptual sense that the two can be present only together. (As I noted early in the first chapter, the relation between having a language and thoughts and having the concept of objectivity is not temporal but conceptual.) That is, I think that conditions of correct application and hence meaning can be present only when the awareness of the semantic distinction between correct and incorrect applications is also present, which it can be only if it has been manifested. As we saw with the second step of the triangulation argument, people who triangulate linguistically with others are in a position to distinguish between correct and incorrect applications of their words, and to deem their applications, and others', to be correct, or incorrect, because they must sometimes acknowledge disagreements between them and negotiate the terms under which these can be resolved.

In short, then, the claim I have construed, on Davidson's behalf, as the claim that meaning determination requires possession of the concept of objectivity is equivalent to the claim that trivial normativity requires semantic attitudinal normativity. This requirement is a consequence of trivial normativity not being analyzable or conceivable in reductive, non-semantic terms. There are those, however, who believe that semantic attitudinal normativity is not constitutive of meaning, though another kind of attitudinal normativity is needed if we are to legitimize the judgments of correctness and incorrectness that we make about people's applications of their words. This is Ginsborg's primitive normativity which, she thinks, has to be added to a mere reductive dispositionalist account of meaning if we are both to make room for the normativity of meaning, that is, a certain kind of semantic normativity, and to account for meaning, in particular, for the semantic notions of correctness and incorrectness, in non-semantic terms (Ginsborg 2010, 1183; 2011a, 247). Furthermore, according to Ginsborg, primitive normativity is needed to explain how one first comes to grasp the meaning of an expression. This explanation, she maintains, is missing both in reductive dispositionalism and, more importantly for our purposes, in non-reductionism, for which the state of meaning is *sui generis*. As I said, examining her account will help me to further define and defend Davidson's non-reductionism. And it will allow me to consider a popular kind of candidate for determinants of meaning I have not discussed so far, namely, dispositions.[14]

4. Primitive Attitudinal Normativity

As just noted, there is a kind of *semantic* normativity that Ginsborg wants to make room for. Which is this? She does accept the claim that meaning is trivially normative—dispositions, she asserts, are what fix the conditions of correct application of our words. (More on this in due time.) But she rejects both the meaning determining and the meaning engendered kinds of semantic normativity. She also rejects the related idea, usually attributed to Kripke, according to which meaning is normative in the sense that, for someone to mean something by her words, there must be facts that guide or justify the applications of those words (Kripke 1982, 24).[15] As we shall see later, she thinks that this rejection allows her to claim that, though the internal entities considered by Wittgenstein cannot serve as determinants of meaning, dispositions, to some extent at least, are perfectly capable of fulfilling this task, since they are not supposed to yield any guidance or justification. The kind of semantic normativity, which, according to Ginsborg, is attached to meaning, is connected to its trivial normativity. If someone genuinely means something by an expression, then we are 'licensed' to apply the concepts of correctness or incorrectness to her behavior (Ginsborg 2011a, 243). As she writes: "The normative significance of [someone's] meaning [something by an expression] is limited to its making intelligible ascriptions of correctness or incorrectness to [her] uses" (Ginsborg 2011a, 246).[16] Thus, for Ginsborg, the kind of semantic normativity that is attached to meaning is of the attitudinal variety. However, contra what I have argued on Davidson's behalf, Ginsborg does not think that a speaker's semantic normative attitudes are constitutive of what she means by her words. These attitudes "are a necessary aspect of the meaningful use of language" (Ginsborg 2011b, 171), but they do not contribute to determining the conditions of correct application and hence the meanings of a speaker's words. They are legitimate, however, only if someone genuinely means something by her words, rather than merely producing sounds as a parrot or an automaton might. Moreover, for someone genuinely to mean something by her words, it is not enough that she has certain kinds of dispositions that have fixed the conditions of correctness of her words' applications. She must also display certain primitive normative attitudes towards the use of her words. Thus attitudinal semantic normativity depends on primitive normativity (on which more shortly), which is essential for Ginsborg's account of meaning not to be circular and to be indeed somewhat reductive. As she says:

> Since I am using the notion of primitive normativity to make sense of meaning and claiming, in turn, that we need to ascribe meaning in order to make sense of the uses of expressions counting as correct as opposed to incorrect, it is crucial that we be able to understand the notion of primitive normativity in a way which does not depend on the notions of correctness or error.
>
> (Ginsborg 2011a, 246–7)

She then proposes to modify the dispositional view in the following way:

> The meaningfulness of expressions on this account is constituted, as on the reductive view, by the fact that we are disposed to use them in

certain regular ways, but with the proviso that, in using them we take our uses to be appropriate in [a] primitive way.

(Ginsborg 2011b, 172)

And for someone to take her response to be 'primitively appropriate' is for that person to take her response to 'fit' the context of utterance, to see it as 'belonging' to a pattern of responses she has previously given, without, however, and this is crucially important, taking the response to be in accord with any meaning it expresses—there may not even be any such meaning for that person. Thus it is for a child who has become competent in sorting out green things to find her pointing to a green thing when her teacher says 'green', appropriate in light of her previous responses to 'green' queries. Or it is for someone to find saying '125', when queried about '67+58', appropriate in light of her previous uses of 'plus' (Ginsborg 2011a, 235).

These are the bare bones of Ginsborg's proposal and they should do for present purposes. One of its features needs to be stressed, however. This is that the thinking and understanding involved in the consciousness of appropriateness are in some sense intentional or contentful—as Ginsborg puts it, the agent thinks or understands that "*this* (what he is now doing) is appropriate to *that* (what he has just heard)." But they are not propositional—the agent can think or understand something with the above content prior to grasping the meaning of the sound he is responding to, indeed, even "prior to thinking of it as so much as meaningful" (Ginsborg 2011b, 171–2). Thus what distinguishes primitive normative attitudes from semantic normative attitudes is that the former are directed at uses of signs, sounds or inscriptions whose meaning, if any, is irrelevant to the attitudes, whereas the latter are directed at uses of signs that are understood in certain ways, i.e., that are meaningful. Ginsborg's account is therefore reductionist, since it explains meaning in non-semantic terms, though it is only partially reductionist, since it involves one intentional notion, that of appropriateness or appropriate fit.

My main question for Ginsborg is of course this: Does her account provide an explanation, in non-semantic terms, of how conditions of correct application are fixed or constituted? More basically, does it say what makes it possible for expressions to be governed by conditions of correct application in the first place? It might be thought that it does since, as I mentioned above, according to Ginsborg, these conditions are provided by dispositions to use words in certain ways. As she writes, "we can retain the idea that the particular meaning that a language-user attaches to an expression . . . is determined by how she is disposed to use the expression" (Ginsborg 2012, 138).[17] Aside from the intentional content involved in the consciousness of normativity, intentional contents (i.e., meanings) are constructed "out of the raw material of our nonintentionally characterized responsive dispositions" (Ginsborg 2011b, 172). At this basic dispositional level, there seems to be no difference between a person and a parrot, an intelligent being and an automaton. It is just that words can become genuinely meaningful, that is, they can be genuinely understood as meaning what they do, only if those using the words connect with their use a certain awareness of doing the appropriate thing. It is not the case, though, that the awareness fixes the meanings of the words—recall, the awareness is not even of something meaningful. The meanings were fixed to begin with, via the dispositions. The awareness is added to make sure that the dispositional uses are not merely automatic and to allow us eventually to make judgments of semantic correctness and incorrectness.

Leaving the details aside,[18] I think the main problem with Ginsborg's account, as with any reductive dispositionalist account, is that, contrary to what I just suggested on her behalf, it fails to give us an explanation of what makes it possible for expressions to be governed by conditions of correct application, for it does not tell us what makes it possible for specific dispositions to determine specific conditions of correct application. Dispositions are of course to be thought of as non-semantically characterized here. For instance, when explaining the meaning of 'green', we are to think of the disposition to apply 'green' to green things, and not of the disposition to use 'green' to mean green or say that something is green. But then Ginsborg does not tell us what it is for a non-semantically characterized disposition to determine the specific condition under which a word is applied correctly and so to determine its meaning. She does not tell us how the condition of correct application and hence the meaning of an expression can be specified in terms of a non-semantically characterized disposition. And so ultimately Ginsborg's account fails to give us an explanation of what makes it possible to mean something by an expression.

The problem with invoking non-semantically characterized dispositions as what determine or specify conditions of correct application and hence meanings is this. In and of themselves, dispositions to use signs in regular ways could be construed as dispositions of different kinds, because the regularities they exhibit could be of different kinds. And, if so, they could be seen as the expression of different meanings. The question then is, how are we to settle on regularities of one kind rather than another? Even granting Ginsborg that dispositions to use words in certain ways constitute, at least in part, what we mean by them, the question she does not address is what puts us in a position to have these dispositions in the first place, that is, what makes it the case that these dispositions, conceived of non-semantically, come to be seen as the expression of some meanings rather than others? The problem with invoking non-semantically characterized dispositions as determinants of meaning is in effect the same problem we have encountered with invoking features of the environment that cause us to respond in certain ways or, for that matter, with invoking Wittgenstein's mental pictures or formulas. If we think of the potential providers of conditions of correct application, and hence of meaning, as not themselves endowed with meaning, then there is always the possibility of their providing different conditions on different occasions, depending on how they are taken, or interpreted. But if they can always provide different conditions on different occasions, then they in fact cannot provide any conditions. If, from one occasion of use to the next, the alleged determinant of meaning can always be interpreted in such a way that the application is correct, or incorrect, as the case may be, then there are no conditions of correctness governing the applications of the expression.

Ginsborg seems to think that dispositions are immune to this problem because, as I mentioned at the outset, they are not supposed to be guiding or justifying the applications of our words. Dispositions are not like pictures or formulas occurring to the mind and telling us what to do. Now, that dispositions are in some respects different from pictures and formulas is undeniable, but I think it is also misleading. Pictures or formulas could after all be said to provide expressions with meaning without being thought of as providing guidance for their applications. Even so, there would still be the question of what makes it the case that a given picture or formula provides an expression with the meaning it does. This suggests that it is not the guiding aspect of the alleged meaning-constituting items that causes the problem. Rather, it is that it is unclear how these items manage to constitute the meanings that they are supposed to constitute. And, again, this is true of any item that is not already itself endowed with meaning. Thus, a fortiori, it is true of dispositions.[19]

I picked Ginsborg as a representative dispositionalist[20] in part because she supplements reductive dispositionalism with dispositions that are to be conceived of as intentional. In doing this she shares an important element of her account with Davidson's in that she takes speakers' contribution to their words meaning what they do as essential to their words being genuinely meaningful, and so to their having a language and thoughts. But I also picked Ginsborg because she tries to respond to someone whose non-reductionism is at least as fierce as Davidson's, namely, Barry Stroud. Ginsborg calls Stroud's brand of non-reductionism "austere", for he, like Davidson, takes meaning facts to be primitive.[21] Turning to Stroud's remarks will help me to nail down the point against reductive dispositionalism and to sharpen my defense of Davidson's non-reductionism.

5. Austere Non-Reductionism

According to Stroud, a reductionist account would be one that explains "the phenomena of meaning and understanding 'from outside' them, as it were, without attributing intentional attitudes or supposing that anything means anything or is understood in a certain way to those whose understanding is being accounted for" (Stroud 2000, viii). Stroud finds the prospects of such a reduction "hopeless": "We could never mean or understand or explain the meaning of something if we had to do so 'from outside' all recognition of what some things mean or what some people mean by them" (Stroud 2012, 24).

"[T]here will be no explanation of the idea of meaning in general solely in terms of regularities non-semantically or non-intentionally described" (Stroud 2000, ix). For instance, if we say that someone regularly applies a word only to things that are green, we are not specifying what the speaker means by the word. To do so, we must say that the speaker uses the word to mean green, or to assert of things that they are green (Stroud 2000, ix). Or if we say that someone regularly responds to 'plus' questions by uttering a numeral that denotes the sum, we are not specifying what the speaker means by 'plus'. To do so, we must say that the speaker uses 'plus' to mean plus. Thus, to describe what someone means by her words, we must describe how she uses her words to say, or assert, or order, etc., things, and not how she uses them to do something non-linguistic, such as getting a green object or calculating.

Ginsborg cannot find any reason to support Stroud's commitment to non-reductionism, especially since he, too, has given up the idea that the determinants of meaning should provide guidance and justification for the ways we use our words. For Ginsborg, this would be a reason to endorse non-reductionism, for, if we were to think of the extra-linguistic determinants of meaning in this way, we would inevitably encounter the interpretation problems I discussed earlier. But she thinks it would be the only reason to endorse non-reductionism. As we have seen, she thinks that once we have abandoned the idea of guidance, we are free to appeal to dispositions as providers of meaning. According to Ginsborg, Stroud fails to realize this because he fails

> to distinguish clearly between two different ideas: the idea that we cannot characterize the meaning of an expression without using that expression or some other expression with the same meaning, and the idea that we cannot characterize the meaning of an expression without using semantical expressions like 'means', 'orders', 'says that' and so on . . . Nothing prevents the dispositionalist from drawing on the notion of addition in characterizing the disposition in which someone's meaning addition by 'plus' is supposed to consist. She can say, for example, that the person's meaning addition by 'plus' consists in her being disposed to give the sum in response to 'plus' questions.
>
> (Ginsborg 2011b, 163)

To characterize meaning in this latter dispositionalist way is indeed not to characterize it altogether from outside language, since expressions that are meant and understood are being used to characterize their meaning or that of other expressions. But it is to characterize meaning from outside language in a "reasonable" sense of 'from outside language', where 'from outside language' means from outside a semantic context. On the other hand, according to the "stronger" sense of 'from outside language', meaning is to be explained without drawing on any concepts or linguistic expressions.

And this, Ginsborg agrees with Stroud, cannot be done. I do not think, however, that Stroud confuses the two senses of 'from outside language', though he sometimes writes as if he did. I think he does this precisely because, according to him, a characterization of meaning that is from outside language even in the reasonable sense, that is, one that merely uses expressions to characterize their meaning, or other expressions' meaning, is inadequate.

Interestingly, the dispute between Ginsborg and Stroud is reminiscent of the dispute Michael Dummett and John McDowell were having, starting in the seventies, as to whether a theory of meaning could be full-blooded or merely modest. The dispute was in fact initially between Davidson and Dummett, with McDowell on Davidson's side.[22] Like Davidson, Dummett thought that the best way to approach philosophical problems about meaning was by asking what form a theory of meaning for a speaker or a community should take, where 'theory of meaning' is to be understood in the technical sense, as a theory, that is, that would enable us to understand any of the speaker's or the community's utterances. The construction of such a theory—an empirical theory—would help us to reach a philosophical understanding of the nature of meaning. (Let us call the empirical theory a semantic theory and the philosophical theory based upon it a meta-semantic theory.) As Dummett put it, we would "arrive at a solution of the problems concerning meaning by which philosophers are perplexed" (Dummett 1975, 96). As Davidson put it, we would answer the question what it is for words to mean what they do "in a philosophically instructive way" (Davidson 1984a, xv). To put it in the present terms, the question of whether the notion of linguistic meaning could be elucidated without any appeal to semantic notions should be answered by asking whether we could specify—describe or characterize—the meanings of someone's utterances from outside semantic contexts. This is connected to the issue between Dummett and Davidson that is most relevant to our purposes. The issue was whether we could construct a full-blooded theory, that is, a theory that would "explain the concepts expressed by primitive terms of the language", or simply a modest theory, that is, one that would "give the interpretation of the language to someone who already has the concepts required" (Dummett 1975, 102). Davidson advocated the latter, hence, I believe, his early non-reductionist stance, which is not surprising as the modesty of the semantic theory goes together with the austerity of the meta-semantic theory.

As I have indeed suggested several times, Davidson's reasons for maintaining modesty and austerity were, I believe, already present when he was considering only one kind of triangulation, viz., radical interpretation, the interpretation from scratch of an unknown language. But they became more apparent with the triangulation argument. When considering radical interpretation, the focus and initial interest are obviously on the semantic theory. One is trying to figure out how any of a speaker's utterances could be understood and so how to specify the meanings of the speaker's primitive expressions, since eventually it is because we understand how the primitive expressions contribute to the meanings of complex ones that we are in a position to understand any of the speaker's utterances. Thus, for Davidson, we eventually specify the meanings of primitive expressions by means of the axioms of the theory of truth we have built for a speaker, which tell us how each primitive expression of the speaker's language contributes to the truth-conditions of the speaker's utterances. As I pointed out in the first chapter, though the axioms may be described as extensional, insofar as they pick out, in the first instance, features of the speaker's environment, still the characterizations of meaning they provide are intensional, insofar as the truth-conditions to which the primitive expressions contribute are to be meaning-giving. Thus, to recall my example, if we are to make sense of someone's saying that he just found out that Hesperus is identical with Phosphorus, we will make sure that the axiom for 'Hesperus' says that this name designates Hesperus, and not Phosphorus. This, I take it, is already a way of saying that characterizations of the meaning of expressions cannot be from outside language at all, not even in the reasonable sense. Considering triangulation more generally takes us a step further or, it might be said, a level higher, as Davidson's focus is now on the meta-semantic theory. Perceptual externalism, the claim that the typical causes of people's basic verbal responses to their environment are what determine the meanings of these responses, can be seen as a philosophical consequence of, or at least a claim that is reinforced by, reflecting on radical interpretation. While focusing on radical interpretation Davidson did not ask how those typical causes are isolated to begin with. It took the triangulation argument to ask that question, the answer to which makes it all the more perspicuous that meaning cannot be accounted for in a reductive way; for it is not just that the radical interpreter cannot specify the meanings of the language of her interpretee outside of semantic contexts—she cannot say how the speaker's primitive expressions contribute to the truth-conditions of the speaker's utterances without saying, in effect, what it is that they mean. When considering triangulators, we also cannot say outside of semantic contexts how the causes, and hence the meanings, of their utterances are fixed. Thus neither a semantic theory nor a meta-semantic theory can be provided without appealing to semantic notions.[23]

To return to Ginsborg's dispositionalism, Ginsborg acknowledges the similarity between the dispute she is having with Stroud and that which Dummett had with McDowell. And she maintains that she is advocating a full-blooded theory when this is properly understood, that is, when this is understood as a theory that describes the meanings of someone's words not from outside language in the stronger sense in which this cannot be done, contra what Dummett seemed to hope initially, but from outside language in the reasonable sense in which he thinks this can be done, that is, from outside semantic contexts. Thus, having conceded that a characterization of meaning in the stronger sense of 'from outside language' could not be obtained, Dummett describes what it is to grasp the concept square (and so the meaning of 'square') saying that it is "to be able to discriminate between things that are square and those that are not" for example by "apply[ing] the word 'square' to square things and not to others" (Dummett 1993, 98). [As] McDowell points out, this sketch "does not hesitate to employ the concept *square*" so could not serve to explain the concept square to someone who did not already have it. But it still counts as a characterization of meaning 'as from the outside' because "it uses the word 'square' in first intention—that is, never inside a content-specifying 'that'-clause" (McDowell 1987, 91; Ginsborg 2011b, 164).

Now, McDowell argued against Dummett that such descriptions could not be meaning-giving, basically for the kinds of reason I have advanced so far. Non-semantically described applications of any given word do not specify what the word means because they do not provide the word's conditions of correct application. Why does Ginsborg not acknowledge this?

Perhaps she conceives of her task in a way different from Dummett's. In Dummett's discussion, we are to describe what it is for a speaker to have the concepts she has on the basis of her applications, which can only be finite and hence compatible with various interpretations. Ginsborg grants that

> [F]acts of meaning cannot be reduced to nonintentionally characterized facts about how a term has been used in the past, since no finite list of its (nonintentionally characterized) uses can determine on its own what the term was being used to mean. But it does not obviously follow that there are no nonintentionally characterized facts to which meaning facts can be reduced. In particular, it does not follow that we could not reduce the fact that someone means addition by 'plus' to the fact that she is disposed to respond to 'plus' questions by giving the sum.
> (Ginsborg 2011b, 155)

We characterize meaning by means of dispositional uses and not just on the basis of past uses. And Ginsborg seems to think that dispositions, contrary to past uses, are not compatible with different interpretations and thus can be used to characterize the meanings of words. But it is far from obvious that non-semantically characterized dispositions are not compatible with different interpretations. Indeed, as I have argued, I believe that this is false. I believe that Ginsborg is reading too much into the distinction between past uses and dispositions. Just what does she take the relevant distinction to be?

On the one hand, when we think of past uses, we think of a limited set of uses. As a result, as Kripke argued, someone's past uses of 'plus' may be compatible with her meaning quaddition, just as much as with her meaning addition, by 'plus'.[24] On the other hand, if we describe the meaning of 'plus' in dispositional terms, it might look as if alternative interpretations are precluded. As Ginsborg says, someone's meaning addition by 'plus' can be reduced to her being disposed to respond to 'plus' questions by giving the sum. Thus, one relevant distinction might be that, if we think of dispositions, we think of all the possible ways in which a speaker may use a word, possible not just in the sense of being the same as previous ones but merely future or potential, but possible also in the sense of being different from the ways in which the word was used previously. Now, to take Ginsborg's other example, which may be more perspicuous, we do not think that characterizing the meaning of 'green' by appealing to past uses of 'green', e.g., to the effect that the speaker has so far applied 'green' to green things, would be adequate. But neither, it seems to me, would the dispositional characterization. To be sure, if we think of dispositions, we do not think of a limited set of uses, such as all past uses. But the point can be taken further than Ginsborg seems to realize, for we also do not think only of all ostensive uses. For instance, we do not think that to mean green by 'green' is to be disposed to apply 'green' only in the presence of green things. Indeed, we do not think that it is to be disposed to apply 'green' only in the circumstances in which it is correct to apply 'green'. Rather, we think that it is to be disposed to apply 'green' only in the circumstances in which one means green by 'green'. How else are we to describe the disposition so as to capture all possible cases and exclude all other possible interpretations? But this way of describing the disposition is no longer non-semantic. And this leads us back to my question, how do dispositions, non-semantically characterized, come to be seen as expressing specific meanings?[25]

In sum, I do not think that Ginsborg has succeeded in giving an account of meaning, in particular of the semantic notions of correctness and incorrectness, in non-semantic terms. Dispositions are no exception to the first step of the triangulation argument, which establishes why the question of how conditions of correct application get to be fixed and how meanings can be specified cannot be answered within the non-semantic realm. As a result, I also do not think that Ginsborg has succeeded in explaining how one first comes to grasp the meaning of an expression. She herself thinks she can do this because she thinks that an account of meaning from outside language in the reasonably full-blooded sense of 'from outside language' can be given. Such an account would enable us to explain a speaker's first grasp of the meaning of an expression, or acquisition of the concept corresponding to an expression, "by explaining how [her] uses of the expression came to stand in [certain] nonintentionally characterized relations [to other expressions or to extralinguistic reality]" (2011b, 165). However, if I am right, explaining this is precisely what cannot amount to explaining grasp of meaning. Grasp of meaning, the exact path from the non-semantic realm to the semantic one, is precisely what cannot be explained if austere non-reductionism is right. But this does not entail that nothing constructive can be said about what is needed to have a language and thoughts. What is needed, in particular, is the presence of semantic normative attitudes towards one's own, and others', uses of words. These are what make it possible for words to be governed by conditions of correct application. Thus only those who display those attitudes can produce meaningful utterances.

As I said at the outset, semantic attitudinal normativity is not the only kind of semantic normativity that the triangulation argument establishes. What also follows from the argument, in particular, from the claim that trivial normativity requires semantic attitudinal normativity, is that meaning is normative in the meaning engendered sense.

6. Meaning Engendered Normativity

The meaning engendered normativity that follows from the triangulation argument is hypothetical. According to it, statements about the meanings of words, describing the conditions under which they are correctly applied, have hypothetical implications about how to use those words.[26] Thus, if I want to tell the truth, I should apply 'green' only to green objects (provided I mean green by 'green', of course). I believe that, though only hypothetical, this kind of normativity is essential to meaning in a way that it is not essential to other things that may also have hypothetical implications. I believe it is essential because, since speakers importantly contribute to what the conditions of correct application of their words are, it follows that they are constrained to use them in the ways dictated by these conditions, albeit contingently on their desires; for, if these implications were not constraining, then the statements about meaning from which they flow would not in fact describe the conditions under which someone's words are correctly applied. Let me explain.[27]

Some non-normativists (i.e., those who deny that meaning is normative in any other than the trivial sense) compare hypothetical obligations implied by statements about the meaning of words with other means/end prescriptive statements such as, "If I want to stay dry, I ought to go outside only if it is not raining". They argue that facts about the weather dictate how I should behave, given my desires, but this does not make these facts normative.[28] This is indeed a complaint non-normativists commonly make about hypothetical normativity: It is uninteresting, for "every fact is normative in that sense" (Boghossian 2005, 207). Similarly to the weather case, my obligation to use my words in certain ways, since it, too, is contingent on my desires, does not make meaning genuinely normative, or so the non-normativists argue. But I believe that there is a significant disanalogy between hypothetical prescriptions involving the weather and those involving meaning. So what does the disanalogy consist in?

To begin with, the weather is not constituted by any conditions of correct application that dictate people's behavior, contingent on their desires. Meaningful expressions are so constituted. However, though conditions of correct application are constitutive of meaning, they do not in themselves dictate, for any particular application of an expression, what it should be like, independently of the speaker's purpose in using it. They only imply which applications will be correct and which incorrect. Thus, so far the disanalogy does not indicate that meaning is normative in a sense other than the trivial one. But there is more to the disanalogy. Facts about the weather do not always dictate how I should behave, say, when planning to go out; they may become irrelevant, as in the case where I no longer care about staying dry. But facts about linguistic expressions, i.e., their conditions of correct application, always dictate how I should behave when intending to produce a meaningful utterance. Indeed, they dictate my linguistic behavior regardless of what my specific desire is, that is, not altogether independently of my desire, but regardless of whether my desire calls for a correct application or for an incorrect one. Thus, depending on my desires, I should apply expressions in certain ways, correctly or not, and this is obviously dependent on what their conditions of correct application are to begin with. For instance, if I want to encourage you to come to Toronto, I might tell you that it is sunny in Toronto, even though it is raining, that is, I might misapply my words—make a false statement. But I cannot make a false statement any more that I can make a true statement if I do not pay attention to what the conditions of correct application of the words I use in the statement are. Again, whether my desire calls for a correct or an incorrect application of my words, their conditions of correct application are relevant.

This observation brings out the following disanalogy between statements about meaning and statements about the weather. Statements about the meaning of words always imply hypothetical prescriptions that, unlike those implied by statements about the weather, speakers *must* take into account. And this reveals how hypothetical normativity is essential to meaning but not essential to just any fact, natural or not. For, if none of the hypothetical prescriptions that flow from statements about the meaning of my words has application to me, then I do not mean by them what the statements say they mean; the statements become false. On the other hand, if none of the hypothetical prescriptions that flow from statements about the weather conditions have application to me, this in no way affects the truth-value of those statements. The weather conditions do not change; they just become irrelevant. In other words, my meaning rain by 'rain' always gives me reason to use (commits me to using) the expression in certain ways, though the particular ways depend on the particular desires I have. I do not have the option to be indifferent to the fact that I mean rain by 'rain'. But I may be indifferent to the fact that it is raining. Its raining does not always give me reason to behave in certain ways (when going out); whether it does or not depends on the desires I have.

Against this, Kathrin Glüer and Åsa Wikforss have recently wondered "whether the cases ultimately really are disanalogous: Just as one might not care whether one gets wet or stays dry, it might seem, one might just not care whether what one says is semantically correct or not—do correctness conditions really dictate anything if all I want to do is say something meaningful?" (Glüer and Wikforss 2015, 11). I find this comment baffling. If I want to say something meaningful, I have to pay attention precisely to the correctness conditions that govern the application of my words, for they are what constitute what I mean by them. If I do not use my words in accordance with these conditions, I do not mean what the meaning statements about my words say they mean. Of course, I may not care if any particular utterance of mine turns out to be correct or not, as when I say that the sun is shining in Toronto, not having checked whether it is or not, but hoping to encourage my friend to come and visit me. But if I want to mean that the sun is shining and be understood by my friend as meaning that, that utterance must be dictated by the correctness conditions governing the applications of its words. I might not care whether the utterance is true, but I do care whether my friend takes it as true. In other words, the correctness conditions still dictate what I must say if I want to be understood as saying something semantically correct. Thus, even though I may not care whether they are met or not, I still intend to be understood as having met them or not, as the case may be.

In short, normative implications, albeit hypothetical, about how to use words are essential to meaning; they indeed follow from expressions having conditions of correct application. But I believe that they so follow because, as demonstrated by the triangulation argument, speakers contribute to these conditions. I do not think they would follow if trivial normativity did not require semantic attitudinal normativity. This point, however, needs a little elaboration.

It might indeed be thought that the claim that the conditions of correctness governing the application of their words should constrain people to use them in certain ways, whether correctly or not depending of course on their desires, just follows from their words being governed by such conditions, and not from those conditions being constituted in a certain way. That is, it might be thought that meaning engendered normativity, of the hypothetical variety, simply follows from trivial normativity. After all, as I just noted, regardless of how my words got to have the conditions of correct application they do have, I should be mindful of them if I want to achieve the goal I have set for myself by speaking. Suppose then that I had no say in what conditions of correctness govern the application of my words. Suppose, to take a popular view, that I inherited them, so to speak, from the community in which I grew up and learned my first language. If so, it looks as if my being indifferent or oblivious to what those conditions are will not falsify statements about what they are. Thus suppose I say, sincerely, "I have arthritis in my thigh". According to this view, I have said something false; I have applied 'arthritis' incorrectly. I did not apply my word in the way dictated by the conditions of correctness that govern its application. But that did not change what I mean by 'arthritis'. Glüer and Wikforss might indeed say that this shows that conditions of correct application do not dictate anything. (Notably, though, the speaker who produced the utterance sincerely intended her utterance to be semantically correct, which indicates that there may be other problems with this view—more on this in the next chapter.) But suppose we hold the view that follows from the triangulation argument, according to which speakers contribute in an essential way to the conditions of correctness that govern the application of their words. Then, in my language, the extension of 'arthritis' may include muscles. If so, I may have said something correct when I said, "I have arthritis in my thigh". Given what I mean by 'arthritis', and that I wanted to tell the truth, this is how I had to speak. This does not entail that I can never make a mistake unintentionally. I could say, "My uncle has arthritis in his thigh", and be wrong (meaning what I do by 'arthritis'). But note again that I intended to tell the truth and thus used my words in the way dictated by their conditions of correct application. One way or another, it looks as if, if I contribute to these conditions, I simply cannot be indifferent to what they are.

7. Conclusion

I have argued that the triangulation argument entails that meaning is normative in two important senses, over and above its being trivially normative. It is normative in a semantic attitudinal sense and in a hypothetical meaning engendered sense. Its being normative in the first sense is what makes its trivial normativity possible and what entails its being normative in the second sense. These claims are of a piece with Davidson's thoroughly austere non-reductionism, which further shows that it is possible to be a non-reductionist without being a total quietist, contrary to what many opponents of non-reductionism, and even some non-reductionists themselves, have thought. What needs to be investigated next is the meaning determining kind of semantic normativity. I already announced that the triangulation argument rules it out. But this needs to be fleshed out in the context of examining the exact kind of externalism the argument leads to, both on its perceptual side and on its social side. Davidson's semantic externalism is the topic of the next chapter.

Notes

1. As before, what is true of words and utterances of sentences is true of the concepts and thoughts they express. But here I shall usually talk only of language.
2. Following Glüer and Wikforss 2009.
3. Following again Glüer and Wikforss 2009.
4. See also, e.g., McGinn 1984, who talks of using a word in the same way as in the past.
5. See again McGinn 1984, who talks of using the "right" word, Millar 2004 and Glock 2005.
6. The example is to be found in Whiting 2013, 8.
7. See also Davidson 1992, 117. Note that, in trying to account for the distinction between thinking that one means something and actually meaning it, Davidson takes himself to be following Wittgenstein. But it is not obvious that this is the distinction Wittgenstein has in mind when he distinguishes between thinking one is obeying a rule and actually obeying it (Wittgenstein 1958, §202). It is

more likely that, by thinking one is obeying a rule (and failing to do so), he has in mind misapplying a rule or a word, as when I say of something blue that it is green, meaning green by 'green'; for Wittgenstein has precisely been trying to show that certain theories of meaning are unable to account for the trivial normativity of meaning. The question both he and Davidson are at bottom interested in is of course what will make it the case that one does mean something by one's words, what will provide one's words their conditions of correct application? And the partial answer for Davidson, as before, but expressed slightly differently in this context, is one's speaking in such a way that one is understood by another person. It is not, as Saul Kripke and the communitarians suggest on Wittgenstein's behalf, one speaking in the same way, that is, applying one's words in the same way, as others. More on this in the next chapter.

8. As just suggested, this is also acknowledged and discussed by Davidson, though he does not always sharply distinguish the "trivial" distinction from the previous one, and indeed sometimes talks of the previous one as embodying the only "norm" that is essential to meaning. This has led some commentators, e.g., Kusch 2006 and Hattiangadi 2007, also not to distinguish clearly between the trivial sense of correctness and the "intention" sense.
9. See Wittgenstein's discussion of ostensive definition in Wittgenstein 1958, §§28–30.
10. Cf. Stroud 2003, 672.
11. Kripke (1982) is of course the one who brought the interpretation problems to the fore, initially asking a speaker who had not computed any number larger than 57 whether she could point to any fact, in her past or present mental life or behavior, that would justify her answering "125" rather than "5" when queried about "57+68". Is there any fact that constitutes her meaning plus rather than quus by 'plus', when 'quus' means plus for additions involving numbers smaller than 57, and otherwise yields 5? Kripke argues that no such fact is to be found, essentially, I think, for the reasons I have given, and so I also think that, when Kripke says that all the facts he considered are inadequate because they do not make room for the normativity of meaning, what he has in mind first and foremost is trivial normativity. (Note that the conclusion is supposed to apply to all expressions of a language and not just mathematical ones. Interestingly, though, features of the external world were not included among the candidate facts for determinants of meaning that Kripke discusses. More on this in Chapter 3.)
12. How about associating words with *semantic* entities, i.e., meanings or Fregean senses? Kripke does consider these and concludes they are subject to the same problem; for, even if they themselves need no interpretation, they must somehow be grasped by the mind, and the question is "how any mental entity or idea can constitute 'grasping' any particular sense rather than another" (Kripke 1982, 54). In his admirable interpretation of Kripke's book, George Wilson describes the problem as that of saying which among the many meanings or "interpretations" that are available determines the conditions of correct application of any given word. (See Wilson 1994; 1998. I have discussed Wilson's interpretation in Verheggen 2003. For a defense of the Platonist idea against Kripke, see Zalabardo 2003.)
13. There are numerous exceptions, that is, many philosophers recognizing that trivial normativity was the central issue, though they are otherwise different in their philosophical outlook and their interpretation of Wittgenstein. See Blackburn 1984; McDowell 1984; Millikan 1984; Luntley 1991; Thornton 1998, among others.
14. The discussion of Ginsborg's views in Sections 4 and 5 is based on Verheggen 2015.

15. Ginsborg, following Kripke, uses 'guiding' and 'justifying' interchangeably, but there are reasons to distinguish between them. See, e.g., Bridges 2014.
16. See also Ginsborg 2011a, 243.
17. See also Ginsborg 2011b, 155.
18. To mention a few other problems that I shall not further elaborate on here, it is not clear how we are to think of the non-semantic understanding that constitutes the awareness of appropriateness. Also, it is not clear how we go from awareness of non-semantic appropriateness to understanding of semantic correctness. For further critical discussion of Ginsborg's view, see Haddock 2012.
19. Contra Ginsborg herself, it might be thought that Ginsborg's appeal to the idea of appropriateness is precisely what enables our dispositions to be the expression of specific meanings. It is our finding our uses of words appropriate that fixes their meaning. After all, we do not find just any uses whatsoever to be appropriate. I think, however, that the same kind of problem recurs here. According to Ginsborg, we do not find our uses to be appropriate on the basis of their propositional content—they have none, at least none that we need to recognize. But then how can they become propositionally contentful? Indeed all past, present, future and potential uses of a word, when these uses are non-semantically described, that is, described without saying what semantic content they are supposed to express, are compatible with their being the expression of different contents. Qua uses, it is indeterminate what content they have. Thus, our finding them appropriate could be based on more than one aspect of the use. Which is it going to be?
20. For further discussion of reductive dispositionalism, see Goldfarb 1985; Ginet 1992; Zalabardo 1997; Horwich 1998, among others.
21. Unlike Davidson, he takes this to entail quietism. More on this in the next chapter.
22. For further discussion of this dispute, see Stroud forthcoming.
23. Needless to say, the previous paragraph further indicates why I take triangulation to be continuous with radical interpretation. More on this in the next chapter.
24. See footnote 9 for an explanation of 'quaddition'.
25. I said that the example of 'green' might make it more perspicuous why the distinction between past uses and dispositions lacks the significance Ginsborg finds in it. It may be that, in the case of 'plus', uses that differ from that described in the dispositional characterization are hard to imagine. I am not sure that is true. But if it were, this would obviously not entail that the meaning of all words can be characterized in terms of non-semantically described dispositions.
26. I have argued against the categorical version of meaning engendered normativity in Verheggen 2011b.
27. The next three paragraphs are taken almost verbatim from Verheggen 2011b.
28. See Wikforss 2001, 205; Kusch 2006, 61.

3 From Triangulation to Semantic Externalism

1. Introductory Remarks

Semantic externalism, broadly understood, is the view that the meanings of thoughts and utterances are determined, at least in part, by factors that are external to thinkers and speakers. Physical externalism maintains that these factors have somehow to do with the physical features of the world surrounding thinkers and speakers. Social externalism maintains that these factors have somehow to do with thinkers' and speakers' relations to others. According to Davidson's brand of physical externalism, which he calls perceptual, what determine, at least in part, the meanings of our basic thoughts and utterances are their typical causes, the features of our environment that we are able to perceive and that typically cause us to have those thoughts or make those utterances. According to his brand of social externalism, which I call interpersonal, what determine, at least in part, the meanings of our thoughts and utterances are our triangular interactions with other people. As we shall see, Davidson's version of each type of externalism is significantly different from other versions. Triangulation, he writes, "corrects and augments both a version of perceptual externalism and a version of social externalism" (Davidson 2001a, xvii). But the most significant difference is that, for Davidson, physical externalism can be secured only through social externalism; for, as we saw in Chapter 1, with the second step of the triangulation argument, it is through triangular interactions that the causes of our basic thoughts and utterances get fixed.[1]

This chapter will proceed as follows: I shall start by tracing Davidson's perceptual externalism back to its origins in his writings about radical interpretation. I shall argue that there is no significant break between the perceptual externalism connected with radical interpretation and that connected with triangulation. Davidson's perceptual externalism is, and always has been, historical and holistic. It is historical in that "the contents of our thoughts and sayings are partly determined by the history of causal interactions with the environment" (Davidson 1991a, 200). It is holistic in that no thoughts or sayings have their meaning determined in isolation from others. I shall then contrast the kind of perceptual externalism that follows from triangulation with one of the more orthodox versions of physical externalism, namely, Hilary Putnam's, whose central idea is that the meanings of natural kind words are determined, at least in part, by the fundamental nature of their extension. I shall argue that triangulation does not privilege any specific aspects of the extension of our words as the causes determining their meaning. Next I shall contrast Davidson's interpersonal externalism with communitarian versions of social externalism, in particular, two versions inspired by Wittgenstein, namely, Saul Kripke's and Meredith Williams's. Both have argued, each in his or her own way, that for trivial normativity to obtain, that is, for meaningful expressions to be subject to conditions of correct application, a social setting is required such that one needs, by and large, to speak like others, that is, to mean the same thing as others do by the same words, in order to have a language and thoughts. They have defended, in effect, a version of meaning determining normativity. I shall argue that Davidson is right in maintaining that all one needs to do is speak with others, that is, be understood by others as meaning what one does by one's words. The triangulation argument further supports Davidson's anti-conventionalism. Finally, I shall argue that the triangulation argument provides us with a way to address the skeptical paradox about rule-following developed by Kripke's Wittgenstein that is different both from Kripke's skeptical solution and from the kind of straight solution sought by the skeptic.

2. Perceptual Externalism and Radical Interpretation

I have so far confined to footnotes my comments on what I take to be the continuity of Davidson's views from radical interpretation to triangulation. But here I should like them to be center stage for a moment, for perceptual externalism has always been a major component of Davidson's views on language and thought. In fact, as we shall see, there is more to be learned concerning Davidson's perceptual externalism by considering his remarks about radical interpretation than by considering those about triangulation. As I noted in Chapter 1, Davidson claims to have advocated perceptual externalism "for some thirty years ... insisting that the contents of our earliest learned and most basic sentences ('Mama', 'Doggie', 'Red', 'Fire', 'Gavagai') must be determined by what it is in the world that causes us to hold them true" (Davidson 1999a, 200). He also explicitly connects perceptual externalism with radical interpretation: "Externalism makes clear how one person can come to know what someone else thinks, at least at the ground level, for by discovering what normally causes someone's beliefs, an interpreter has made an essential step toward determining the content of those beliefs" (Davidson 1989b, 195). Some commentators have thought, however, that there is at least a tension between Davidson's early externalist views, connected with radical interpretation, and his later externalist views, connected with triangulation, in that the latter, but not the former, have a historical element attached to them.[2] Davidson himself never recognized such a tension. In fact, he once declared that a "precursor" of his triangulation thesis and his externalism is Quine's account of radical translation, which is of course acknowledged by all parties to be a precursor of radical interpretation.[3] Indeed, Davidson describes radical translation in a very triangular way, as involving "two interacting people, their interaction mediated by the external objects, situations, and events they mutually observe" (Davidson 2001b, 11).[4] I shall come back to this when I consider interpersonal externalism and another alleged break between radical interpretation and triangulation, according to which Davidson went from claiming that only interpretability is necessary for the possession of language and thoughts, to claiming that it is actual interpretation that is necessary. For now I focus on the perceptual externalist thesis associated with radical interpretation. Quine, Davidson continues, "teaches us that what a speaker means by what he says, and hence the thoughts that can be expressed in language, are not accidentally connected with what a competent interpreter can make of them, and this is a powerful externalist thesis" (Davidson 2001b, 11).

As I said in Chapter 1, perceptual externalism is the basic premise of the triangulation argument. As I also said, the triangulation argument vindicates perceptual externalism, since answering the question of what the typical causes of our thoughts and utterances are leads us to realize that the determinants of meaning, at least the meaning of our basic thoughts and sayings, could only be fixed by triangulators, and hence only external physical factors could serve as determinants of meaning, since only they can be triangulated upon. Before he developed the triangulation argument, Davidson merely assumed perceptual externalism to be true, at least insofar as he assumed that language and thoughts are essentially public.[5] This assumption is what justified his reflecting on radical interpretation as a non-question-begging and illuminating way to answer the question what it is for words to mean what they do and thus as the best way to investigate philosophically the nature of meaning. There was no doubt in Davidson's mind that, by reflecting on how meanings and thoughts could be attributed to someone from scratch, that is, without the help of bilingual speakers or dictionaries,[6] we would learn all there is to be learned about how they get to be constituted or determined. As he says, "there can be no more to meaning than an adequately equipped person can learn and observe" (Davidson 1990b, 62).[7] What we find by reflecting on radical interpretation is that the physical environment of the interpretee, in particular the causes of her basic verbal responses, plays a crucial role in our discovering their meaning, and hence it must play a crucial role in determining what she means and thinks to begin with. Thus, perceptual externalism can also be seen immediately to follow from reflection on radical interpretation. Moreover, as I suggested above, reflecting on radical interpretation helps us to fill out at least some of the details of perceptual externalism. So how is radical interpretation supposed to proceed?

2.1 The Historical Aspect of Perceptual Externalism

The aim of radical interpretation is to construct a theory of interpretation for a speaker, that is, a theory that would eventually enable us to understand any of her utterances as well as attribute propositional attitudes to her.[8] And the idea is to do this starting with no knowledge of the speaker's language and a very limited knowledge of her propositional attitudes, limited since knowing in any detail what her beliefs, intentions and other attitudes are would require that we also know what her utterances mean (Davidson 1974a, 144). Thus all we may assume is that the speaker has by and large the same basic desires and beliefs as we do, given that we have the same kind of physical constitution and that we share her environment (Davidson 1993a, 81). The evidence initially available to the interpreter is that of sentences held true by the speaker and of features of the environment she shares with the interpreter and which cause her to hold her sentences true. The idea, roughly, is to accumulate enough evidence of particular sentences held true in particular circumstances at particular times and, on that basis, assuming, in the first instance, that sentences held true are true, come up with sentences that give us, for any particular sentence, the conditions under which it is in fact true. Eventually the interpreter should be able to extract from the evidence of sentences held true, as well as from pieces of information gathered about the speaker and her circumstances, and from background information of various sorts,[9] the role that each semantically primitive expression of the speaker's language plays in contributing to the truth-conditions of the speaker's utterances. This in turn should enable her to derive, for any utterance of the speaker, the conditions under which the sentence uttered is true, and thus its meaning. For, if the theory is constructed properly (on which more shortly), the truth-conditions should be meaning-giving.[10] Even leaving further details aside,[11] interpreting another radically would evidently be an enormous endeavor, even if it is plausible to think that learning a second language *in situ* goes faster than learning a first language. (Presumably, though, learning a second language without the help of bilingual speakers or dictionaries would not unfold in the way radical interpretation is supposed to unfold, by keeping track of sentences held true and coming up with axioms on their basis, from which in turn T-sentences—sentences describing the truth-conditions of a speaker's utterances—would be derived, that is, in effect, by building a theory of truth for the speaker.)[12] Repeated observations of connections between the speaker's utterances and objects or events in her environment, and repeated interactions between the speaker and the interpreter, would be necessary. It would take some work to determine whether, to take Quine's example, 'gavagai' means there goes a rabbit, or a furry animal, or a yellowish brown thing, or tonight's dinner. This is to say that some extended causal history must be available to the interpreter before she can start understanding any utterances of the speaker. It may not be the very causal history that the speaker went through when she first acquired her language. But the causal histories are likely to be similar. The main point here is that there is no way to interpret an alien language on the spot, so to speak. But then it is not clear why it has been thought that there is a tension between the kind of perceptual externalism Davidson held when he was considering radical interpretation and the kind he held when considering triangulation. In each case, the central idea is that the meanings of someone's thoughts and utterances are determined, at least in part, by features of the physical environment that have caused her to use words in certain ways. Ernie Lepore and Kirk Ludwig insist, however, that this does not "require us to think that there is any historical element at all in what fixes thought content." They continue:

> From the standpoint of the radical interpreter, what is important is what the speaker's environment is like, and what his dispositions are to respond to changes in his environment. These are the facts that determine the correct interpretation theory. Since we do not have magical access to nomic facts, in practice, to discover a speaker's dispositions, we must observe his interactions with his environment. But this no more means that what we thereby discover is a historical fact about him than does the use of induction in science generally show that the dispositional properties of things are really historical properties of them.
> (Lepore and Ludwig 2005, 337)

I believe, however, that the analogy drawn concerning dispositions is faulty.[13] The disposition to mean what one does by any given word is significantly different from, say, the disposition to dissolve in water. Semantic dispositions are not ready-made, so to speak, but constituted through speakers' interactions with their environment, as reflecting on radical interpretation teaches us. Thus one question we seek to answer is, what must these interactions be like for someone to have a language and thoughts? What we want to know is what makes it possible for a speaker to have the semantic dispositions that she has, what constitutes the meanings of her words and thoughts, to begin with. This, to repeat, is the ultimate goal in considering radical interpretation. If, on its basis, we conclude that we get to know what someone means and thinks by observing her and interacting with her in various environmental contexts, we should also conclude that the various environmental contexts in which she developed her language play an essential role in determining the meanings of her words and thoughts to begin with. She already had her language when she started being interpreted. What she thinks and means is not determined simply by what currently cause her thoughts and utterances. Indeed, suppose that the interpreter we are imagining lives on Twin Earth, where the chemical composition of the liquid referred to by 'water' is XYZ and not H_2O, as it is on Earth. It would be wrong, it seems to me, for her to interpret a speaker who acquired her language on Earth, and has just arrived on Twin Earth, as speaking about XYZ, rather than H_2O, when she uses the word 'water'. The H_2O environment is the environment in which the meaning of 'water' for the speaker was determined. (Matters here are more complicated than this suggests; for one thing, after living on Twin Earth for a while, the meaning of 'water' may change for the speaker—more on this in Section 4 below.) This indicates that knowledge of historical facts is relevant to correct interpretation. There is no reason to confine the interpretive data to those "readily observable" to the interpreter; rather, there is reason not to do that. The only demand "is that the evidence for the theory be in principle accessible, and that it not assume in advance the concepts to be illuminated" (Davidson 1990a, 314). Thus, the interpreter has no knowledge of the speaker's language and no detailed knowledge of her propositional attitudes. But she "has the concepts of truth, of intention, of belief, of desire and of assertion (and many, many more). She knows a lot about the world and about how people behave in various circumstances" (Davidson 1993a, 81). Needless to say, she knows her own language. And she knows the relevant history of the person whose thoughts and utterances she is seeking to interpret.[14]

What some commentators claim has led them to think that, or at least wonder whether, Davidson changed his views about the historical character of perceptual externalism is his Swampman thought-experiment,[15] which he himself came to see as "embarrassing" (Davidson 2006, 1061). Swampman, recall, is a physical replica of Davidson, created out of a tree while Davidson, standing nearby, is destroyed by lightning. Swampman, Davidson tells us, acts and talks exactly as he, Davidson, used to. Davidson has maintained that Swampman cannot "be said to mean anything by the sounds he makes, or to have any thoughts. It cannot mean what [Davidson] means by the word 'house', for example, since the sound 'house' Swampman makes was not learned in a context that would give it the right meaning—or any meaning at all" (Davidson 1987b, 19). But commentators have begged to differ, even on Davidson's behalf. "After all, on the assumption that Davidson is radically interpretable, the Swampman is, too" (Glüer 2011, 124, fn 9).[16] Thus, commentators have continued, insofar as interpretability is all that is required for the possession of language and thoughts, Swampman has a language and thoughts.

Leaving aside the claim that interpretability is all that is required for the possession of language and thoughts, let us ask whether Swampman truly is interpretable and whether the claim that Swampman has a language and thoughts truly is based on how we would go about interpreting him. Davidson was of course radically interpretable. Not only did we have access to some of what he said and the surroundings in which he said it, we also had access to some of his past surroundings, and to some of the events connected with his past; in short, we had access to some of his past history, even though none of it was directly observable, so we could be confident that we interpreted him correctly. This of course cannot apply to Swampman, not just because we have no access to his past, but because he has no past. Is Swampman indeed really interpretable? What could make us confident that our imagined interpretation of his English sounding utterances is correct? Since Swampman has no past, what fixed the meanings of the utterances we are now allegedly interpreting? He utters the sounds 'house', and 'table', and 'water', and we understand him as meaning house and table and water, because this is what Davidson meant by these words. But what reason do we have to think that this is what Swampman means? The reason cannot be simply that he can be interpreted in that way. We need a reason to think that the interpretation is correct. All of this strongly suggests that, when we conclude that Swampman has a language and thoughts, it is not because we have imagined our engaging in the process of radically interpreting him. I think, rather, that the intuition, which I do share, when I read about Swampman, that Swampman has a language and thoughts, indeed, that he means by and large what we do by our words, is based on the fact that, as we are told, he speaks English. Swampman, as we conceive of him, does not need to be interpreted; he is immediately understood. Which is why, as I noted in Chapter 1, the thought-experiment is, strictly speaking, question-begging with regards to the question of the possession of language and thoughts, though it may be useful to reflect on it in order to get clearer on the question of interpretability. What the brief foregoing remarks suggest is that either Swampman is not properly interpretable or, if he is, interpretability is not sufficient for the possession of language and thoughts, since it may be just the result of a fluke.

I turn to the holistic aspect of Davidson's perceptual externalism, which I also take to have been a permanent component of his view.

2.2 The Holistic Aspect of Perceptual Externalism

Holism applies to several aspects of Davidson's views, but I shall focus here on those aspects that are directly relevant to perceptual externalism.[17] Before embarking on radical interpretation, Davidson assumes semantic holism, according to which "what one sentence means depends on the meanings of other sentences", and by which "radical interpretation is constrained" (1993a, 80). His reasons for assuming this kind of holism, though prima facie plausible, are not entirely convincing—he mentions for one the "holistic nature of linguistic understanding" (Davidson 1984a, xv), and for another the fact that "a given sentence in someone's language can't express a certain proposition unless it occupies a place among other sentences that reflect the logical relations among those sentences" (Davidson 1993a, 79). The latter is really an aspect of what Davidson has called the "holism of the mental", according to which, most importantly for our purposes, "beliefs [and the meanings of the sentences that express them] are individuated and identified by their relations to other beliefs," including, in addition to the logical relations, relations of evidential or inductive support (Davidson 1999a, 124–6).[18] Kathrin Glüer thinks the two kinds of holism are quite different, but this, I think, is because she focuses on a consequence of the claim that beliefs come in clusters, which is that "it is impossible to have just one belief about any subject matter whatsoever" (Glüer 2011, 117). This is indeed a consequence of the holism of the mental, but this does not impeach the claim that thoughts are identified, and hence their meaning determined, "only as they can be located within dense networks of related beliefs" (Davidson 1982, 98).[19] This is the kind of holism I have been talking about all along so far, which I expressed above by saying that no thoughts or sayings have their meaning determined in isolation from others.

Davidson, however, does not merely assume this kind of holism; it is also vindicated by reflecting on radical interpretation. The meanings of a speaker's utterances cannot be attributed or discovered individually; hence meanings are not determined or constituted individually. There is no way an interpreter could interpret 'gavagai', the first time the speaker utters the sound, as meaning rabbit, even if the speaker points at a furry animal as she exclaims, "Gavagai!" She could be reacting to the rabbit's skin, or to its size, or to its speed, or . . . The sound will have to be produced on different occasions, in different contexts, and be sometimes associated, sometimes contrasted, with others, before the interpreter can narrow down a meaning for it and start building sentences describing the conditions under which "Gavagai" and other utterances of the speaker are true. The holistic aspect of radical interpretation is what in the end makes it possible for the T-sentences to be interpretive. "A T-sentence . . . can be used to interpret a sentence [uttered by a speaker] . . . provided we also know the theory that entails it, and know that it is a theory that meets the formal and empirical criteria" (Davidson 1973, 139). Thus, on the formal side, we must know that the theory is finitely axiomatized, that is, that there is a finite number of axioms—a finite vocabulary and a finite set of modes of composition—describing the contribution each expression makes to the truth-conditions of any given utterance the speaker may make. And we must know that the T-sentences are entailed by these axioms. On the empirical side, first, to know the theory, we must know its axioms. And these we get to know if we have checked against the evidence many different T-sentences, each of which describes the truth-conditions of an utterance that is related to other utterances in virtue of sharing primitive expressions with them, not to mention in virtue of being inferentially related to them. Second, we must know that this checking has been done by respecting the empirical constraints. To respect these constraints is, in a nutshell, to apply the principle of charity, in all its complexity, in a holistic way. This means, to begin with, that we attribute beliefs to the speaker when she holds sentences true in the circumstances in which we would ourselves hold them true, and thus that we start by attributing a number of true beliefs. But this is only what enables us to get started. What we must also pay attention to are the ways the speaker acquires beliefs and the ways she supports them. We must pay attention to the ways her beliefs cohere with each other and are logically related. In all, we strive for an interpretation that respects these different norms of rationality, trying also to attribute reasonable desires and coherent patterns of preferences. But this does not mean that a speaker's beliefs will ever be all true, or perfectly justified and consistent, or that her desires and preferences will ever be perfectly reasonable. That is, this does not mean that a speaker will ever be perfectly rational and reasonable. What the principle of charity dictates is neither that we maximize agreement, nor that we maximize rationality, but that we maximize intelligibility. And this sometimes requires that we attribute only a modicum of rationality to the speaker.[20]

Once more, I must insist that what is true of the interpreter is true of the speaker. The constraints that apply to the interpretation of an alien language also apply to the constitution of the meanings of any language's expressions. A speaker no more attaches a meaning to an expression in isolation, or has a single thought, than an interpreter interprets an alien expression in isolation, or attributes a single alien thought. This should come as no surprise to those of us who have been impressed by Wittgenstein's remarks on ostensive definition. But reflecting on radical interpretation makes the holistic conclusion vivid. Now there is the question (answered affirmatively by Glüer 2011, 136) of whether the radical interpreter is just a "dramatic device", which can be left behind once we have gathered our philosophical fruits. This might be the case if Davidson thought that interpretability is sufficient for the possession of language and thoughts and actual interpretation not required. But he certainly never said that he thought of the radical interpreter in that way,[21] and shortly after having introduced the idea of radical interpretation he did make clear that he did not think interpretability is sufficient for the possession of language and thoughts.[22] There are those who will insist that, even so, he did not believe that actual interpretation is needed for meaning determination but only for possession of the concept of objectivity. I have tried to make my case against this in Chapter 1. But I do want to stress that the answer to the question of whether Davidson believed from the very beginning that actual interpretation is needed for the possession of language and thoughts cannot conclusively be answered. The topic was simply not broached by Davidson himself for a couple of years. However, he promptly came to say that he did believe it, and this is perfectly compatible with his remaining initially silent on the topic. As I mentioned in Chapter 2, we may regard the reflections on radical interpretation as establishing that the meanings of our basic thoughts and utterances are determined, at least in part, by what cause us to have and make them. We can then ask the next, obligatory question: How are these causes in turn identified or individuated? Then the interpreter, of necessity since only a triangulator can fix meaning-determining causes, reenters the scene, if she ever left it. (Of course those who insist that interpretability is enough for the possession of language and thoughts might also insist that radical interpretation establishes nothing concerning the constitution of meaning, a claim which, to repeat, is not Davidson's and which would make reflecting on radical interpretation much less interesting.)

I have spent some time discussing perceptual externalism in the context of radical interpretation in part because I think Davidson's externalism has always been both historical and holistic. There has been no change of mind on that score, and there is no related tension between his views that Davidson himself failed to notice. But I have also examined radical interpretation because it is after all a species of triangulation. Now, what more can be said about the kind of perceptual externalism that emerges from triangulation considered in a broader way?

3. Perceptual Externalism and Triangulation

The short answer is: not much. When Davidson gives examples of people triangulating, it is usually of teachers and children acquiring a first language. He is always clear, however, that his intention is not to describe the process of language acquisition, just as he was always clear that his intention in discussing radical interpretation was not to describe what actually goes on when people communicate with each other.[23] It is just that reflecting on the triangulating aspect of language acquisition may help us better to understand how the causes, and hence the meanings, of basic thoughts and utterances are fixed. What does get reinforced in light of triangulation is the historical side of perceptual externalism, as what determine the meanings of someone's thoughts and utterances are, in the first instance, the objects and events on which she triangulated with others while learning her first language. It is not the case, of course, that, for every expression of her language, even for those words that refer to features of her environment, she must have triangulated on the relevant features in order to mean something by them. "Of course very many words and sentences are not learned this way" (Davidson 1988b, 45). It is just that, for every thought or saying, for instance, "for someone to think or say that the cat is on the mat there must be a causal history of that person that traces back, directly or indirectly, to triangular experiences" (Davidson 2001c, 293).

In the end, there is in fact little that Davidson says even about triangulating children, or about the triangulating process more generally. Here is the most elaborate passage, about a child learning 'table':

> Involved in our picture there are . . . three similarity patterns. The child finds tables similar; we find tables similar; and we find the child's responses in the presence of tables similar. It now makes sense for us to call responses of the child responses to tables. Given these three patterns of response we can assign a location to the stimuli that elicit the child's responses. The

> relevant stimuli are the objects or events we naturally find similar (tables) which are correlated with responses of the child we find similar. It is a form of triangulation ... Where the lines from child to table and us to table converge, 'the' stimulus is located.
>
> (Davidson 1992, 119)

Recall, however, that, according to Davidson, all we have done so far is "give a meaning to the idea that the stimulus has an objective location in a common place" (Davidson 1992, 119). But nothing yet shows that we or the child have the idea. For this to happen, Davidson continues,

> [t]he interaction must be available to the interacting creatures. Thus the child, learning the word 'table', has already in effect noted that the teacher's responses are similar (rewarding) when its responses (mouthing 'table') are similar. The teacher on his part is training the child to make similar responses to what he (the teacher) perceives as similar stimuli ... [Thus a] condition for being a speaker is that there must be others enough like oneself.
>
> (Davidson 1992, 120)

What more is needed to have the concept of a table?

> [T]o have the concept of a table ... is to recognize the existence of a triangle, one apex of which is oneself, the second apex another creature similar to oneself, and the third a ... table ... located in a space thus made common.
>
> The only way of knowing that the second apex of the triangle—the second creature or person—is reacting to the same object as oneself is to know that the other person must also know that the first person constitutes an apex of the same triangle another apex of which the second person occupies. For two people to know of each other that they are so related, that their thoughts are so related, requires that they be in communication. Each of them must speak to the other and be understood by the other. They don't ... have to mean the same thing by the same words, but they must each be an interpreter of the other.
>
> (Davidson 1992, 121)

What does it take to be the interpreter of another? Here, in effect, we are back to where we started, for if we want further to illuminate the philosophical nature of meaning in a non-question-begging way, we have to ask what it would take to interpret someone from scratch, that is, we have to reflect on radical interpretation. But this we already have done. Only, this time, there is no question of getting rid of the interpreter. She is an indispensable contributor to the determination of meaning, since fixing causes, and hence meanings, requires having the concept of objectivity, which only triangulators are in a position to have. (Note that this further shows how reflecting on triangulation, since it forces us eventually to reflect on radical interpretation, does illuminate the philosophical nature of language and thought, even though, again, no reductionist account is in the offing.)

Strangely enough, however, it has been said that there might be a tension between the perceptual externalism connected with triangulation, on the one hand, and holism, on the other hand. Thus Sven Bernecker has written that "[t]here is nothing about triangular externalism that speaks against the atomistic view whereby a belief can have content independently of the web in which it is embedded" (Bernecker 2013, 447). What may have led him to make this baffling assertion? Perhaps the following: When Davidson gives examples of triangulation such as the one above, he focuses on a single word or concept and thus makes it sound as if its meaning could be determined independently of others'. This mistake is not uncommon. Goldberg writes that, on Davidson's view, "'table' . . . means table for the learner because she learned 'table' via triangulating a table in her environment" (Goldberg 2009, 266), suggesting that nothing more is needed.[24] However, as I have just emphasized with my step-by-step presentation of the example, even though the learning triangular situation is necessary to fix particular meanings, it is not sufficient. The learning triangular situation is after all but an advanced instance of primitive triangulation. It is but one step towards attaching a meaning to 'table'. Eventually, for the child to have the concept of table, she will have to engage in full-blown linguistic triangulation with another, that is, she will have to interpret and be interpreted by another. And this, as we have also seen, cannot be done in an atomistic way. Indeed, we have by now accumulated several reasons to think that the meaning-determining task can be achieved only holistically.

Thus, to recapitulate: First we noticed that the particular aspects of the causes that determine the meanings of one's thoughts and utterances cannot be fixed by single associations, say, single acts of ostension, between one's utterances and features of one's environment. As Wittgenstein first pointed out, ostensive definitions can succeed in endowing a word with meaning only against the background of a language. This in itself already indicates that some degree of holism will be required. We then noticed that what is true of an individual is also true of a group. Shared ostensive acts will not do either. (This is why there is no way the child has learned the meaning of 'table' just by triangulating on tables—on what is she supposed to have triangulated?) Nor will repeated ostensive acts, no matter how regular. For someone to fix the aspect of a meaning-determining cause she must come to realize that the aspect is shared by another person, that the aspect is the same for her as it is for her interlocutor.[25] But to realize this requires that she have the concept of objectivity, of the distinction between what is the same and what merely seems to her to be the same, and thus between correct and incorrect ways to respond to the environment. And this in turn requires a great many linguistic exchanges in numerous contexts.

In short, there is no escaping holism, whether we focus on triangulation or on radical interpretation. I also believe that this is in part why there is no escaping the historical aspect of perceptual externalism. And I believe that the holistic aspect of Davidson's perceptual externalism is the central element that distinguishes it from other versions of perceptual externalism, to which I now turn.

4. Davidson's vs. Putnam's Physical Externalism

Once upon a time, physical externalism was all the rage, with Putnam and Kripke the main stars of the show, soon to be followed by Burge, who eventually declared the debate to be over and their brand of externalism to be the received view.[26] I do not wish to revisit the numerous replies and discussions that orthodox versions of, and arguments for, physical externalism generated. All I want to do is to expound one of them sufficiently, so that the distinctive character of Davidson's version is brought to the fore and his view further clarified. I shall focus on Putnam's view and argument.

The view applies, in the first instance, to natural kind words, words like 'water', 'lemon', and 'gold', but is extended to many other words, including "the names of artifacts—words like 'pencil', 'chair', [and] 'bottle'," (Putnam 1975). In short, it applies to words that refer to macroscopic features of our environment, features that we may be able to perceive. Here I shall focus on natural kind words, which are the words that Putnam himself focuses on when he develops his argument. According to Putnam, the extension of natural kind words plays an essential role in determining their meaning.[27] This sounds much like an expression of the view every physical externalist endorses, but here is the twist: The relevant aspect of the extension that determines the meaning of those words is its "actual nature", as established, or at least establishable, by the scientific experts of one's linguistic community. What is Putnam's argument for this?

It is of course the famous Twin Earth thought-experiment I alluded to earlier. Suppose there is somewhere in the galaxy a planet—call it Twin Earth—which is exactly like Earth except that the liquid called water on Twin Earth, which tastes like water and quenches thirst like water, is not composed of H_2O molecules but of XYZ. "[S]uppose that the oceans and lakes and seas of Twin Earth contain XYZ and not water, that it rains XYZ on Twin Earth and not water, etc." (Putnam 1975, 223). If we were to visit Twin Earth, Putnam tells us, we may suppose at first that their 'water' means the same as our 'water', but upon discovering that their 'water' refers to XYZ we would change our mind. The extension of the words is different in English and Twin English, hence their meaning is different. This was true even in 1750, when no one could have yet discovered that the liquids' chemical compositions are different. Or so Putnam further tells us. Now, you may well ask, as Putnam does, "why should we accept it that the term 'water' has the same extension in 1750 and 1950 (on both Earths)" (Putnam 1975, 224)? I would also like to ask, why should we accept that 'water' has a different extension on Earth and Twin Earth even in 1950? Putnam's answer is that, if he were to explain the meaning of 'water' to someone by means of an ostensive definition, he would assume that the liquid he is pointing to is the same kind of liquid as the liquid that he and other speakers in his linguistic community have called water on other occasions. But what does it take to be the same kind of liquid? This "may take an indeterminate amount of scientific investigation to determine" (Putnam 1975, 225). There is one thing of which Putnam is certain, though. This is that what kind of liquid it is is determined by its actual nature, and once it is discovered that the actual nature, i.e., the microstructure, of what we call water on Earth is H_2O, "nothing counts as a possible world in which water isn't H_2O" (Putnam 1975, 233). According to Putnam, natural kind words are rigid designators; they refer to the same kind of stuff in every possible world in which they designate (Putnam 1975, 231). How does Davidson's version of physical externalism compare to this?

As is to be expected, Davidson "is persuaded that Putnam is right [in so far as] what our words mean is fixed in part by the circumstances in which we learned, and used, the words" (Davidson 1987b, 29). But he does not think Putnam's thought-experiment is needed to establish this. "[T]he case can be best made by appealing directly to obvious facts about language learning and to facts about how we interpret words and languages with which we are unfamiliar" (Davidson 1988b, 44). Nor does he think that microstructure necessarily is the aspect of a natural kind that determines the meaning of natural kind words. Pressing the claim that it is might even lead to the denial of knowledge of what one means and thinks. This would certainly seem to be the case of Earthlings in 1750, who failed to know that H_2O determined the meaning of 'water'.[28] It is possible to insist, Davidson contends, "that 'water' doesn't apply just to stuff with the same molecular structure as water but to stuff enough like water in structure to be odorless, potable, to support swimming and sailing, etc." (He admits: "I do not know a rigid designator when I see one" (Davidson 1987b, 29).) How is this possible? How, according to Davidson, do we decide what someone means by 'water' and so what properties of water are relevant to determine the meaning of 'water'? To begin with, we pay attention to how that person uses the word in various contexts. We also pay attention to how she uses other words in those contexts, centrally, perhaps, to how she uses 'liquid' and 'wet'. We pay attention not only to her surroundings but also to her background, education, desires and interests. This is pretty basic, indeed, I should say, simplistic, but already much more complex than Putnam's suggestion that we pay attention only to the microstructure of the stuff people intend to refer to by using 'water'. So, let us do a little (not very) radical interpretation of people using 'water', starting with Putnam.

We know that Putnam lives on Earth, that he is a scientifically minded philosopher who presumably drinks, bathes and swims in what he calls water. We also know, because he tells us, that when he ostensively defines 'water' he intends the word to be applied to whatever liquid is of the same kind as the one he is pointing to. And we know that he thinks that what determines what kind a liquid belongs to is its microstructure.[29] This is perhaps enough for us to say that Putnam means something different from Twin Putnam by 'water'. But let us now imagine someone at the other side of the spectrum, so to speak, someone, call her Pamela, who is scientifically ignorant and uninterested, wondering how long the drought will last and when she will be able to wash her clothes. We may again assume that she drinks, bathes and swims in what she calls water. Now, keep in mind that, for Davidson, the meaning of any word is to be identified on the basis of the many utterances one makes using the word, that is, the many beliefs one expresses about whatever the word refers to. It is also in this holistic way that the meaning of any given word can be seen to be constituted or determined, via of course, in the case of a natural kind word, the features of the environment that the word is about. Why then should we interpret Pamela as meaning the same thing as Putnam does by 'water'? She has no beliefs whatsoever about the microstructure of water. Why should beliefs she does not have play a crucial, indeed essential, role in determining what she means by 'water'? Note that I am not suggesting that one has to know that 'water' refers to H_2O in order to mean the same thing as Putnam does by 'water'. I shall presently suggest two scenarios under which one would fail to know that and yet one might still mean the same as Putnam.

Even in 1750, someone might be mindful of the hidden causal powers things in nature have, powers which perhaps best individuate natural kinds, and think that 'water' should designate whatever has the hidden structure the stuff she calls water has. In this case, given other beliefs she shares with Putnam about what she calls water, she may well mean the same as Putnam does by 'water'. At the very least she does not mean the same as her Twin on Twin Earth means by 'water'. Or suppose someone is mindful of how scientists in her community classify the stuff in their natural environment. She thus takes 'water' to be about whatever they say it is, though she has no knowledge of this herself. Again, given other beliefs she shares with Putnam about what she calls water, she may well mean the same as Putnam does by 'water' or at the very least not mean the same as her Twin on Twin Earth. What she means all depends in the end on which beliefs we (and of course she as well) take to be determining what she means by 'water', but there is no particular set of beliefs that we know in advance we should privilege. As Davidson puts it, having given up the analytic-synthetic distinction, "we have no [firm] way of distinguishing between the relations [among beliefs] that define the state of mind (or the meaning of an utterance) and those that are 'merely' contingent, and so do not touch content" (Davidson 1995a, 15).[30] Still, a line has to be drawn between those beliefs that determine meaning and those that do not.

And, as usual, maximizing intelligibility is our guide in drawing it. But it is not the case that, as some have suggested,[31] all the beliefs someone expresses with 'water' will play this determining role. Nor, accordingly, is it the case that every new belief someone acquires about water will change what she means by 'water'. As Davidson continues:

> [G]iving up the idea of a firm line between the analytic and the synthetic does not mean giving up the idea of a continuum in which some connections among thoughts are far more important to characterizing a state of mind than others. Thus my belief that it is raining today probably contributes essentially nothing to the content of my other beliefs about rain except those that are logically related, while my belief that rain is caused by the condensation of drops in water-saturated air contributes a great deal.
>
> (Davidson 1995a, 15)

None of the above is to suggest that there is a great fluctuation among us about what we mean by 'water'. Enough of the beliefs we have about what we call water overlap, and a core of them determines the meaning of 'water' for most of us. What I am emphasizing, though, is that one single belief will not do to determine the meaning of 'water', or of any other word, for that matter. A fortiori the single belief one may have about the particular kind of liquid one's word designates will not do to determine the meaning of that word.[32] Neither will any belief a speaker lacks contribute to the meaning of any word. In this way, contra Putnam, there is no danger of our failing to know fully what we mean by our words.

It might be pointed out that, even for Putnam, there is more to the meaning of words than their extension (and thus more than a single belief relevant to their meaning), where the extension is to be given in terms of the actual nature of the features of the world words referred to (in what follows, I shall restrict 'extension' to hidden structure or "actual nature", and use 'referent' to designate any kind of external feature a word may be about). To describe the meaning of a word, one has to include, in addition to its extension (as well as to its syntactic markers, such as mass noun, concrete, and its semantic markers, such as natural kind, liquid), the stereotype associated with the referent of the word, such as colorless, transparent, tasteless, thirst-quenching, etc. (Putnam 1975, 269). Someone counts as being competent with a word if she knows at least some of the stereotypical properties of the referent of the word (Putnam 1975, 248). These properties may also help us initially to identify a given kind and thereby fix the extension of the word that refers to it. But the properties so used are neither necessary nor sufficient for something to fall under the kind in question, and so for the word to have the meaning that it has. In the end, the only external determinant of meaning is the extension of the word (Putnam 1975, 234). And thus, as I have been suggesting we might say, the only relevant meaning determining belief is the belief about the extension. Thus what we have, on Putnam's side, is the intention to refer to, or the assumption or belief that one's word refers to, its extension and a bunch of descriptions that may help us to acquire the word, as he puts it, and to fix its extension, but which are not essential to its meaning. And, on Davidson's side, what we have is a bunch of beliefs about its referent that help us to identify and therefore constitute the meaning of one's word. There is no predicting which beliefs in particular may contribute to determining the meaning of a word, but there is no ruling out the possibility that a belief about its extension is not crucial to it. What significant difference does it make to side with Davidson?

I have already mentioned one crucial difference, which is that nothing of which a speaker is ignorant will contribute to determining the meaning of her words.[33] But Putnam's insistence that the intention to refer to the extension be present for the word to mean what it does for the speaker might be thought to take care of that worry.[34] Thus what may play the essential role in determining the meaning of 'water' is not the belief that water is H_2O but the belief that water has a certain molecular structure. However, there is a much more profound difference between the two accounts. As I see it, Putnam's account of meaning is guided by a desire to describe the world around us as it really, naturally is. The dominant belief is that many things in nature have hidden structures that scientists are to discover and that our language is to reflect. I have no qualm with the former, scientific claim, but I am wary of the latter, linguistic one, even if many speakers do rely on scientists and try to talk accordingly.[35] Whereas Putnam's primary goal is to give an account of meaning that matches his metaphysical motivations, Davidson's primary goal is to give an account that pays first and foremost attention to communication, both the source and the purpose of meaning. I do not think that Putnam gives a general answer to the question what it is for words to mean what they do, or the question what determines meaning. He tells us only how the meanings of some words are fixed once we already have a language. Now it might be thought that he is no different in this respect from Davidson. Davidson, too, does not explain how the meaning of any particular word is fixed by someone who has no language yet. But this thought would be misguided. Davidson's reflections on what makes having a language possible lead him to realize not only that the meanings of words cannot be fixed by means of direct connection between words and their referents, but also that they can be fixed only in a holistic way by people who interact linguistically with each other. Many words need to be used in triangular situations for their referents to be fixed. And no particular referent can be fixed unless it has been triangulated upon repeatedly and in connection with other words that have also been used in triangular situations. This is how the meanings of words are fixed. Change the connections among many triangular situations and the meanings involved may change as well. Putnam has given no alternative story and so no reason to favor his externalism in the end.[36]

At this stage, it may be protested that there is a side of Putnam's account that I have so far neglected and which may better support it. This is the social side of externalism, to which I now turn.

5. Social Externalism

There are a great variety of views about language and thought that incorporate a social element. There is, to begin with, a big divide between, on the one hand, those that maintain that there is a social factor that is essential for anyone to have a language and thoughts—there can be no solitary language—and, on the other hand, those that maintain that there is a social factor that applies only to socially situated individuals—a solitary language is at least metaphysically possible. I shall focus on views of the first type, of which Davidson's is obviously an instance. But I do want to comment briefly on the social aspect of Putnam's view, which may be thought to belong to the second type, and which may seem to make his version of physical externalism more attractive.[37]

5.1 *Putnam's Social View*

Putnam emphasizes, in his account of meaning, what he calls the division of linguistic labor, according to which in every linguistic community there are at least some words "whose associated 'criteria' are known only to a subset of the speakers who acquire the terms, and whose use by the other speakers depends upon a structured cooperation between them and the speakers in the relevant subsets" (Putnam 1975, 228). Thus someone may be able to mean water by 'water' without knowing its chemical composition, let alone being able to recognize it. She is able to do this because she relies on the experts of her community to tell her, if needed, whether something is water. She indeed intends her word to be about whatever it is that the experts may know better about. This is the kind of intention that, as I have conceded above, may make it the case that she means the same as the experts by 'water'. At the very least, she shares with them the referent of 'water'. Now, this might be thought to show that, according to Putnam, there is a social element that is essential to the determination of meaning. But I do not think this is the case. The experts actually play no role in determining what we mean by our words. They just know better than we do what our words are about, because they have better access to their extension, which is still the fundamental determinant of meaning. This is shown by the fact that even in 1750, in the absence of any people we could regard as experts, people may have meant the same as we do now by 'water'.[38]

Still, might not the fact that people do rely on others who know better tell in favor of Putnam's version of physical externalism? I do not think so. For one thing, I doubt that the phenomenon of reliance is as ubiquitous in ordinary communication as it is sometimes suggested. For another, even when reliance is undoubtedly present, it is far from obvious what role it should play in the determination of the meaning of the words involved in the reliance. Take Putnam's own case of his relying on experts for what he means by 'elm' and by 'beech'. The only description he associates with each word is 'deciduous tree', and presumably, though he fails to mention this, 'elm trees are different from beech trees'. It might be argued that, though his 'elm' and 'beech' have the same extension as the experts' 'elm' and 'beech', his do not have the same meaning as theirs. He shares too few of the beliefs they have about those trees. Or take Burge's example of the patient who is reported to utter statements such as, "I fear I now have arthritis in my thigh, I'm too young to be suffering from arthritis, my father was riddled with arthritis, arthritis deforms one's hands and feet", etc. We are told that he also intends to use 'arthritis' in the same way as the medical experts of his community. Does he mean the same as they do by 'arthritis'? At the very least, Burge came to claim (Burge 2003b, 358) he shares the referent of 'arthritis' with the experts, that is, he is talking about inflammations of the joints exclusively. Davidson has disagreed, repeatedly.[39] In this case, both the referent and the meaning of the word are, or at the very least may be, different for the patient from what they are for the experts. Here is how I would explain this, briefly: Though the patient intends to talk like the experts, he also intends 'arthritis' to cover inflammations that may affect muscles. So here we have two conflicting intentions. Why should we give more weight to the meta-semantic one—he intends his word to have the meaning it has for the experts—than to the semantic one—he intends his word to be about the ailment he has in his thigh? Surely communication will better proceed if we pay attention to the intentions that are revealed in the speaker's use of his words than to those that do not show up in his behavior. I think that what in the end should settle what the patient means by 'arthritis' is a triangular situation involving him and his doctor. A rheumatologist once told me that he does not always try to change his patients' use of words, such as the above patient's use of 'arthritis'. Sometimes it is just easier to interpret them as meaning something different from what he means—it makes for smoother conversation. What explains communication, what is essential to it, has always been Davidson's primary concern in developing an account of meaning. And his primary claim has always been that people do not have to mean the same thing by the same words in order to communicate, hence sameness of meaning, or conventional meaning, is not essential to meaning. This claim is further supported by the triangulation argument.

5.2 Interpersonal Externalism

The other big divide among those who think that language and thought incorporate a social element involves those who think that this social factor is essential for anyone to have a language and thoughts. On the one hand, there are those who believe that having a (first) language essentially depends on meaning by one's words what members of some community mean by them—call this the communitarian view. Some think that this is true of most words of one's language; others think that this is true of at least a particular subset of them.[40] And the relevant community may be either the one that the speaker belongs to or the one that is considering the speaker.[41] On the other hand, there are those who believe that having a (first) language essentially depends on having used (at least some of) one's words to communicate with others. This is of course Davidson's interpersonal view, according to which the possession of language and thought essentially depends on having triangulated linguistically with others. Linguistic triangulation, no more than communication in general, does not require that the triangulators assign the same meanings to the same words. Recall that, at bottom, the reason why we can say only of people who have triangulated linguistically with others that they have a language and thoughts is that only linguistic triangulators can distinguish between causes that are the same and causes that merely seem to be, between responses to their environment that are correct and responses that are not. And so, since the ability to make this distinction is needed for someone's expressions to be governed by conditions of correct application, only expressions used by linguistic triangulators can be governed by conditions of correct application and hence be meaningful. The triangulating situation makes it possible to have the concept of objectivity through the disagreement, negotiation and eventual settlement that interlocutors may have with each other as to which causes are the same as which, which responses are correct or not. However, the meanings that get fixed through triangulating do not have to be shared by interlocutors. All the triangulators have to do is agree on what the causes of their respective responses are. It is not the case that, for any given response, each interlocutor must respond as the other does. So it is not the case that, for any given expression, it must have the same conditions of correct application, and hence the same meaning, for both interlocutors. This is not to deny that many meanings will be shared—after all, interlocutors share the environment that many of their thoughts and utterances are about. It is only to say that no particular meaning must be shared.[42]

It might, however, be objected that there are reasons to think that at least some subset of meanings must be shared. After all, though this must have happened once upon a time, people do not now develop their first language together, by responding to each other and their shared environment. They acquire it with those who already have one. Are they not, then, per force speaking the language of others? Indeed, as long as they do not have the concept of objectivity, they could not be in a position to distinguish between the correct and incorrect applications of their words. It might thus be thought that their conditions of correctness would have to be the conditions that govern the applications of those they got the words from. Does this not show that language is essentially communitarian after all? Here is John McDowell's way to express the worry:

> Davidson is sceptical about whether speaking a language requires doing as others do . . . I think this scepticism would make it hard for him to acknowledge the importance, in acquiring a conception of the world with oneself and others in it, of simply learning what to say at that fundamental level, which to begin with—before light has dawned—surely cannot be anything but learning to vocalize in ways that pass muster in a group that one is being initiated into.
> (McDowell 2003, 679)

The worry is shared by Williams, who maintains that a version of the communitarian view is defended by Wittgenstein, to whom she attributes a version of the triangulation argument:

> For Wittgenstein, the individuation of the stimulus and response (and so what counts as the same or not) is a function (in part) of our shared reactions to stimuli in the environment and our shared response to training. Since "the same" and "different" can't get a conceptual hold without the correlation in response, shared responses are required.
> (Williams 2000, 312)

Williams argues that there are judgments that a child acquiring a first language and her teachers must share.[43] These are "bedrock judgments of the obvious—judgments like Moore's 'This is a hand' or 'This is red' said of a fire engine." Such judgments "constitute the norms by which objects are individuated and understanding the game can be assessed. Such judgments are bedrock judgments of similarity, of what is the same as what and of what it is to go on in the same way. Such judgments are made blindly; that is, they are not made from an application of a rule, concept or hypothesis" (Williams 2000, 311). If these are the judgments that the child is making when she first acquires a language, it looks as if she cannot but make the very bedrock judgments that her community fellows make. And this, Williams seems to think, entails that the child must mean the same as they do by their basic words.

Davidson of course accepts, and indeed, as we have seen, presses, the claim that some judgments or beliefs must be shared. He even quotes approvingly Wittgenstein's claim that "if language is to be a means of communication there must be agreement not only in definitions . . . but also in judgments" (Wittgenstein 1958, §241). However, Davidson continues, "these theses . . . have nothing to do with . . . lexical norms. They tell us nothing about how people should or must speak to be understood" (Davidson 1993b, 146). The sharing of beliefs that makes understanding of another possible at all does entail that communicators also share many meanings or concepts. This is something Davidson does not stress, making it sound perhaps as if communication requires only the sharing of beliefs and not at all the sharing of language.[44] But it should go without saying that beliefs cannot be shared unless concepts are, too, and hence the meanings of the words that express them. Here Davidson actually says it: "I know of no one who denies [that we could not understand someone with whom we did not share a large number of (fundamental) concepts], for how could an interpreter grasp, much less formulate, the truth conditions of an utterance which she lacks the resources to conceive" (Davidson 1993b, 145–6)? What Davidson does emphasize is the much less trivial claim that there is no obligation that any particular beliefs or meanings be shared nor any guarantee that shared ones will continue to be shared, including bedrock judgments of the obvious; for Davidson's claim is the even more radical one that, precisely because speakers and thinkers contribute to determining what the conditions of correct application of their words and concepts are, because, in effect, meanings are to some extent created rather than discovered, the fact that languages are learned, far from lending support to the communitarian view, actually reinforces the interpersonal view.

Davidson writes:

> Someone who is consciously teaching a beginner the use of a word may think of herself as simply passing on a meaning that already attaches to the word. But from the learner's point of view, the word—the sound—is being *endowed* with a meaning. This is why doubt [about an application] makes no sense at the start. The first examples, the first things ostended, must, from the learner's point of view, belong to the application of the expression. This is so even if the teacher is at fault from society's point of view . . . The question what others besides the learner, even his teacher, mean by the sound is irrelevant . . . and we will misinterpret the learner if we assume that for him it has any meaning not connected with that process.
>
> (Davidson 2001b, 14–5)

This is not to deny that, at this basic level, it is likely that the child will end up meaning by her words what her teachers mean by them. Nor is it to deny that the first language-learning process, in addition to the necessary sharing of beliefs, gives us all the more reason to think that people's languages overlap a lot. But, again, there is no saying in advance which particular meanings will be shared because no particular ones must be. In short, it is not that language is not often communitarian; it is only that it does not have to be. And this is the case even though, initially, the conditions of correctness governing the applications of the child's words really are those imposed on them by her teacher; for the teacher does not have to assign to the child's words the same meanings as she does to her own—this is the point of Davidson's saying that the question what even the teacher means by the sound is irrelevant. Ultimately, the important part of the learning process lies not in the particular ways in which the child draws the distinction between correct and incorrect applications of her words but in her acquiring the very idea of the distinction. (Note that Davidson's anti-communitarian remarks are in exact parallel with his anti-conventionalist ones. Davidson does not deny the existence and utility of linguistic conventions. What he denies is that conventions are necessary to communication and hence to language. He also does not deny that regular uses of words are necessary to language—how else could conditions of correct application and hence meanings be determined to begin with? What he denies is that any particular words must be used in a regular way for them to be meaningful.)[45]

We may conclude, then, contra Williams, that the fact that languages are learned yields no reason to think that language is essentially communitarian. But Williams has further worries about Davidson's interpersonal view. She thinks that it can be made a target of Wittgenstein's interpretation argument since, she says, Davidson pays no attention to Wittgenstein's claim that there is "a way of grasping a rule which is not an interpretation" and instead maintains that "interpretation can go all the way down, that is, applies to everything that is said or presupposed by what is said" (2000, 309). The problem here, as we know, is that, if this were so, everything that is said could always be interpreted in such a way that it is correct, or not—statements could always be said to be true, orders to be obeyed, etc.—making the distinction between correct and incorrect applications, and hence meaning, impossible. Williams's worries are, however, unfounded.

Recall, to begin with, that Davidson does not construe "interpretation" in the way Wittgenstein does, viz., as the explanation of the meaning of an expression by means of other words. Rather, by 'interpretation', he simply means the understanding of another's words, which of course can only be described by using words, but these are "not offered as the interpretation" (1994, 112). So, trivially, interpretation does go all the way down, much as understanding obviously does. Now, Williams's contention that Davidson ignores Wittgenstein's claim that there is a way of grasping a rule which is not an interpretation is taken care of by Davidson's stressing that the child, when acquiring a first language, is not grasping a meaning already attached to the word. Rather, the word is being endowed with meaning as she starts using it, hearing it and observing it used by others. From the child's point of view, there is no rule there to be grasped. Indeed, even from the teacher's point of view there may be no rule there to be grasped, if it turns out that the child is creating one different from that attached to the word by the teacher. Of course there is a difference here between the child and the teacher who alone, at this early stage, can tell what rule or meaning is being attached to the word. So Davidson can call these early judgments, or, better, protojudgments, blind, just as much as the communitarian can, since there are no rules there from which the judgments proceed. There is indeed no reason to think that the shared judgments, which, for Davidson, constitute the background for communication, are any more the result of interpretation than

Williams's bedrock judgments. Such judgments, Williams reminds us, are made with right but without justification. All we can say in their defense is that we understand English (Williams 2000, 311). In a similar vein, Davidson would say, all we can say in defense of our shared judgments is that we have successfully communicated by means of them.

Williams has however recently reiterated her complaint that Davidson's view is subject to Wittgenstein's paradox of interpretation (Williams 2010, 162 ff.). Davidson's answer to Kripke, to the effect that the paradox Kripke finds in Wittgenstein is really an instance of the problem of induction and should be treated accordingly (Davidson 1992, 111), has hardly helped matters. What can we say on Davidson's behalf in response to Kripke's skeptical problem?

The problem, in a nutshell, is that of finding, for any expression of a speaker's language, a "fact", as Kripke calls it, that determines the meaning, that is, the conditions of correct application, of the expression for the speaker. Kripke examines a variety of facts, all connected to the speaker, from mental pictures she is entertaining to her dispositions to use the expression in certain ways, and finds them all lacking for what comes down to the same basic reason: None of the facts he considers can provide expressions with conditions of correct application, because each of them needs to be taken or interpreted in a certain way before it could do so. Hence the skeptical problem: If there are no facts determining meaning, how else can we account for it? If there are no facts providing an individual's expressions with conditions of correct application, how else can we distinguish between correct and incorrect applications? This is perhaps the shortest way ever to describe the detailed exposition of the problem articulated by Kripke, and it certainly does not do justice to the richness and complexity of the arguments he deploys.[46] I believe however that Kripke can be interpreted as taking the problem of accounting for the trivial normativity of meaning as the fundamental one, though I shall not attempt to defend this interpretation here. More importantly, for our purposes, this is the problem that Wittgenstein and Davidson can be understood as taking as the fundamental one. As we saw in Chapter 1, it is the problem Davidson unravels in the first step of the triangulation argument and solves in the second step. One significant difference between Davidson and Kripke is that, whereas Davidson does not even mention "facts" other than those to be found in the environment of the speaker, these external facts are the only ones Kripke does not mention. This difference is significant because focusing on external facts is what provides Davidson with a solution to the problem of meaning determination. But first I wish to make clear why the skeptical problem, as expounded by Kripke, is not just an induction problem.

Davidson sees it this way because he sees it as the problem of saying what evidence is adequate in order to determine how a speaker is going to go on—this much might have been inspired by Kripke, who starts by stressing that the speaker's past behavior—her answering 'plus' queries with the sum—is compatible with her meaning quaddition rather than addition by 'plus'. But Davidson misunderstands the problem Kripke is grappling with; for, as Kripke continues, we do not know how she will go on, and so what she means by 'plus', because there is no fact she can point to that determines what she means. It is not just that she does not know what fact that might be, but that there is no such fact to be found. Davidson answers that we do have reason to believe that a speaker means one thing rather than another by an expression:

> The longer we interpret a speaker with apparent success as speaking a particular language, the greater our legitimate confidence that the speaker is speaking that language—that is, that she will continue to be interpretable as speaking that language. Our strengthening expectations are as well founded as our evidence and ordinary induction make them.
> (Davidson 1992, 111)

But this is to assume that what the speaker means is determined by some fact, and that the only problem is to figure out what that fact is. However, in the absence of a fact to point to, apparent success in interpreting the speaker will not cut it—we would have been equally successful if we had interpreted her as meaning quaddition rather than addition. In short, Kripke's skeptical problem arises over and above the induction problem. As he himself says, the skeptical challenge is not epistemological, but constitutive (Kripke 1982, 21).[47] But I believe Davidson can meet it, and that he can do so in a more satisfactory way than Kripke.

The key, as I noted above, is to focus on external things as determinants of meaning. Recall once again that, as acknowledged by Davidson in the first step of the triangulation argument, invoking features of the world around us, when considered by themselves, yields the interpretation problem just as much as invoking any other entities. That is, invoking external features is subject to the aspect problem, which is left over even if speakers can be seen as responding to distal causes rather than to proximal ones. The skeptic may insist that external features will therefore not do as meaning-determining facts, any more than any of the facts considered by Kripke. The reply should be that external features will not do only insofar as we think of the relation between them and our utterances in a certain way. There is indeed no way, without a language, to isolate the aspect or part of the world any particular expression used by a speaker is about. As I stressed in Chapter 2, it is a certain conception of how meanings should be determined, through sheer association between expressions and extra-linguistic items, that is the source of the skeptical problem, that is, the source of the claim that no fact determines meaning. If the skeptic insists on this conception, as Kripke seems to, the solution she has available can only be skeptical—since no facts determine meaning, an alternative account of meaning must be provided. But it could also be urged that insisting on this conception is incoherent, that it is hopeless to try to ground meaning on sheer associations between expressions and extra-linguistic items, because the associations could only proceed by means of language. In other words, we would need a language in order to develop one.[48] One way or the other, however, we are still left with the task of explaining how meanings are determined, or what makes it possible for expressions to mean what they do, if this cannot be explained in the way urged by the skeptic.

Kripke's answer is that ascriptions of meaning to a speaker's utterances have assertibility conditions rather than truth-conditions. They are justified if the speaker's applications of her words agree consistently with those made by competent members of her community. (They are also justified in terms of the role and utility they have in people's lives.) Thus, in effect, the meanings of a speaker's words are determined by what the members of her community mean by those words. Correct applications are applications that conform to the conditions of correctness at play in her community. Kripke's answer is thus communitarian, and I believe that, like any communitarian answer, it has serious limitations; for we are not told how the members of a community get to mean what they do by their words, how their conditions of correct application are determined.[49] We are just told that the correct applications are those that they agree on—going on in the right way is going on in the same way as others. But there is no story as to how this agreement is achieved. I think of Davidson's triangulation argument as supplying this story. The meanings of speakers' words are determined, in the first instance, by the features of their environment on which they have triangulated linguistically and which they have agreed to take as the relevant aspects determining the meanings of their words. Thus the external facts, if they may be so called, that serve as determinants of meaning are those that triangulating speakers agree to take to be so. They do not have to agree to take the same facts to determine the meanings of both interlocutors' words. But they have to agree as to what facts determine the meanings of the speaker's words. What is crucial, indeed, indispensable, is the three-way interaction, contra Kripke, who thinks that a solitaire could have a language insofar as she would be considered by a linguistic community whose expressions' conditions of correctness would govern the application of her words.[50] Meanings cannot be imposed on an individual's words by others any more than they can be imposed by the world around her.

6. Conclusion

We have seen that the brand of semantic externalism entailed by the triangulation argument is highly distinctive. And this is due to the fact that the meanings of at least some of our thoughts and utterances are fixed through triangulating linguistically on the features of the environment that cause us to have those thoughts and make those utterances. Perceptual externalism can be secured only through interpersonal externalism. The resulting kind of semantic externalism is historical and holistic, and it is anti-normative in the sense that there are no norms or conventions that determine the meanings of an individual's words. In other words, the triangulation argument entails the denial of meaning determining normativity. This chapter further supports the claim that it is possible to be non-reductionist without being quietist about meaning. Indeed, it also shows that a much more robust and constructive answer can be given to the semantic skeptic than that suggested by Kripke. But it is not just semantic skepticism that can be overcome with the triangulation argument. In the next chapter I explore the consequences of the argument for skepticism about the external world.

Notes

1. I would rather not call Davidson's externalism "transcendental" (Bridges 2006) or "triangular" (Amoretti 2013; Bernecker 2013), though each label has a point. Davidson's externalism may be described as transcendental insofar as Davidson's aim is to provide necessary conditions for the possession of language and thoughts; but "transcendental" also has connotations that do not apply to Davidson's view. Davidson's externalism could be called triangular, for obvious reasons; but the label may be misleading since Tyler Burge, as we saw in Chapter 1, describes solitary creatures as triangulating visually on features of their environment.
2. See Hahn 2003, 43; Lepore and Ludwig 2005, 338; Glüer 2011, 124; Bernecker 2013, 446. (Glüer calls Davison's early view semantic behaviorism, Bernecker calls it interpretationism, but each recognizes the externalist element.) For extended discussion, see Goldberg 2008.
3. As Davidson often emphasized, there are numerous differences between his radical interpretation and Quine's radical translation, differences that need not concern us here. But the key idea is the same: to give a philosophical account of meaning by considering what it would take to understand the utterances of an alien speaker. See Quine 1960, especially Chapter II.
4. See Quine 1996, 160, for an externalist description of his approach, which he did not hold initially.
5. See, e.g., Davidson 1979, 235.
6. This might not be the only way to understand what makes radical interpretation radical, as Davidson himself recognized (Davidson 1993a, 77), in reply to much misunderstanding of his views on the topic (by Fodor and Lepore 1993). Davidson's views and terminology, he admits, have not been "absolutely steady" over 27 years of writing. I shall myself stick with this understanding of radical interpretation. See also Davidson 2001b, 13.
7. See also, e.g., Davidson 1979, 235. One may call this into doubt and say that what is true of attribution is not true of constitution. But then reflecting on radical interpretation would have a rather limited purpose. Indeed, it is hard to see how it could be used to answer the question what it is for words to mean what they do.
8. As this has sometimes been missed (see section 5.2 of this chapter) it is worth stressing that by 'interpretation' Davidson just means understanding, specifically, understanding someone's linguistic and intentional behavior. Thus it is not

to be confused with Wittgenstein's notion, according to which an interpretation is an explanation of the meaning of an expression in other words.
9. As Myers will discuss in Chapter 5.
10. Cf. Chapter 1, Section 1.
11. To be found in numerous articles, most importantly Davidson 1973, 1974a, 1976, 1990a and 1993a.
12. Note that Davidson never claimed that the kind of theory we imagine building through radical interpretation is the kind of theory we do have or use when we communicate with others, or the kind of theory we have acquired by learning a first language—see Davidson 1974a, 141, and Davidson 1986, 95–6.
13. Davidson has often denounced the related analogy drawn by commentators on radical interpretation "between how we come to know what others mean and think and how we come to know [natural facts, such as] how the blood circulates or how planets are formed" (Davidson 1993a, 83). See also, e.g., Davidson 1974a, 154.
14. What Nathaniel Goldberg suggests, that "[a]n utterance is meaningful whenever and only whenever a radical interpreter could determine that it is meaningful given the speaker's utterances at the time of interpretation and the conditions that prompt them" (Goldberg 2008, 366), is based on an understanding of radical interpretation that simply makes it impossible.
15. See, e.g., Hahn 2003 and Goldberg 2008.
16. See also Lepore and Ludwig 2005, 338 and Goldberg 2008, 364.
17. See Davidson 1995a, 9–17, for a survey of varieties of holism.
18. According to Davidson's holism of the mental, not only are there no beliefs without many related beliefs, there are "no beliefs without desires, no desires without beliefs, no intentions without both beliefs and desires. Conceptually, actions themselves belong to the realm of the mental" (Davidson, 1999a, 126).
19. Davidson himself says that semantic holism follows from the holism of the mental (Davidson 1993a, 80).
20. There is another facet of the holism of the mental that I have not mentioned and which is really a consequence of what I have discussed so far. This is that, given the holistic constraints on interpretation, there is sometimes no telling whether it is someone's concepts or beliefs that are different from ours. (See Davidson 1974b, 197.) More on this in Section 3 below.
21. He does not say this in Davidson 1974c, contra what Pagin suggests (Pagin 2013, 231).
22. See, again, Davidson 1975.
23. He has this to say, though: "Though radical interpretation cannot, of course, explain or describe how a first language is learned, it is hard to believe it does not throw light on what helps make that accomplishment possible" (2001c, 294). See also Davidson 1991b, 210.
24. See also the 'house' example in Goldberg 2008, 368.
25. '[W]hat makes the particular aspect of the cause of the learner's responses the aspect that gives them the content they have is the fact that this aspect of the cause is shared by the teacher and the learner" (Davidson 1991a, 203).
26. What Burge declared, to put it less provocatively, is the acceptance, by most philosophers, of the thought-experiments on which he and Putnam ground physical externalism (Burge 1992, 48). This is not to say that they agreed on all matters. In particular, some philosophers thought that the externalist component of mental content has to be supplemented by an internalist one in order to account for the role that content plays in the explanation of behavior—see, e.g., Loar 1982 and McGinn 1982. Strikingly, in his 1992 "state of the art" article, there is no mention by Burge of Davidson as a participant in this externalism debate. For

Kripke's defense of physical externalism, see Kripke 1972. For Burge's defense, see Burge 1982 and 1986, among others.
27. I shall focus on language since Putnam, initially at least, did not think that the view applies to thoughts or psychological states (Burge did). However, as before, the claims I make on Davidson's behalf apply to both the meanings of words and utterances and the concepts and thoughts they express.
28. See Davidson 1987b, 21. Putnam seemed to be happy to accept this, at least as far as meaning is concerned. As I said in the previous note, his view does not apply to concepts.
29. Of course there might be exceptions to this, that is, there might be kinds without a hidden structure. See Putnam 1975, 241.
30. This is part and parcel of the holism of the mental I mentioned in note 18.
31. See, e.g., Williams 2000, 305–6. I further discuss Williams's complaint in Verheggen 2006.
32. Putnam himself does not talk about beliefs determining meaning—after all, one might say, it is extension that does so. However, as I already noted, he does talk about the "presupposition", in ostensively defining 'water', that the liquid pointed at is of a certain kind, and the "intention" to refer to what has a certain nature (Putnam 1975, 243). Thus I think that talk of beliefs determining meaning is acceptable here. For Putnam, the relevant belief concerns the nature of the external stuff talked about, whereas for Davidson the relevant beliefs are varied though they, too, of course concern the external things talked about. After all, external things, too, for Davidson, determine meaning.
33. This is not to say that we never attribute to someone's word a meaning she does not fully understand. But we do so for purely pragmatic reasons, because nothing turns on making the fine distinctions that would require assigning to her word a meaning different from the one we attach to it.
34. In a very interesting article, William Child (2001) has emphasized the role played by speakers' intentions in Putnam's account to argue that Putnam and Davidson share a realist view about kinds.
35. Note, though, that, as Putnam himself insists, the scientists themselves may be (temporarily or permanently) in a state of ignorance. Even then, our words are supposed to be about the features of the world around us individuated in terms of their actual nature.

Muhammad Ali Khalidi has suggested to me that Putnam's account of meaning is more radical than I have been intimating, in that it is guided, not by the idea that our language is to reflect the real nature of the world around us, which scientists are to discover, but by the idea that language by itself, and independently of language users, somehow reflects the nature of reality, making the connection between words and world utterly mysterious. This may be the standard way to understand Putnam's view, but I do not think it is right. I think that, according to Putnam, there is an intention, on the part of the speakers, to talk about the real features of their environment, which scientists are in a better position to discover. Even if they do not, our words still refer to those real features, because we intend them to do so, making the connection between words and world not quite so mysterious—which does not mean, of course, that the view is then unproblematic. (My reading of Putnam is strongly indebted to Child's article, mentioned above, which made me pay closer attention to aspects of Putnam's view that are often neglected. Before reading it, I was inclined to agree with Khalidi.)
36. For a related discussion, see Amoretti 2007.
37. Dummett 1974 and Burge 1979 defend views of the second type.

38. As Davidson says, "[w]e could get along without" the division of linguistic labor (Davidson 1994, 114).
39. See, e.g, Davidson 1987b, 27–8.
40. Kripke 1982 is usually understood as a representative of the first group, Williams 1999 as a representative of the second.
41. See McDowell 1992 and Williams 1999 as representatives of the first group, and Kripke 1982 and Stroud 2000 as representatives of the second group. The latter makes it possible for there to be solitary speakers but not solitary languages. (I have discussed McDowell in Verheggen 2000 and 2003, and Stroud in Verheggen 2005.)
42. This claim is reinforced by the holistic nature of meaning determination.
43. The discussion of Williams's views in the next five paragraphs is taken almost verbatim from Verheggen 2006.
44. Another one of Williams's complaints against Davidson—see Williams 2000, 307.
45. For Davidson's views on convention, see Davidson 1984b and 1986. For an excellent overview and discussion, see Glüer 2013.
46. See Kripke 1982, Chapter 2.
47. Cf. Kusch 2006, 88, for a similar criticism of Davidson's interpretation of Kripke.
48. Rather than calling for a skeptical solution to the problem, we may then declare the problem dissolved, following McDowell 1992 and Williams 1999, since it is based on an untenable assumption. There then remains the question whether anything philosophically constructive can be said about meaning. Williams thinks it can. McDowell thinks not.
49. Cf. Stroud 1996, 189.
50. Kripke writes: "Our community can assert of any individual [including an isolated one] that he follows a rule if he passes the tests for rule following applied to any member of the community" (Kripke 1982, 110). Martin Kusch has suggested that "a triangulation of sorts is also central to [Kripke's] skeptical solution" (Kusch 2006, 83). But the triangulation he envisages does not seem to have to involve linguistic interaction between interlocutors. Indeed, how could this be required, since, according to Kripke, a solitaire could have a language? (I discuss Davidson's treatment of the rule-following paradox further in Verheggen forthcoming b.)

4 From Triangulation to Global Anti-Skepticism

1. Introductory Remarks

"*[I]f* you accept perceptual externalism, there *is* an easy argument against global skepticism of the senses" (Davidson 1991a, 200). Davidson describes this "fallout" from externalism as "revolutionary. If words and thoughts are, in the most basic cases, necessarily about the sorts of objects and events that commonly cause them, there is no room for Cartesian doubts about the independent existence of such objects and events" (Davidson 1988b, 45). "If externalism is true, there can be no further general question how knowledge of the external world is possible" (Davidson 1989b, 196).

As the above quotations indicate, insofar as Davidson endorsed externalism prior to making the triangulation argument, he also believed that his earlier views about meaning deliver anti-skeptical goods. Some commentators have understood the goods they deliver to be different depending on whether they are based on considerations concerning radical interpretation or considerations concerning triangulation. Moreover, among those who take them to be stronger when they are based on the latter, there is no agreement on how strong exactly they are. Just what then is the conclusion of Davidson's argument against global skepticism of the senses? In what sense exactly is there no room for Cartesian doubts about the independent existence of external objects and events? Is it that these doubts "cannot even be formulated" (Davidson 1988b, 45) or "coherently entertained" (Davidson 1988b, 52), or that they are "empty" (Davidson 1995a, 5)? Is it that skepticism is "unintelligible" (Davidson 1995a, 5), or "untenable" (Davidson 1995a, 17), or that no "constructive answer" to the skeptic can be provided, so that skepticism cannot be "refuted" but only "dismissed" (Davidson 1995a, 5–6)? Davidson himself came to acknowledge that he had "vacillated over the years on how to describe [his] attitude toward skepticism":

> Do I think that if I am right about the nature of thought scepticism is false, or that scepticism simply can't get off the ground? The two poses can be reconciled . . . Reflecting on the nature of thought and interpretation led me to a position which, if correct, entails that we have a

basically sound view of the world around us. If so, there is no point in attempting, in addition, to show the sceptic wrong . . .[We can] show that we know enough about the world to be able to say that it is pretty much as we think it is. On my understanding of scepticism, this is to show that it is false.

(Davidson 1999e, 163)

I shall proceed by tracing Davidson's treatment of skepticism about the external world to its sources. This will help us to appreciate how he can be regarded as addressing it in different ways at different stages of the development of his views about meaning. And it will help us better to understand why some commentators do not take his final answer for what it is. But before I proceed, I must say a little about Cartesian or "global" skepticism of the senses.

The Cartesian skeptic starts by asserting that I could have all the thoughts and beliefs I currently have about the world around me, as well as all my current experiences seemingly of the world around me, even if all of those thoughts and beliefs were false and none of those experiences were veridical. So I could, for instance, be mistaken in thinking that I am now writing this on my computer, that my computer says it is 4:53 in the afternoon, that it has stopped raining and that it is getting dark outside. None of these thoughts may be true, and I could simply be dreaming that I am having them. It may be retorted that dreaming would not prevent me from having at least true general beliefs and even some knowledge about the objects and events that surround me, such as computers and rainy days. But that would be assuming that the distinction I am making between dreaming and waking states of mind and experiences is not itself the product of my imagination, that I have reason to think that my states of mind and experiences sometimes are waking states of mind and experiences. However, the Cartesian skeptic maintains that I have no such reason, for what could it be? I could not appeal to any aspect of my sensory experiences, since their reliability is precisely what is in question. Besides, those experiences as well as all of my thoughts and beliefs could have been caused by an evil demon in such a way that they may in fact correspond to nothing in the world around me, indeed, in such a way that this world may not even exist. Thus the hypothesis from which stems the Cartesian skeptical challenge: All of my beliefs about the world around me could be false.

The Cartesian skeptic, however, never doubts that he has the very thoughts and beliefs he has, with the very contents they have (I shall sometimes use 'content' rather than 'meaning' in this chapter as the term seems to fit beliefs better). He never doubts, that is, not only that thoughts and beliefs exist, but also that we know what they are about. So what the Cartesian skeptic, in particular Descartes, never does when he is entertaining the hypothesis and its consequent doubts, is pause to ask what might make it possible for him to have all those beliefs seemingly about things beyond him—as far as he cares, they could have been produced by some other unknown "faculty" of his, or have been directly implanted in him by some supernatural being. This, of course, is where Davidson (after Kant) departs from Descartes. Ironically, he says, his "starting point is the same as Descartes': what I know for certain is that thought [with propositional content] exists, and then I ask what follows" (Davidson 1995a, 5).[1] A "great deal" follows, he continues, from answering the question how we can have the thoughts we do have about the world around us. Indeed, if Davidson's answer is right, it follows that the skeptic's hypothesis that I could have all the beliefs I have about the world around me even if they were false is mistaken. Such beliefs can only be by and large true beliefs; otherwise I would not have them. As Davidson famously wrote, "Belief is in its nature veridical" (Davidson 1983, 146). Moreover, for this very reason, "simply because beliefs are by nature generally true", I do know that my beliefs are generally true (Davidson 1983, 153).

I shall therefore take Davidson's conclusion against the skeptic to be the denial of the skeptic's hypothesis: It is not the case that all of my beliefs about the world around me could be false; rather, such beliefs are by and large true. Moreover, I have reason to believe that they are by and large true. In short, I have knowledge of the external world. How did Davidson reach these strong conclusions?

2. Radical Interpretation and Skepticism

Davidson thought that he first reached his anti-skeptical conclusions on the basis of his considerations concerning radical interpretation. As he wrote when he first introduced these conclusions, "Successful communication proves the existence of a shared, largely true, view of the world" (Davidson 1977, 201). Recall that the purpose of those considerations is to illuminate philosophically the nature of meaning by asking how an interpreter could come to understand the utterances of an alien speaker, and to attribute to her thoughts and propositional attitudes without the help of bilingual speakers or dictionaries. The only way for the interpreter to get the process started is by assuming that many of the beliefs the speaker expresses about objects and events in her immediate environment are the same as those the interpreter is having in the circumstances. Thus the only way for the interpreter to get the process started is by attributing to the interpreter many of the beliefs she herself thinks are true, which is one of the many demands imposed by the principle of charity. This does not mean, however, that interlocutors must agree on all matters. "We can make sense of differences all right, but only against a background of shared beliefs" (Davidson 1977, 200). In short, successful interpretation depends on the interlocutors by and large agreeing on matters about their surroundings. If so, however, it looks as if the most we can conclude by reflecting on radical interpretation is that successful communication proves the existence not of a largely true but of a largely agreed-upon view of the world; for what is agreed upon does not guarantee its truth. Radical interpretation may require that the interpreter attribute many of her beliefs, which she takes to be true, to the speaker, but, as Duncan Pritchard recently put it, this "does not in itself give us any more reason to think that the speaker's beliefs are in fact true than it does for thinking that our beliefs are true" (Pritchard 2013, 523). Or does it?

I think it does (barring a serious caveat I shall discuss shortly). But to recognize this requires that we take seriously Davidson's motivation when he first embarked on the project of radical interpretation. As I have indicated in previous chapters, Davidson was not interested merely in figuring out how we can come to understand another person's thoughts and utterances from scratch. He was interested in figuring this out because he thought that it would reveal much of philosophical importance about the nature of meaning. As he said, it would answer the question what it is for words to mean what they do, and what it is for thoughts and beliefs to have the content they have, in a philosophically instructive way, which I take to be tantamount to saying that it would answer the question of what determines the meanings of one's thoughts and utterances, and thus the question of what makes it possible to have a language and thoughts. In other words, reflecting on radical interpretation is meant to yield, not just the conditions under which meanings and beliefs are attributed to others, but also, and more importantly, the conditions under which meanings and beliefs are constituted. Thus, it would seem that the very features that make attribution of meanings and beliefs possible also are the features that fix them. As the process of radical interpretation makes explicit, what makes these attributions possible are features of the environment that interpreter and speaker share and jointly respond to. But this is to say that many of our beliefs about the world around us must be true, since it is the world around us, what makes many of our beliefs true, that determines their content to begin with.

I do not think that Davidson immediately realized the force of the epistemic conclusion he had reached simply on the basis of considerations of radical interpretation. He initially thought that, in order to make his anti-skeptical point, he needed to appeal to the idea of an omniscient interpreter, an interpreter who, though omniscient, attributes beliefs to others and interprets their utterances in the way we do, thus through having to find others much in agreement with herself. However, Davidson argued, in this case, "what is agreed is by hypothesis true", and this makes it "plain why massive error about the world is simply unintelligible" (Davidson 1977, 201). No one was convinced by the omniscient interpreter argument, for a variety of reasons, which I shall not review here, in part because I believe that they have mostly to do with unclarities in the idea of an omniscient interpreter and not much to do with Davidson's actual point.[2] In any case, Davidson himself came to acknowledge that the case against the skeptic can be better made without the omniscient interpreter (Davidson 1999c, 192). And it is pretty obvious that he soon took the case to be made on the basis of considerations of (non-omniscient) radical interpretation alone:

> What stands in the way of global skepticism of the senses is, in my view, the fact that we must, in the plainest and methodologically basic cases, take the objects of a belief to be the causes of that belief. *And what we, as interpreters, must take them to be is what they in fact are.* Communication begins where causes converge: your utterance means what mine does if belief in its truth is systematically caused by the same objects and events.
>
> (Davidson 1983, 151, my emphasis)

As I warned above, however, there is a reason to worry that the methodology of radical interpretation causes the case against the skeptic to be begged after all. Recall that one of Davidson's reasons for engaging in the radical interpretation thought-experiment is his assumption that meanings and beliefs, and more generally propositional attitudes, are necessarily public. Thus what someone means and thinks is necessarily discoverable by others and therefore must depend on features of the world that are accessible to interlocutors. This is an assumption that may already be objected to when inquiring into the nature of language and thought, though pre-theoretically it is hard to separate meaning and linguistic communication. But it is definitely an assumption that must be objected to when inquiring into the possibility of knowledge of the external world; for the assumption is tantamount to asserting the existence of the world of objects and events surrounding us. As Michael Williams once put it, if, "in the context of the sceptic's question, we grant ourselves this access [to objects in the world], the game is over before it begins" (Williams 1988, 188).[3] Unless perceptual externalism is independently motivated, it in effect begs the question against skepticism.[4] As I argued in Chapter 1, however, when Davidson reflects on triangulation more generally, he can be understood as vindicating perceptual externalism and thus as no longer begging the question against the skeptic. The train of thought that leads to this conclusion is worth reiterating at this stage.

As we saw in Chapter 1, the kind of argument Davidson uses against the individual externalist can also be deployed against the internalist, who denies any essential contribution from the external world to meaning and thinks that the determinants of meaning may be items that are internal to the mind, such as mental pictures or abstract entities grasped by the mind. As we saw, these items will not do as determinants of meaning because, considered in and of themselves, they are no better off than the external objects and events causing our thoughts and utterances, when these are considered in and of themselves. (As we saw in Chapter 2, items internal to the brain, such as dispositions, will not do either, for the exact same reason.) We saw that it is only when external items are taken in certain ways that they can be seen as determining the meanings of our thoughts and utterances. Similarly, it is only if internal items could be taken in certain definite ways that they could be said to determine specific meanings. However, as we also saw, if the triangulation argument is successful, in order to succeed as determinants of meaning, the potential determinants of meaning need to be taken in certain ways by *triangulating* individuals; indeed, only triangulating individuals are in a position to take them in certain ways. If this is right, then the considerations against individual externalism hold against internalism as well. It takes two to triangulate—this tells against individual externalism; and items internal to the mind cannot be triangulated upon—this tells against internalism. And if what prompts interpersonal externalism can be understood as also prompting the rejection of internalism, no question has been begged against the skeptic. There are those, however, who think that even considerations of triangulation do not warrant the claim that belief is in its nature veridical and thus the denial of the skeptic's hypothesis. They think that the anti-skeptical claim should be interpreted in a weaker way, such that the answer to the skeptic is not that the skeptic's hypothesis can be denied but that it cannot be entertained. I turn to this criticism.

3. Triangulation and Skepticism

Barry Stroud is one of the most formidable challengers of the anti-skeptical claims that Davidson contends follow from the triangulation argument.[5] Even when he focuses on triangulation rather than merely radical interpretation, Stroud still does not think, to begin with, that Davidson is in a position to tell the skeptic that his beliefs about the world around him are by and large true. According to Stroud, all that Davidson has established is a claim about belief-attribution, namely, that it is largely truth-ascribing. What follows from this, Stroud argues, is simply that the skeptic cannot ask whether his beliefs about the world around him are by and large true, for he cannot coherently entertain the thought that all or most of those beliefs could be false since from the conditions of interpretation it follows that he can think of himself as having the beliefs he has only while thinking that most of these beliefs are true. Not only, Stroud further argues, does the claim that belief is in its nature veridical not follow from the claim that belief-attribution is in its nature largely truth-ascribing, making the stronger claim would in fact involve adopting a standpoint on our knowledge of the world that Davidson has shown does not exist. Moreover, Stroud continues, the stronger claim would not imply that anyone knows or has any good reason to believe anything about the world. Even if it were the case that most of our beliefs about the world are true, we might still lack any good reason to believe this. And so the stronger claim would not refute the skeptic insofar as he precisely denies that we have any knowledge of the world (Stroud 1999, 154). I believe that Davidson meant to establish the stronger claim, so the first question to consider is why exactly Stroud thinks that Davidson failed to do so.[6]

3.1 Belief-Attribution Is in Its Nature Largely Truth-Ascribing

As I said, Davidson takes his anti-skeptical claim already to follow from considerations about the nature of interpretation, considerations he advanced before developing the triangulation argument. Though he is well aware of the triangulation argument, Stroud nonetheless focuses on radical interpretation and thus on the question what it takes for someone fully equipped with a language and thoughts to understand from scratch another person's utterances and attribute to her beliefs and other propositional attitudes. Strictly speaking, when investigating the anti-skeptical consequences of Davidson's views about meaning, there is nothing wrong with focusing on radical interpretation, provided that it is understood as a species of triangulation, and thus provided that focusing on it is prompted by the same considerations that prompted focusing on triangulation more generally. The answer to the question of what it takes to understand someone's thoughts and utterances from scratch is, to repeat, that, since the interpreter could not get interpretation started unless she assumed that the speaker has by and large the beliefs she, the interpreter, would have in the circumstances, the interpreter is forced to attribute to the speaker beliefs that she herself takes to be true. According to Stroud, the crucial claim that follows from this is that one could not first attribute beliefs and then ask whether these beliefs are by and large true. As Stroud writes, if Davidson "is right about the conditions of interpretation, no interpreter will be in a position to find all or most of the beliefs he ascribes to people false . . . one's finding most or all of those attributed beliefs to be false is inconsistent with one's having found the people in question to have those very beliefs" (Stroud 1999, 146). But this means that "our having [the beliefs we now have] and their being all or mostly false is not a possibility we could consistently believe to be actual, so it is not a possibility we could be pressed to explain how we know is not actual" (Stroud 1999, 157). Thus, according to Stroud, the weaker claim, according to which belief-attribution is in its nature largely truth-ascribing, is sufficient to keep the skeptic quiet, but not to negate his contention that we lack knowledge of the world. This would require, to begin with, that the stronger claim, according to which belief is in its nature veridical, be established.

I think we must agree with Stroud that the stronger claim does not immediately follow from the conditions of interpretation considered as such. But, as I emphasized above, Davidson does not mean to provide only conditions of interpretation but also conditions of the possession of language and thoughts, something which, to those who missed it,[7] is made entirely clear by the triangulation argument, and something of which Stroud is aware. After all, he does write that "on Davidson's view, *thoughts with propositional content are present* only if there is communication or reciprocal interpretation" (Stroud 1999, 153, my emphasis).[8] The question then is: Does focusing on triangulation as an account of the possession of language and thoughts make any difference to the anti-skeptical claim that can be drawn? Does triangulation add anything to the conditions of interpretation? Stroud himself asks this question and considers specifically the role of causality in triangulation. But he concludes that this cannot strengthen the anti-skeptical claim, for, as I also emphasized above, ultimately the causes of triangulating interlocutors' utterances are what they take these causes to be. And Stroud takes this to imply that these causes could be other than what they take them to be. Only, he writes, if there were "no possible difference between what in fact cause verbal responses and what an interpreter takes their causes to be" could the stronger claim be supported (Stroud 1999, 151). But now, on the face of it, Stroud seems to be expressing a flat contradiction here. If the causes of interlocutors' utterances are what they take these causes to be, how could the causes of their utterances be different from what they take them to be? (Perhaps it is worth recalling here that the causes in question are the causes at play "in the plainest and methodologically basic cases", that is, the meaning-determining, or "typical", or "systematic" causes; there is no suggestion that we can never be wrong about what cause our utterances.) What could Stroud have in mind here? I think that his (at least apparently) contradictory claim belies a failure fully to take on board the fact that triangulation is supposed to provide conditions of the possession of language and thoughts, and that it thus amounts to a rejection of Davidson's externalist account of content.

Stroud quotes Davidson as saying, in support of the stronger claim, that "we do not first form concepts and then discover what they apply to; rather, in the basic cases the application determines the content of the concept." But he chooses to focus on what Davidson says next: "An interpreter who starts from scratch . . . cannot independently discover what an agent's beliefs are about, and then ask whether they are true" (Davidson 1991a, 195). However, Stroud then argues, the truth of most of an agent's beliefs is not needed to explain that. "That is explained by the fact that interpreters attribute beliefs only by correlating the utterances they interpret with conditions which they believe to hold in the world they share with their speakers; they cannot discover what those speakers' beliefs are without also believing certain things to be the causes of those utterances." But it does not follow from this "that interpreters must take the utterances to mean whatever in fact causes them" (Stroud 1999, 151–2). And so, according to Stroud, considering triangulation in addition to the conditions of interpretation makes no difference to how we treat the skeptical problem. It does seem to me, however, that, once we acknowledge that Davidson aims to provide not just conditions of interpretation but also conditions of the possession of language and thoughts, we are in a stronger position against the skeptic.

3.2 Belief Is in Its Nature Veridical

Suppose indeed that Stroud is right in thinking that we could be wrong about the (typical) causes of our beliefs. What becomes clear, once we keep in mind that the causes of our basic beliefs determine the content of these beliefs, is that this possibility does not entail simply the possibility that our beliefs are false; it entails the possibility that our beliefs have a content that is different from the content we think they have. Thus the thought the skeptic cannot consistently entertain is not just, "I have all these beliefs and these beliefs are all false", but "I have all these beliefs and I am wrong about their content, which is to say, in effect, I do not have all these beliefs". This suggests two ways of dealing with the skeptic that are different from Stroud's: Either we tell the skeptic that he must produce an alternative account of what does provide our beliefs with content, if it is not what we take to be their causes.[9] Or we push skepticism one step further and become skeptical, as Nagel has put it, "about whether we are really capable of significant thought, while at the same time admitting that [such skepticism] is inexpressible and strictly unthinkable, since it is equivalent to saying, 'Perhaps the sentence I am uttering right now means nothing at all'" (Nagel 1999, 205).

Another way to see that the considerations of triangulation cut more deeply against the skeptic than Stroud maintains is suggested by an observation of Ernest Sosa's. Sosa points out that from the fact that 'Not p but I believe p' cannot be coherently believed, it does not follow that 'It is possible that both: not p and I believe p' cannot be coherently believed (Sosa 2003, 171).[10] Now, when we focus on the content of beliefs rather than on their truth-value, what cannot be coherently believed is 'I believe p but I do not believe p'. But in this case neither can 'It is possible that both: I believe p but I do not believe p' be coherently believed. And this, it seems to me, shows again that the skeptic is more deeply challenged by the considerations regarding the possession of language and thoughts. After all, we, philosophers, discussing philosophical skepticism, may observe, as Stroud repeatedly does, when reflecting on the conditions of interpretation, that there may be a gap between what we take to be the causes of our utterances and what these causes in fact are, that is, that the beliefs that we per force take to be true could in fact be false. This may not be something the skeptic could consistently assert, but it is something that could be the case. (Hence, in effect, Sosa's disappointment with Stroud's conclusion.) But triangulation offers the Cartesian skeptic something that, as I mentioned at the outset, he has simply neglected to give, viz., an answer to the question what makes it possible for us to have the beliefs we have. Now, when discussing philosophical skepticism, what may the skeptic observe at this stage? That he may not have the beliefs he thinks he has? This does not seem to be an acceptable starting point for Descartes (or anyone, for that matter—as Pritchard says, "even the skeptic is committed to the possibility of there being contentful thought" (Pritchard 2013, 527)). But this indicates that what the skeptic owes us is indeed an alternative account of the content of our beliefs. As Davidson reminds us, following Wittgenstein, "it is only after belief has a content that it can be doubted" (Davidson 1999b, 165). Stroud is in fact still conceding too much to the Cartesian skeptic by taking content for granted, an assumption which, ultimately, is revealed by his willingness to conceive of a possible gap between what triangulating interlocutors take the causes of their utterances and thoughts to be and what these causes actually are. Let me return to this possible gap.

When I initially introduced this contention of Stroud's, I noticed that it was at the very least puzzling that Stroud could conceive of such a gap, but I then proceeded to grant it to him and ask how granting it would affect how we reflect, not just on the truth-value of our beliefs, but on their content. As we have seen, the answer has been twofold. Either the skeptic is left with no starting point; if he cannot be sure of what it is he believes, he a fortiori cannot discuss the possibility that most or all of his beliefs could be false. Or the skeptic insists that he has the beliefs he thinks he has but owes us an account of their content that is different from that provided by triangulation. Either way, it has now become plain that what the skeptic, and Stroud with him, is doing is simply denying Davidson's externalist account of content. Allowing for there to be a possible gap between what interlocutors take the causes of their thoughts and utterances to be and what these causes actually are is in effect denying Davidson's semantic externalism. Throughout, Stroud simply fails to ascertain what anti-skeptical implications would follow if Davidson's account, as an account of belief-possession, and not just as an account of belief-attribution, was right. A further way to realize this is to recall Stroud's choosing to focus on Davidson's claim that "An interpreter who starts from scratch . . . cannot independently discover what an agent's beliefs are about, and ask whether they are true", and then arguing that the truth of an agent's beliefs is not needed to explain that, hence the possible gap. Let us now focus on the other claim Stroud quotes but which he then chooses to ignore: "we do not first form concepts and then discover what they apply to; rather, in the basic cases the application determines the content of the concept" (Davidson 1991a, 195). If Davidson's externalist account of content is right, the correctness of an agent's applications, that is, the truth of her beliefs, *is* needed to explain that. If the application determines the content of the concept, there is no possible gap.

I believe that denying that there might be a gap between what triangulating interlocutors take the causes of their basic thoughts and utterances to be and what these causes actually are is of a piece with the rejection of semantic reductionism, a rejection which, as we saw in Chapter 2, Stroud fully endorses, making his assertion that the above gap is possible all the more puzzling. As we are about to see, however, this apparent inconsistency indicates another possible option that one may take with regards to the theory of content and its consequences for skepticism, which I think dissipates, at least in part, the puzzle created by Stroud. The relevant options, in a nutshell, are these: Either Davidson's theory of content is right or it is not. If it is right, then either many of our beliefs about the world around us are true or we do not know what we believe. If it is wrong, then either an alternative theory of content is called for or no theory can in fact be provided—the call for a theory is illusory. I believe the latter is the option advocated by Stroud. I elaborate below.

4. Semantic Non-Reductionism and Skepticism

Recall the non-reductionist claims I made on Davidson's behalf in Chapter 2. First I stressed that, if the truth-conditions described by T-sentences are to be meaning-giving, we, as radical interpreters, cannot say how the speaker's primitive expressions contribute to these truth-conditions without in effect saying what they mean. As Stroud puts it, we cannot describe the meanings of a speaker's expressions outside of a semantic context. The theory of meaning for a speaker, what I called in Chapter 2 the semantic theory, can only be modest. As a result, and as becomes clearer with triangulation, we cannot say, outside of a semantic context, how the causes, and hence the meanings, of a speaker's expressions are fixed. Indeed, to say that the causes of their basic thoughts and utterances are what thinkers and speakers take them to be is to say that they cannot be fixed outside of semantic contexts. The meta-semantic theory can only be austere. I suspect that it is this non-reductionism, which, to repeat, he fully endorses, that leads Stroud to see no significant difference between radical interpretation and triangulation and to fail to recognize that the latter in particular provides an account of the possession of language and thoughts. Davidson's account of triangulation is ultimately an account of language and thought within language and thought. It does not provide an explanation of how specific utterances or thoughts get connected with specific causes; as long as these connections are not recognized by interlocutors as connections of given kinds, they cannot be meaning-determining. Thus we do not get a reductive account of how they come to mean what they do by their thoughts and utterances, as we might do if we could account for this simply by observing and describing non-semantically their responses to their environment. Rather, we might say, the triangulating interlocutors we are reflecting on are just as full of thoughts as the radical interpreters we were reflecting on. But saying this may be misleading, and it may mislead us into quietism, that is, the claim that nothing philosophically constructive can be said about meaning, which I believe is Stroud's ultimate stance on the matter. However, as I have stressed before, non-reductionism is in fact compatible with non-quietism.

True, we cannot give non-circular sufficient conditions for people meaning what they do by their thoughts and utterances. But we certainly can give illuminating necessary conditions for the possession of language and thoughts. To be speakers and thinkers, people have to interact with the world surrounding them and with one another. To talk and think of external objects and events, they have to interact with at least some of these objects and events at the same time that they interact with others who react to the same objects and events. We cannot say, in non-semantic terms, how any particular thought or utterance gets to have the meaning it has. But we can say of basic thoughts and utterances in general how they get to mean what they do. In short, given semantic non-reductionism, we cannot think of triangulating interlocutors as speakers and thinkers unless we describe their utterances and thoughts as having determinate causes and hence meanings. But this should not blind us to the fact that triangulation is also the process through which they get to determine what the causes and hence the meanings of their utterances and thoughts are. If we are so blinded, we may, like Stroud, underestimate the force of Davidson's claim that triangulation provides conditions of the possession of language and thoughts, and, like Stroud, we may then miss the anti-skeptical goods that reflecting on triangulation delivers. As we shall see below, I believe a similar kind of blind spot influences John McDowell's assessment of Davidson's anti-skeptical claims. But first I wish to address one more complaint that Stroud makes against Davidson's stronger claim that belief is in its nature veridical. This complaint also has, I think, a non-reductionist motivation: Just as we cannot describe how the causes of our beliefs affect us outside of a semantic context, so we cannot assess our beliefs outside of an epistemic context.[11]

Stroud argues that drawing the stronger claim involves adopting a standpoint on our knowledge of the world that Davidson himself has shown does not exist. Davidson has indeed shown that we cannot step outside our body of beliefs in order to assess them. As he writes, "There is no going outside this standard [provided by communication] to check whether we have things right, any more than we can check whether the platinum-iridium standard kept at the International Bureau of Weights and Standards in Sèvres, France, weighs a kilogram" (Davidson 1991b, 217–8). However, Stroud retorts, the skeptic wants us to reach our conclusion concerning the beliefs we have about the external world without appealing to any of the beliefs in question. This complaint of Stroud's is of course a variation on the idea that, if Davidson is right, the skeptic's question of whether his beliefs about the world around him are by and large true cannot be raised. And, if it cannot be raised, it cannot be addressed. Davidson answered this objection directly, noting that from the fact that it makes no sense to question the adequacy of a standard, it does not follow that it also makes no sense to assert its adequacy: "when the standard for the kilogram was a weight kept in Sèvres, there was no point in checking whether that weight weighed a kilogram. It does not follow that that weight was not the standard" (Davidson 1999e, 164). I think that Stroud's complaint belies again a failure fully to acknowledge that the stronger claim is grounded on an account of the content of our beliefs. This precludes us from asking whether all or most of them could be false. But it does not preclude us from asserting that many of them must be true. Stroud however insists that this way of dealing with the skeptic is "too quick" or, in fact, "unsound" (Stroud 1999, 155).

Stroud claims that it violates "the abstract possibility of a set of beliefs' being all or mostly false in the minimal sense that the truth of all or most or even any of them does not follow simply from their being held ... It would be to deny that, considered all together, the truth or falsity of the things we believe is independent of their being believed to be so" (Stroud 1999, 155). But, as Davidson has argued, "the assumption that the truth of what we believe is logically independent of what we believe is . . . ambiguous" (Davidson 1991b, 214). Thus, the truth of any one belief about the world does not follow from its being held. But the truth of a large number of them does so follow. Again, this is grounded on Davidson's account of content. Beliefs could not by and large be false since what makes many of them true is what makes many of them contentful to begin with. Furthermore, as Davidson has also argued, this does not threaten the objectivity of truth in the sense that what we believe to be true is so independently of our believing it. Davidson's view does not commit him to the anti-realist claim according to which what the world is like depends on what we believe it is. To be sure, Davidson also does not think that there is no connection whatsoever between our beliefs and the world they are about and so between beliefs and truth. But the connection goes the other way around, so to speak. It is, rather, that what we believe about the world depends on the way the world is. (This is why he eventually preferred to call his view neither realist nor anti-realist (Davidson 1988a, 185).)

In sum, I believe that Davidson is in a position to tell the skeptic that the hypothesis that gives rise to the skeptical challenge is mistaken: It is not possible for all or most of our beliefs about the world around us to be false. If our beliefs are contentful, that is, if we do have the beliefs we have about the world around us, then they are by and large true beliefs.[12] Hence the skeptical question whether they are true is addressed. It is, however, one thing to claim that our beliefs are true; it is another thing to claim that they are justified. This leads us to Stroud's last complaint about drawing the stronger claim and to Davidson's last step in his refutation of Cartesian skepticism.

5. Beliefs are Known to be Generally True

According to this objection, even if we could draw the stronger claim, it would not refute skepticism because it would not imply that we know or have any good reason to believe anything about the world. This, presumably, would be so because, again, we could not step outside all of our beliefs in order to assess them. But in fact, as I quoted him at the outset of this chapter, Davidson does believe that, precisely because belief is in its nature veridical, it does follow that beliefs are generally known to be true. Davidson has made it clear that he took his "account of how many of our perceptual beliefs come to have the contents they do . . . also [to explain] why we are justified in accepting them" (Davidson 1999f, 106). Thus, if Davidson's account of content is right, there are many things we know about the world since how our knowledge-claims about the world come to have the content they have both ensures the truth of many of them and explains how they are justified. As Davidson says, someone "who wonders what reason he has to think his beliefs are mostly true . . . has only to reflect on what a belief is [something which may be true or false, which is identified, directly or indirectly, by its cause] to appreciate that most of his basic beliefs are true, and among his beliefs, those most securely held and that cohere with the main body of his beliefs are the most apt to be true" (Davidson 1983, 152–3). This may make it look as if only philosophers, who correctly reflect on the nature of belief, are privileged enough to have knowledge. Consequently, prompted by Nagel, Davidson acknowledged that the above remarks were a mistake and that "The right thing to say is rather this: we are *justified* in taking our perceptual beliefs to be true, even when they are not, and so, when they are true, they constitute knowledge" (Davidson 1999g, 208). "We are justified in holding them not because they rest on something more secure or fundamental, but because they are the kind of beliefs they are and because they are supported by many other beliefs" (Davidson 1999e, 163).[13]

To the Cartesian skeptic who remains unsatisfied with this because he is seeking an assessment of our body of beliefs as a whole, Davidson keeps replying that this is precisely what cannot be done. We cannot step outside all of our beliefs in order to assess them. There is thus no way we can know that we have the knowledge we do have. If this is the kind of knowledge the skeptic is seeking, he is "demanding more of knowledge than is justified" (Davidson 1999e, 162). More accurately, I would add, he is demanding more of knowledge than is intelligible. If we take seriously the claim that triangulation provides conditions of the possession of language and thoughts and not just conditions of interpretation, we can no longer point out, from a philosophically skeptical point of view, that all or most of our beliefs could be false after all, or that we could be wrong about all or most of the causes of our beliefs. Rather, we have to remain silent. Not being able to assess our beliefs from outside means not being able to discuss them from outside either.

Another forceful critic of Davidson's claim that he has shown the skeptic that many of our beliefs about the world around us are justified is McDowell, whose *Mind and World* is, among other things, a sustained attack on Davidson's account of knowledge. McDowell applauds Davidson's rejection of the scheme/content distinction, that is, the idea of there being a neutral world, reality or universe, or some kind of neutral stuff, raw data or whatnot, waiting for us, as it were, to structure or organize it by means of a conceptual scheme. As Davidson (1974b) argues, such a distinction is unintelligible. Without going into the details of Davidson's argument, it is interesting to note here that the unintelligibility of this distinction is also of a piece with the unintelligibility of the gap between the typical causes of interlocutors' basic responses to features of their environment and what they take these causes to be. In each case, what makes no sense is the idea of the world standing completely apart from our beliefs. It is the idea that the world could contribute in different ways to our system of beliefs. But McDowell does not seem to understand the rejection of the scheme/content distinction in the exact terms that Davidson understands it, since he does not think that Davidson's view yields the anti-skeptical results Davidson takes it to yield. What McDowell applauds is, as he puts it, Davidson's rejection of the Myth of the Given, which is also the idea that we could conceive of experience in non-conceptual terms and yet invoke it in the justification of our beliefs, "the idea that truth and knowledge depend on rational relations to something outside the conceptual realm" (McDowell 1994, 16). On this much Davidson and McDowell are in agreement: Only something that has conceptual content could justify a belief. Davidson actually takes this a step further by maintaining that only a belief could count as a reason for holding another belief (Davidson 1983, 141). In the rejection of the scheme/content distinction, we can see again Davidson's non-reductionism, stressing, as we might put it, how we cannot make sense of the idea of something devoid of content providing content. What McDowell stresses here in addition, but in tandem with Davidson, is that we cannot make sense of the idea of something devoid of conceptual content providing justification for something that has conceptual content. Still, we do want our empirical beliefs to be justified, and we want this justifying to be based on how things are in the world. How is this to be done if the world cannot be seen to cooperate, that is, if only beliefs can justify beliefs? This is McDowell's question for Davidson. McDowell thinks that, by renouncing the Myth of the Given, Davidson renounces any "rational constraint from the world":

> Davidson recoils from the Myth of the Given all the way to denying experience any justificatory role . . . Davidson's picture depicts our empirical thinking as engaged in with no rational constraint, but only causal influence, from outside . . . I think we should be suspicious of his bland confidence that empirical content can be intelligibly in our picture even though we carefully stipulate that the world's impacts on our senses have nothing to do with justification.
> (McDowell 1994, 14–15)

It is true that in the essay McDowell focuses on, "A Coherence Theory of Truth and Knowledge" (Davidson 1983), Davidson labels his view, misleadingly, as he acknowledged four years later in "Afterthoughts" (Davidson 1987a), coherentist. And Davidson certainly is a coherentist insofar as he insists that "all that counts as evidence or justification for a belief must come from the same totality of belief to which it belongs" (Davidson 1987a, 155). But as I noted earlier, already in the essay, which is prior to any developed view concerning triangulation, Davidson also insists that "belief is intrinsically veridical"—as he says in the afterthoughts, he took that to be the main thesis of the essay (Davidson 1987a, 155). And the grounds he provides for this claim—that "belief can be seen to be veridical by considering what determines the existence and contents of a belief" (Davidson 1983, 146)—are provided in the essay as well. This leads me to conclude that McDowell, like Stroud, is not paying sufficient attention to, or taking seriously enough, the account of content that Davidson is giving and the fact that it is this account that grounds his argument against the skeptic.

McDowell's own solution to the problem he poses to Davidson—how can our empirical beliefs be justified if we renounce the Myth of the Given?—is to say that "the relevant conceptual capacities are drawn on *in* receptivity. It is not that they are exercised *on* an extra-conceptual deliverance of receptivity . . . The conceptual contents that are most basic . . . are already possessed by impressions themselves, impingements by the world on our sensibility" (McDowell 1994, 9–10). That is, the Given, the contribution from the world that provides the rational constraint that is needed if our beliefs are to be justified, has to be thought of not as "given", but as structured, organized or conceptualized, or, we might say, as full of conceptual content. Now it seems to me that Davidson's solution is very similar to McDowell's. As we have seen repeatedly, according to Davidson, the causes that "influence" our thinking are not to be thought of as mere causes, to be considered in and of themselves. But they are to be thought of as what we take to be the causes, that is, they are to be thought of within a semantic context and thus, as we might say again, as imbued with content. Davidson's non-reductionist claim, which insists that content cannot be explained "from outside" content, or in terms that do not use the notion of content, is indeed tantamount to giving up the myth of the Given. But it does not preclude a "rational constraint from the world". As Davidson writes: "There must be 'friction' between the world and our thoughts if our thoughts are to have any content at all, and I find this friction right here, in the external causes of our perceptual beliefs" (Davidson 1999f, 106).[14]

I take it that in answer to this McDowell would say that external causes, conceived of as mere causes, may provide friction, but it cannot be friction of the right kind, that is, it cannot be the kind of friction that yields justification. But this would be to forget again that the causes that provide content are the causes that we have taken to do so. The external causes' friction does yield justification, and it is a genuine friction in that we have no choice but to accept our basic beliefs. (Recall that "we do not first form concepts and then discover what they apply to; rather, in the basic cases the application determines the content of the concept" (Davidson 1991a, 195).) In other words, at the basic level there can be no distinction between friction and justification. What provides our basic beliefs with content is also what justifies them, in the sense that what provides our basic beliefs with content cannot do so unless we take it in a certain way. Once more: What we take the causes of our basic beliefs to be is what these causes are. To this it could in turn be replied that our involvement in the fixing of the causes is what deprives the world of its constraining role. But this would in a way be a call for reintroducing the Myth of the Given, that is, it would be to deny that the world can play any such role if we conceive of it as conceptualized. To say that the causes of our basic beliefs are what we take them to be is not to say that we make up these causes. It is only to say that the causes cannot be seen as providing content unless they are recognized as the causes that they are, that is, as providing the contents that they do. It is an expression of the inescapability of semantic non-reductionism. The causes that provide content are out there all right, but we cannot describe how they affect us outside of a semantic context.[15]

There is another worry McDowell expresses concerning Davidson's view, a worry that has often been voiced by others. McDowell in fact recognizes that Davidson's "coherentist framework" is supplemented by the "reassuring thesis" that belief is in its nature veridical. However, McDowell wonders how reassuring the thesis may be,

> if we are worried about whether Davidson's coherentist picture can incorporate thought's bearing on reality. Suppose one feels the worry in this familiar form: so far as the picture goes, one might be a brain in a mad scientist's vat. The Davidsonian response seems to be that if one were a brain in a vat, it would be correct to interpret one's beliefs as being largely true beliefs about the brain's electronic environment . . . The response does not calm the fear that our picture leaves our thinking possibly out of touch with the world outside us. It gives us a dizzying sense that our grip on what it is that we believe is not as firm as we thought.
>
> (McDowell 1994, 16–7)

Suppose indeed that I am now wondering about the causes of my beliefs and thus about whether they are grounded in the world of objects and events around me, as I take them to be, or in the states of a computer injecting thoughts in my brain. As we have seen before, if we accept Davidson's account of content, doing that is not tantamount to wondering whether all of one's beliefs might be false. It is tantamount to wondering what the contents of one's beliefs might be. McDowell seems to acknowledge this—"our grip on what it is we believe is not as firm as we thought"—but he fails to acknowledge how radical the skeptical position here has become. The belief I allegedly have as a skeptic is in fact a belief that cannot be expressed or thought, since as soon as I wonder whether I am a brain in a vat I am in fact depriving myself of any belief, insofar as my beliefs no longer have content for me. But if they do have content, then they have the same old content I always took them to have, that is, they are about what I take to be their causes.

The brain-in-a-vat scenarios are varied and it may look at first as if they could not all be dealt with in the same way. There are, to be sure, slight variations in the answers. Thus I do not think that the answer McDowell attributes to Davidson (cited by Rorty 1986), according to which "it would be correct to interpret one's beliefs as being largely true beliefs about the brain's electronic environment" is the right answer if it is given from the first-person point of view. To repeat, if I am wondering whether I am a brain in a vat, I am wondering whether I am really thinking of the world of objects and events, and not whether my thoughts are by and large correct. And either I keep wondering, which becomes nonsensical, or I stop wondering and acknowledge that many of my thoughts, which are about the world around me, are correct. However, if the brain in the vat we are imagining is external to us and we are wondering what it is thinking, then we may conclude that, insofar as we think of ourselves as interacting with the brain and its electronic environment, it is thinking about the states of the computer, which are after all the typical causes of its thoughts.

Trickier cases seem to be provided by brains that started off in the way we did, triangulating with others on features of our environment, but were subsequently envatted. Here we may distinguish between cases where the brain remains envatted and cases where the brain first is envatted, then is unenvatted, and this switch keeps happening at a rate that does not allow the brain to establish causal relations with its environment (Amoretti 2011, 63). Could I not be one of these brains, in which case what would I be thinking? In the first case, it might be tempting to say, following Amoretti, that perhaps I would retain some of the beliefs I had about my previous surroundings, but some of them would obviously be false, though coherent. Perhaps I would eventually develop beliefs about my new environment, if I were in a position to triangulate with others on some of its states. The second case seems harder to deal with—it is extremely tempting to invoke Davidson's declaration that he has "a general distrust of thought-experiments that pretend to reveal what we would say under conditions that in fact never arise" (Davidson 1991a, 199). But the difficulty afforded by the second case reveals the danger that threatens brain-in-a-vat scenarios as well as thought-experiments in general. As we have seen several times by now, we must be careful, when considering thought-experiments, that they are not expressed in such a way that the question is begged in favor of the case they seem to establish. Thus, we must be careful that the brain-in-a-vat scenarios do not assume the falsity of the view they are supposed to address, in the present case, the view that the contents of our basic beliefs are determined by the objects and events on some of which at least we have triangulated with others. What all the brain-in-a-vat scenarios have in common is that they assume the skeptic's hypothesis that I could have all the beliefs I have about the world around me even if they were false. They assume that, envatted or not, I am thinking about the world around me. But this is precisely what Davidson's triangulation argument has been meant to deny.

6. Conclusion

I have argued that Davidson is right in maintaining that it follows from the triangulation argument, and thus from his particular brand of semantic externalism, that both many of our beliefs about the world around us are true and that we know them to be true. There might still be a question, however, of what kind of an answer to the skeptic this precisely amounts to. As has been debated,[16] is the answer direct or therapeutic? It cannot be direct, if a direct answer involves accepting the skeptic's terms, in particular a commitment to a non-externalist theory of content. But I do not think that it is merely therapeutic either, where this means that Davidson "gives us a good reason for regarding [the skeptical problem] as a *pseudo-problem*, one that does not require a direct philosophical response" (Pritchard 2013, 529). Davidson's response may not be direct, but it is still philosophically constructive and challenging. Contra Pritchard, the philosophical picture that Davidson presents—his theory of content—is not on a par with the philosophical picture the skeptic is relying on—"the claim that we can even make sense of the idea of beliefs as being genuinely contentful and yet massively false" (Pritchard 2013, 529). This picture is not on a par with Davidson's because the skeptic has provided no support for his claim. Davidson, on the other hand, has offered philosophical considerations that the skeptic cannot ignore simply because he is "already sold on the skeptical problem" (Pritchard 2013, 529). I think that the failure to acknowledge this makes Davidson's achievement look less impressive than it really is. If the skeptic wants to cultivate his skepticism, he now has work to do to undermine the "conclusion that I know that the world, both in general and in many particular ways, is as I think it is" (Davidson 1999g, 209).

Notes

1. As Thomas Nagel has aptly put it, Davidson's argument is not the Cartesian "*je pense, donc je suis*, but *je pense, donc je sais*" (Nagel 1999, 196).
2. For the numerous discussions and criticisms the omniscient interpreter argument generated, see, e.g., Foley and Fumerton 1985, Klein 1986, Williams 1988, Brueckner 1991, Ludwig 1992, Genova 1999 and Stroud 1999.
3. See also Genova 1999.
4. Thus I do not think that, e.g., Putnam's argument for externalism, discussed in the previous chapter, has any consequences for skepticism.
5. The discussion of Stroud's views in Section 3 is based on Verheggen 2011a.
6. Where I talk of two claims, one weaker, according to which belief-attribution is in its nature truth-ascribing, and one stronger, according to which belief is in its nature veridical, Stroud talks of two readings, one weaker and one stronger, of "belief is in its nature veridical". As it is obvious that Davidson endorses the stronger reading, I prefer to refer to it as the stronger claim.
7. Bjørn Ramberg is one of the philosophers who does not recognize the continuity of Davidson's thought and who, as a result, contends that significant progress on the anti-skeptical front is made when we move from the considerations of radical interpretation to those of triangulation (Ramberg 2001, 228). This is of course because he takes radical interpretation to be an account of thought-attribution exclusively, where the question what constitutes the content of thoughts does not arise, and thus it makes sense to think of all the attributed thoughts as possibly mistaken. If, however, triangulation is constitutive of the thoughts of interlocutors, "we have to conclude that we can no longer make sense of the idea of a radically mistaken radical interpreter" (Ramberg 2001, 231).

114 Language, Thought and Knowledge

8. Stroud's talk of 'reciprocal interpretation' suggests that he is still not fully acknowledging the focus on conditions of possession, rather than attribution, of language and thoughts, which, as we shall see, he indeed is not.
9. This is the answer proposed by Ramberg 2001, 234.
10. Sosa goes on to conclude that Stroud's reading is not much of an answer to the skeptic. For "even if, *only for the sake of the argument*, it is granted that I cannot coherently think or say the following: <although I believe that p, it is, compatibly with that, possible that not p>, nevertheless it does not follow from that, nor is it true, that I cannot coherently think or say *this*: <I might be massively wrong in my beliefs>" (Sosa 2003, 171). In other words, for Sosa, the skeptical hypothesis remains alive and well.
11. The next two paragraphs are taken almost verbatim from Verheggen 2011a.
12. Has Davidson provided, as has been suggested repeatedly, a transcendental argument? This is a rather vexed question, which can only be answered with "it depends". If a transcendental argument is one that lays out the necessary conditions for the possibility of a phenomenon, in the present case, the possibility of having beliefs about the world around us, then Davidson's argument may be called transcendental. However, as I hope I have shown, it does not suffer from the shortcomings that transcendental arguments have been said, initially by Stroud (1968), to suffer from. As Pritchard puts it, "Very roughly, Stroud's charge is that transcendental arguments demonstrate what we are committed to thinking is the case, but fall short of actually showing what *is* the case" (Pritchard 2013, 528). (See also Genova 1999, 187.) This indeed sounds like Stroud's charge against Davidson's argument, according to which what it has shown is that we must think that many of our beliefs are true, but not that these beliefs are in fact true. In other words, a necessary condition for having the beliefs we have about the world around us is that we must think that these beliefs are true. Davidson is spelling out "what we must think, believe, or experience if we are to think, believe, or have experiences at all" (Pritchard and Ranalli 2013, 364). I have argued that this is precisely not what Davidson is doing. He is not telling us what we must think is the case, but what in fact must be the case, in order for us to have the beliefs we have about the world around us. Thus he is not saying that, if I believe that there are external objects and events, then I must think that these beliefs are true. Rather he is saying that if I am to have these beliefs, then they must be true. Davidson himself has expressed reservations about attaching the label "transcendental" to his argument in so far as the argument depends "in part not on purely a priori considerations but rather on a view of the way people are" (Davidson 1999c, 194) and "on the fact that I have just the beliefs I do" (Davidson 1999g, 209). (Others, e.g., Putnam, see nothing wrong with calling an argument transcendental even if it includes empirical assumptions (Putnam 1981, 16).)
13. Davidson, in his reply to Nagel, continues in the following way: "since our only reasons for holding [our perceptual beliefs] true are the support they get from further perceptual beliefs and general coherence with how we think things are, the underlying source of justification is not itself a reason. We do not *infer* our perceptual beliefs from something else more foundational" (Davidson 1999g, 208). This has led Cristina Amoretti, following Sosa, to label Davidson's theory of justification externalist (Amoretti 2011, 61). I would be wary of doing this, however, as Davidson has always be adamant that only a belief could count as a reason for holding another belief (more on this shortly). But if this is just another way of saying that we do not have to know that we are justified in order to have knowledge, then I have no problem with it.
14. 'Friction' is the term McDowell sometimes uses to characterize the constraint from the world. See, e.g., McDowell 1994, 11.

15. The worry that our involvement in the fixing of the causes of our basic beliefs is what deprives the world of its constraining role is, I think, what in part has recently led McDowell to claim that the kind of conceptual content that allows us to avoid the Myth is not propositional but intuitional. Contra Davidson, according to McDowell, "experiencing is not taking things to be so" (McDowell 2008, 10). "Though they are not discursive, intuitions have content of a sort that embodies an immediate potential for exploiting that same content in knowledgeable judgments. Intuitions immediately reveal things to be the way they would be judged to be in those judgments" (McDowell 2008, 9). I have several worries about McDowell's claims. In particular, I wonder about the kind of isomorphism between world and mind that seems to be involved here, about how things can be revealed, non-propositionally, to be the way they can (propositionally) be judged, and, more generally, about what kind of theory of content may ground McDowell's claims. More importantly, in any case, if I am right in thinking, contra McDowell, that once we think of the causes of our beliefs in a semantic context, they can be seen as constraining, McDowell's notion of intuitional content is not needed.
16. See Pritchard and Ranalli 2013.

Part Two
Desires, Reasons and Morality
Robert H. Myers

5 Triangulation and Normative Skepticism

Are there normative truths—truths about what people have reasons, in the normative sense, to do? For someone to have a reason in the normative sense to Φ, there must be some consideration that counts in favor of her Φ-ing. Clearly people often believe they have such reasons; but are such normative beliefs ever actually true? Davidson thinks they are. My aim in the second half of this book is to consider how strong his case for this claim is.[1]

We have just seen how important the triangulation argument is for Davidson's response to Cartesian skepticism, turning what would otherwise be conclusions only about our attributions of beliefs into conclusions about the real nature of beliefs and their presumptive veridicality. My claim in this chapter will be that the triangulation argument is equally important to Davidson's response to normative skepticism, but that in this case it also raises several difficult questions that will have to be tackled down the road.

1. Some Preliminaries

Before introducing Davidson's arguments, let us take a few moments to get clearer about the conclusion he hopes to defend.

The first point we need to underline turns on the distinction between normative reasons and motivating reasons. Whereas a normative reason for someone to Φ is a consideration counting in favor of her Φ-ing, a motivating reason for someone to Φ is a psychological state potentially appropriately explanatory of her Φ-ing.[2] Famously, Davidson maintains (1963, 5) that primary reasons for action are always constituted by suitably related pro-attitudes and beliefs. He also maintains (1963, 8) that someone's pro-attitude towards Ψ-ing and her belief that she could Ψ by Φ-ing could appropriately explain her Φ-ing because they would reveal her Φ-ing to be at least minimally rational. This can make it sound as if he is trying to get normative truths on the cheap, by simply assuming that normative reasons are somehow determined by the fact that people have such and such pro-attitudes and that these pro-attitudes could be satisfied by their acting in so and so ways. As we shall soon see, however, this is not at all Davidson's view of the matter.

His claim about the constitution of primary reasons is a claim about the constitution of motivating reasons, and these reasons rationalize actions only by revealing what agents are trying to achieve in performing them. Davidson recognizes that the normative question is whether there is anything people *should* be trying to achieve. So even if he wanted to establish that people's normative reasons are somehow determined by their pro-attitudes, he recognizes that this would take something more than an argument about the structure of motivating reasons. But in point of fact this is not the sort of view that Davidson wants to defend. His view is that people's normative reasons typically obtain both prior to and independently of their pro-attitudes, and that, if anything, it is their reasons that shape their attitudes, not their attitudes their reasons.

This is also potentially misleading, however, for it seriously complicates Davidson's relation to internal reason theories. If the question is whether people's normative reasons are in principle accessible to them via internal reasoning—as Bernard Williams (1980, 104) puts it, via sound deliberative procedures that take off from their initial motivational sets—Davidson's inclination is to answer by allowing that this could very well prove to be the case. He does not himself have very much to say about what such sound deliberative procedures would look like, but because he believes normative truths play an important role in determining what people's pro-attitudes are, he does not believe it is possible for anyone's pro-attitudes to be systematically off the mark. And this makes it perfectly plausible to suppose that sound deliberation taking off from their initial motivational sets could at least in principle lead any agent to the truth about what her normative reasons are. But of course, on Davidson's view, this is not because normative truths are mere constructions of reason. They are not determined by sound deliberative procedures but instead determine what deliberative procedures count as sound. Although Davidson does not believe normative truths and people's pro-attitudes are fully constitutively independent of one another, it is important to remember that it is still a kind of realism he is defending, for, as he sees things, it is people's pro-attitudes that are partly constitutively dependent on normative truths, and not, as internal reason theorists think, normative truths that are partly constitutively dependent on people's pro-attitudes. Invoking Christine Korsgaard's (1996, 35) terminology, his realism about normative reasons could be described as substantive rather than procedural. But it is a version of substantive realism that procedural realists or constructivists like Korsgaard often overlook, one that makes it almost as difficult for skepticism to take hold as their own views do.

At the risk of getting ahead of ourselves, we should also note another respect in which Davidson's version of normative realism is somewhat unusual. Normative realism is often associated with the idea that normative properties play a role in causing people to have the particular pro-attitudes they have.[3] And this, when combined with the assumption that causal relations are nomological, can seem to commit normative realists to the existence of normative laws. But the idea that there are strict laws linking the existence of normative properties to the acquisition of corresponding pro-attitudes is surely not plausible—certainly no more plausible than the idea that there are strict laws linking the possession of particular pro-attitudes to the performance of corresponding actions. It is important to remember, therefore, that Davidson (1967) distinguishes sharply between relations and explanations and holds that only the latter can be nomological. If two events are related as cause and effect, he insists that there must be *some* description under which they are linked by laws, but he allows that there may be other descriptions under which the one still explains the other even though there is no law involved. Famously, he holds (1970) that this is the case with pro-attitudes and actions; under these descriptions, explanations are possible, because possession of some particular pro-attitude can make it understandable that the agent would perform the corresponding action, but it would be a mistake to think such explanations are nomological. My claim will be that Davidson's view of normative properties is similar—under that description, they can explain, because they can make it understandable that a person would have acquired one pro-attitude and not some other, but these explanations are not going to involve applications of any laws.

One final cautionary note before we start looking at Davidson's actual arguments. You might suppose that anyone arguing for normative realism must be hoping to establish that specifically moral reasons obtain prior to and independently of people's pro-attitudes and hence have an inescapable and perhaps even overriding authority. It is worth noting, therefore, that this is not Davidson's goal. He in fact has remarkably little to say about specifically moral reasons. However, he does make it clear that he thinks the normative landscape is too complicated to be captured by any single ultimate principle.[4] In his view, reasons for action are captured in what he calls, somewhat misleadingly, prima facie principles, not ultimate or all things considered principles.[5] All things considered judgments are formed by ascertaining which prima facie principles are applicable to the case and weighing their verdicts against one another. As we shall see, this makes it extremely unlikely that specifically moral reasons could possess an authority that is in every case fully overriding. In fact, it raises some interesting questions about how specifically moral reasons might actually be identified and about what ultimately distinguishes them from others. My suggestion towards the end of the book will be that Davidson's normative realism is best combined with a sort of contractualism about morality. People's first-order reasons for action, though real, put them in conflict, thereby giving them second-order reasons to negotiate a mutually acceptable morality. Be this as it may, however, the point for now is just that Davidson does not have a horse in this race. He does not defend any particular view of the content of morality, let alone the view that the authority of morality is always overriding.

So it is in several quite important respects a very modest version of normative realism that Davidson will be defending, one that does not have anything directly to say about either the content or the authority of specifically moral reasons, one that does not involve any commitment to the existence either of strict normative laws or of nomological normative explanations, and one even allowing that people's normative reasons might in principle always be accessible to them via sound internal reasoning. For all that, however, Davidson's version of normative realism still does involve commitments that many readers will find untenable. Rather than taking the easy and popular way out and regarding people's normative reasons as mere constructions of their pro-attitudes, Davidson holds that at least in typical cases people's normative reasons obtain both prior to and independently of their pro-attitudes, and in fact that they have an important role to play in causing people to have the pro-attitudes they do. So let us now turn to the task of identifying the arguments by which Davidson hopes to establish these claims.

I believe it is helpful to view Davidson's arguments for these claims as coming in two distinct stages or steps, beginning in what I will be calling his interpretation argument and culminating in what we have been calling the triangulation argument. Logically speaking, the triangulation argument is actually further upstream, offering support for claims that the interpretation argument treats as premises; but Davidson defends the interpretation argument first, and I think for expository purposes it is best to begin with it. I should note that I do not believe these two arguments are always so very sharply distinguished by Davidson himself. My aim in this chapter is not to trace the historical development of Davidson's various claims concerning interpretation and triangulation, but to organize them in a manner that will highlight their strengths and weaknesses as an argument for normative realism. By sharply distinguishing the interpretation argument from the triangulation argument and starting our discussion with it, we get a clearer view both of the worries the triangulation argument seeks to address and of the doubts it raises in its turn.[6]

2. Davidson's Interpretation Argument

As I understand it, Davidson's interpretation argument contains four claims—two premises and two conclusions about what follows from them. I shall begin by explaining what these four claims are, then take up a number of common objections to them.[7]

One premise upon which the argument rests involves a claim about the essentially public character of beliefs and the other propositional attitudes. Propositional attitudes are to be thought of as theoretical states of a sort, not known by direct observation but inferred in the attempt to explain and predict behavior. (To be sure, one typically has non-inferential knowledge of one's own attitudes, but even this is not the product of direct observation.)[8] But this is not to be taken as opening a possibly unbridgeable gap between people's behavior and their propositional attitudes, as in the traditional problem of other minds; for minds require contents, and Davidson's claim is that minds would not have contents if they were not interpretable as having them. What he means by this is not simply that the contents of people's minds must in principle be accessible to anyone who has sufficient evidence at their disposal. A general commitment of this sort to empiricism would not guarantee the essentially public character Davidson is claiming for the propositional attitudes. That involves the stronger claim that people must be interpretable solely on the basis of evidence concerning observable features of their behavior and their relations to their environment.

This claim might seem misguided because it might seem to suggest that background information has no essential role to play in interpretation. It might seem to suggest that a person would have to be interpretable even by someone who knew nothing about how prior interpretations of other people had fared. Yet, as Jerry Fodor and Ernest Lepore (1993, 65) have remarked, the possibility of any such "first linguistics" is surely something we should dismiss. Surely, in our endeavor to interpret any one person, we must be guided by what we believe to be the lessons of previous endeavors to interpret other people. I think this is clearly right; but for that very reason I also think Davidson's claim is not meant to deny it. His claim speaks only to questions about the sorts of evidence we need regarding the particular person who is at the particular moment the subject of our interpretation. He is not denying that other sorts of information, including information gleaned from interpretations of other people, will be necessary as well. He is simply maintaining that all we need regarding the particular subject of any particular interpretation is evidence regarding her observable behavior and her relations to her environment.[9]

Now the fact that background information has an essential role to play in interpretation might seem to indicate that interpretations can be constructed in a straightforwardly empirical manner.[10] This illusion is shattered, however, by the second cornerstone of the interpretation argument, to wit, by the holism of the mental. The thought here is that the content of any one of a person's propositional attitudes depends on the contents of many of the other propositional attitudes she has. And Davidson's claim is that this creates an obstacle to interpretation that no amount of background information can be expected to overcome; for it means we cannot advance a hypothesis about any one of a person's propositional attitudes without simultaneously advancing supporting hypotheses about many of her other propositional attitudes. Yet it is difficult to see how publicly accessible evidence could justify us in making such a complex attribution of propositional attitudes. There will undoubtedly be many isolated respects in which our subject's behavior and circumstances match the behavior and circumstances of people whose propositional attitudes we are familiar with. But inevitably these matches will be too fragmentary to justify us in postulating a broad match between her propositional attitudes and theirs.

Some believe Davidson's holism commits him to the extreme claim that the content of every one of a person's propositional attitudes depends upon the content of every other.[11] And because they believe this extreme claim to be patently absurd, they believe his consequent worries about interpretation to be largely unfounded. It seems to me, however, that the extreme nature of this claim should again make us wonder whether it can really be what Davidson intends to convey.[12] Moreover—and perhaps more importantly—I think a considerably less extreme claim suffices to generate the problem he envisions for interpretation; for the strict matches to be found between one person's behavior and circumstances and the behavior and circumstances of other people are rarely going to be very extensive. Bits of hers will undoubtedly match bits of theirs, but broader swaths of her behavior and circumstances will typically lack strict precedents. It follows, therefore, that the holism of the mental does not have to be taken very far before background information starts becoming of doubtful help to interpreters. For how, once again, can fragmentary matches among people's behavior and circumstances possibly justify us in postulating broader matches among their attitudes?

The third main tenet of the interpretation argument, the unhappily named principle of charity, constitutes Davidson's solution to this puzzle.[13] The claim is that interpretation can and must proceed on the assumption that others see things largely as we do. We are to begin the process of interpretation by provisionally assigning our subjects pro-attitudes and beliefs roughly like our own; we can then tailor this assignment to fit the facts about their actual behavior and their relations to their environment.[14] We can count on receiving help here from the information we have gleaned from previous attempts to interpret other people, from our empirically conditioned sense of the ways in which different histories and circumstances correlate with different pro-attitudes and beliefs. Applying this knowledge to the case at hand, we will justifiably expect our subjects to harbor certain disagreements with us, and this will help us decide how our provisional assignment of pro-attitudes and beliefs should be adjusted to fit them. One must not conclude from this, however, that no limits exist on the form that these disagreements could take. It is one thing to allow that the subjects of our interpretation might deviate somewhat from the precedent we set. It would be another thing altogether, however, to suppose that the precedent we set is not relevant to them. One must not suppose that the existence of rival precedents is something previous interpretations of other people could have revealed.

Before introducing the fourth major tenet of the interpretation argument, we need to be a little clearer about the sense in which our own pro-attitudes and beliefs must be assumed to set a precedent for other people's pro-attitudes and beliefs. The claim here is not simply that we must assume every person to share in a common nature or psychology, so that we set a precedent for others only in the sense of providing instances of that nature or psychology.[15] The claim is rather that we must assume every person to be influenced or shaped by that which is true, so that we set a precedent for others in the different sense of providing indications of what those truths are. In order to highlight this idea, the principle of charity may be usefully reformulated by saying that we must begin the process of interpretation by provisionally assigning our subjects roughly the pro-attitudes and beliefs we take to be correct. Since we typically take our own pro-attitudes and beliefs to be correct, this reformulation will make little difference in practice; but its implications for theory are extremely important, for it indicates that we are committed to thinking in objective terms. By putting the principle this way, we bring to the fore Davidson's contention that in our interpretations of one another we necessarily reveal ourselves to have real convictions about both the descriptive and the normative properties of our shared environment.

Thus we are led to the conclusion that interpretation requires us to exhibit real convictions about both descriptive and normative properties and to find others largely in agreement with them. The fourth and final step in the interpretation argument is meant to take us to the further conclusion that these convictions upon which we must largely agree must be largely true. To this end, we are asked to imagine an "omniscient" interpreter who knows all there is to know about both descriptive and normative matters.[16] How is this interpreter to make sense of us, if its knowledge of us concerns only our behavior and our relations to our environment? Only, Davidson famously claims, by following the very same procedure—that is, only by assuming us to have pro-attitudes and beliefs roughly like the ones it takes to be correct. And since it is, by hypothesis, fully knowledgeable about both these matters, it follows that the pro-attitudes and beliefs we actually do have approximate the ones we really should have. Thus, summing up the interpretation argument, we can successfully interpret one another only because we have real convictions about both descriptive and normative properties, which convictions, by the same argument, can be successfully interpreted in their own right only because they are largely true to how things are.

Various critics have complained that this final step in the argument is hopelessly question-begging. Why should we suppose an omniscient being would be able to interpret us correctly? If a successful interpreter would have to share many of our convictions about descriptions and norms, isn't this simply to assume that our convictions about such matters are largely true? Why couldn't the skeptics simply reply by speculating that an omniscient being might not share our manifold illusions either about descriptions or about norms, and so might prove constitutionally incapable of interpreting us solely on the basis of evidence concerning our behavior and our relations to our environment? It should be clear, however, that by allowing the argument to reach this stage, these critics have given Davidson all the ammunition he needs to deal with their complaint. For the publicness condition, after all, stipulates precisely that people must be interpretable by anyone who has at their disposal both sufficient behavioral and environmental evidence and adequate background information. Pretty clearly, an omniscient being would have such information at its disposal, so there would be nothing preventing it from succeeding as an interpreter. And so, if that would require it to share many of our convictions, it just does follow that our convictions must be largely true.[17]

More discerning critics are therefore careful to get their objections in earlier, often directing their fire against Davidson's claim that interpretation depends upon charity. Why, they will ask, must interpreters assume that their subjects have roughly the pro-attitudes and beliefs that they—the interpreters—take to be correct? They may well grant that the holism of the mental poses a problem for interpretation, and indeed that interpreters must make some substantive assumptions about their subjects' pro-attitudes and beliefs. But they will insist that there are many different forms these substantive assumptions could take, and hence that Davidson must explain why the principle of charity should always be favored.[18] Moreover, they will say, the explanation cannot simply be that there are too many different forms alternatives to the principle of charity could take. It might be thought that this prevents interpreters from having any reason to set aside the principle of charity in favor of something else. But that cannot be the explanation that Davidson himself means to give, especially not if I am right in maintaining that he wants to allow interpreters access to background information; for why couldn't their background information have a bearing on this choice, precisely by revealing that one alternative to the principle of charity has been successfully employed in earlier interpretations?

The simplest way to respond to this is to argue by reductio. Thus suppose we somehow have accomplished what Davidson believes to be impossible: We have interpreted a group of people—call them the As—and found them to have pro-attitudes and beliefs radically different from our own. Now suppose we encounter another group of people—call them the Bs—and try to interpret them following not the principle of charity but the precedent set by the As. That is, we begin by assuming them to have pro-attitudes and beliefs not even remotely like our own but at least roughly like the pro-attitudes and beliefs possessed by the As, then try to tailor this assumption to fit their behavior and circumstances. Could some such method as this have any chance of actually succeeding? The problem is that what we take their behavior and circumstances to be will of necessity depend on what our pro-attitudes and beliefs are. So the challenge will be to determine how behavior and circumstances viewed from our perspective could call for adjustments to the sorts of pro-attitudes and beliefs possessed by the As. And given how radically different those sorts of pro-attitudes and beliefs are supposed to be, it is difficult to see any grounds for confidence that this challenge could be met.

If this argument seems too quick, that is probably because one is surreptitiously supposing that the pro-attitudes and beliefs provisionally assigned to the Bs are not *so* different after all. Gopal Sreenivasan, for example, invites us (2001, 21) to image that the As believe themselves to be inherently superior to everyone else, and that, in consequence, their pro-attitudes differ markedly from ours. That clearly is imaginable. So why should it not also be imaginable that, upon encountering the Bs, we might set about interpreting them following the precedent set by the As? The problem with this, however, is that the As' pro-attitudes could be markedly different from ours without being different in the radical sense we are trying to isolate here. If we simply imagine the As to have more or less the pro-attitudes we think they would be correct in having if they actually were inherently superior to everyone else, then it is indeed easy to imagine using them as our model for the Bs, but only because the precedent they would set would not be radically different after all. Our convictions about descriptions and norms would still be guiding our interpretations of the Bs; the As would just be illustrating how one kind of mistake can lead to others. That might be a real aid to us in our efforts to interpret the Bs, but it in no way suggests that an alternative to charity is in fact possible. That requires us to imagine the As as having pro-attitudes markedly different from our own, where the differences are not regarded as consequences of mistakes we think they have made. But once our understanding of their pro-attitudes is cut loose from our convictions about norms, it becomes doubtful that the As could be used as our model for the Bs. How could we possibly tailor pro-attitudes to fit the Bs in light of their circumstances, if our understanding of their circumstances is of necessity shaped by our convictions about norms, yet the sorts of pro-attitudes out of which we are seeking to fashion our interpretation are precisely ones that do not have any connection whatsoever to our convictions?

Now it might be wondered why our understanding of the Bs' circumstances would have to be shaped by our convictions about norms, as I have been assuming it would be. Given that we are trying to interpret the Bs following the radically different precedent assumed to have been set by the As, shouldn't we be appealing to their convictions instead? That is to say, shouldn't we be asking what pro-attitudes the As would think the Bs should have, and what mistakes the As would think the Bs are prone to? The problem, however, is that, since we do not share the As' convictions about norms, most of what they would believe about the Bs would strike us as deluded. Elaborating upon Sreenivasan's example, for instance, suppose many As would acknowledge that the Bs are just as superior as they are and so should possess pro-attitudes roughly like their own. At the same time, however, suppose something about the Bs' circumstances would leave many As wondering whether the Bs really appreciate their inherent superiority and possess the appropriate pro-attitudes. So, if the As were doing the interpreting, they would often end up assigning the Bs pro-attitudes that they—the As—would regard as missing the mark in various ways. But of what relevance is this to us, given that we regard the As as deluded both about their superiority and about the sorts of pro-attitudes superior people should possess? Our brief as interpreters is to identify pro-attitudes and beliefs that are intelligible in light of the Bs' circumstances and such as to make the Bs' behavior intelligible in turn. So if we take the As' pro-attitudes and beliefs to be deeply deluded, not just badly mistaken, they can't be of any assistance in our attempts to interpret the Bs.[19] And of course what follows from this is not just the fact that we could not possibly interpret the Bs if we invoked the model provided by the deluded As. It also follows, contrary to the supposition with which we began, that the As could never have been interpreted as being so deluded in the first place. Hence the reductio.

If the interpretation argument is to be blocked, therefore, it will have to be even further upstream, at either or both of the publicness and holism assumptions. For example, if holism were rejected, the principle of charity would no longer be necessary for interpretation, even if publicness were still accepted. Interpretation would be able to proceed in a more incremental fashion, more bottom-up than top-down, and radical differences among people's pro-attitudes and beliefs would become possible. Alternatively, if publicness were rejected, the principle of charity might still be necessary for interpretation, since holism might still be accepted, but it would no longer follow that everyone's pro-attitudes and beliefs are largely correct. Everyone interpretable by us might have to have pro-attitudes and beliefs similar to ours, but some people's pro-attitudes and beliefs could be uninterpretable by us, and our pro-attitudes and beliefs could be hopelessly off the mark. The picture would be very much as Barry Stroud painted it in Chapter 4.[20] The interpretation argument might tell us something important about the attribution of propositional attitudes, but nothing that would show them actually to be largely correct, and so nothing that would show Cartesian skepticism to be false.

I suspect many readers will think that Stroud is actually being too charitable here, and that the interpretation argument is even less successful than he thinks it is. They might be prepared to admit that, for purely pragmatic reasons, our interpretations of one another should often be guided by charity. We often have little choice, as interpreters, but to treat our subjects' propositional attitudes as if their contents had been holistically determined by factors that are publicly available. Our knowledge of their behavior and circumstances is rarely very extensive, so we assume charity and get on as best we can. As these readers see things, however, this is justified solely on pragmatic grounds; it should not be regarded as a necessary truth about the nature of interpretation, and thus does not tell us anything terribly important even about the attribution of propositional attitudes, let alone about their essential nature. To suggest otherwise is, in this view, not just to conflate epistemology and metaphysics; it is to get the epistemology wrong, and then to talk nonsense on those stilts. Although rarely put so bluntly, I think worries of this sort lie behind much of the current hostility towards Davidson's later writings.

Given that so much so obviously turns on publicness and holism, Davidson initially had surprisingly little to say in their defense. He seemed to think they were just obviously true in the case of meaning, and for that reason could not be denied in the case of content either. Even if we confine our attention to beliefs, however, I think we must acknowledge that this inference is much too quick. If we find it hard to resist, that is perhaps only because we have no clear sense of what beliefs are to get in the way of it. But of course this is no argument, and it hardly puts us in a position to fend off attacks from the skeptics. Moreover, bad as this is, the situation is very much worse when it comes to pro-attitudes, for many of us do have views about what pro-attitudes are—and many of these views make it very difficult to see how both publicness and holism could possibly be true of them.[21] When it comes to normative questions, therefore, many people are going to wonder how the interpretation argument could possibly yield the sorts of conclusions that Davidson wants.

Now it is the triangulation argument that, in Davidson's later philosophy, is supposed to provide support for the publicness and holism assumptions, ensuring that the principle of charity represents not simply a possible method of interpretation, which may or may not get at the actual truth about people's propositional attitudes, but something more like a constitutive feature of those truths themselves, which makes them truths about propositional attitudes in the first place. I will therefore begin the next section with some general remarks about how the triangulation argument is supposed to provide support for the publicness and holism assumptions. The main aim of the section, however, will be to introduce three worries about the argument's relevance to specifically normative matters. The first worry concerns the need for the argument in the case of pro-attitudes. The second worry concerns the intelligibility of the claims it makes about normative properties. And the final worry concerns the overall plausibility of those claims, given other things that we believe about people's reasons for action. Chapters 6 through 8 will then take up each of these questions in turn, endeavoring to show in each case that Davidson has the resources to answer them.

3. Davidson's Triangulation Argument

As we move upstream from Davidson's interpretation argument to his triangulation argument, the flow of his ideas becomes less clear.[22] He evidently advocates a form of social externalism. But why? And how does this lend support to publicness and holism?

The rough direction of Davidson's argument is not so difficult to discern. He begins (e.g., 1992, 117 ff.) with a simple question: What makes it the case that a person's particular propositional attitudes possess the specific propositional contents they do? He then somehow concludes that this is explained by the causes that gave shape to the person's attitudes, and further that these causes must be understood to include more than the person's reactions to external things. He claims that they must also be understood to include the person's reactions to other people's reactions to those same external things and her own reactions to them. It is, he maintains, only by triangulating in this way with other people as well as external things that a person can acquire content-bearing attitudes at all. Apparently it is the fact that the record of these triangulations consists only of observable occurrences that prompts Davidson to conclude that this person must be interpretable solely on the basis of evidence that is public. Similarly, it must be some consideration about the manner in which these triangulations are conducted that prompts him to conclude that the contents of this person's attitudes necessarily end up being fixed not individually but jointly. And it certainly is true that the parties to these triangulations will at any given moment be reacting to many different aspects of the environment that they share. So perhaps it does follow that the content fixed through this process for any one of a person's attitudes must depend on the contents fixed for many others.

But what are the arguments Davidson gives in support of these conclusions? Insofar as he actually does argue for his perceptual externalism, the considerations he advances are reminiscent of Wittgenstein's remarks concerning ostensive definition. The thought seems to be that no objects, whether public or private, whether abstract or concrete, could by themselves give content to people's attitudes, since by themselves they could not determine which contents they were giving. As Wittgenstein (1958, §§28–30) puts the point, any object will have a multitude of different properties, and so could in principle give a multitude of different contents to people's attitudes. So if people's attitudes have determinate contents, that is because those contents are determined not by people's passive relations to objects but by their active engagements with them. This is not to deny that people's attitudes will often be incorrect; to say that the contents of people's attitudes are determined by their practices is not to say that they never depart from those practices. But it is to say that practices are what makes content possible; it therefore entails that people couldn't have content-bearing attitudes if objects didn't exist with which they could engage in content-determining practices. And I think Davidson, much like Wittgenstein, wants to maintain that neither private objects nor abstract entities are the sorts of things with which people could appropriately engage. He regards causal interaction as prerequisite for the sort of engagement that determines content, and so concludes straightaway that some form of perceptual externalism must be true.

Why must these content-determining practices involve triangulations among two or more different people? Why couldn't a person's solitary engagements with objects give determinate content to her attitudes? Here again the argument advanced by Davidson seems to have been anticipated by Wittgenstein, although this time I think Davidson is the one who puts it most forcefully. His thought is that the practices through which the contents of people's attitudes are determined must be of a sort that could at the same time generate in people some understanding of the concept of objectivity; for it is only if a practice gives people some occasion to wonder whether their attitudes are out of place that it can succeed at giving any determinate content to those attitudes in the first place. As Davidson sees things, only practices involving groups of triangulating people can do this, because only such practices oblige people to work through actual clashes of divergent perspectives. No matter how much a solitary person's engagements with objects might change over time, they would never oblige her to work through an actual clash of divergent perspectives. So they would never oblige her to entertain the possibility that her attitudes towards objects might be mistaken. But then, Davidson argues, they would never oblige her to consider what her attitudes towards objects actually are. And that, he concludes, would rule out the possibility that her attitudes towards objects do have determinate content; for the contents of people's attitudes become determinate only as they refine their practices to make them so.[23]

Reviews of this argument have been harsh, but often because its ambitions are misunderstood. Most critics recognize that it doesn't aim to give a reductive explanation of content. But that is not to say that it doesn't aim to give any explanation; and that is a fact that many critics of the argument seem to overlook. Too often, for example, one finds it said that a solitary person could have occasion to entertain the possibility that her attitudes towards objects might be mistaken because she could imagine being contradicted by other people. Another, similarly common suggestion is that a solitary person could recall that her attitudes towards objects have not always been what they now are and so come to wonder what they should be next time around. The problem here, of course, is that a solitary person would need already to have acquired the concept of objectivity before she could imagine or recall such things. She would need already to understand that differing utterances or actions could be contradictories, not just differing noises or movements but actually competitors for the same logical space. Davidson is hoping to explain how people come to understand this by pointing to their experiences of triangulation, whereas his critics too often simply presume that people understand this and hence beg the question against him. Either that, or they simply assert that there could be other explanations without saying what they could be—in which case they avoid begging the question against Davidson only because they don't answer it themselves.[24]

As I indicated a moment ago, I think Davidson believes this social externalism leads pretty straightforwardly to his publicness condition. If the contents of a person's attitudes really are determined by her triangulations with other people, then it simply follows, he seems to think, that anyone with sufficient knowledge of these triangulations would be in a position to interpret her. However, it might be objected, against this, that it is actually only a very much weaker conclusion that follows—something to the effect that a person would in principle be interpretable by anyone who was not only sufficiently knowledgeable about the history of this person's triangulations with other people but also fully capable of triangulating with this person herself. The worry might be that people couldn't triangulate with one another if they didn't share ways of reacting to things, and that it is not inconceivable that radically different groups of people could react to things in radically different ways, ways perhaps so different that members of the one group would not be able to interpret members of the other. But then it would not be inconceivable that an omniscient person would react to things completely differently than ordinary people, in which case we would have no guarantee that ordinary people could be interpreted by a person who was omniscient, and so also no guarantee that everyone's propositional attitudes must in fact be at least roughly what they should be.[25]

But is it indeed conceivable that radically different groups of people could react to things in radically different ways? Davidson (1974b) famously denies that it is, arguing that conceivable differences are not radical and that radical differences are not conceivable. For example, it is easy enough to imagine that different groups of people might come equipped with different sensory mechanisms. But differences of such a purely mechanical sort would not prevent members of the two groups from interpreting one another, since each side could find indirect ways to pick out the secondary qualities that the other side picks out directly, if only by referring to them as the secondary qualities that are picked out by those people in that way.[26] For the two groups to be unintelligible to each other, the differences separating them must be not mechanical but conceptual. If we try to imagine this, however, we are bound to run afoul of Davidson's perceptual and social externalism, for we will be trying to imagine that these people's reactions to things are conditioned by their different conceptual schemes, whereas we are meant to be supposing that it is their reactions to things that give content to their concepts. Thus Davidson argues that, given his perceptual and social externalism, the very idea of a conceptual scheme makes no sense, and hence that every person is interpretable by every other—even by the omniscient person introduced downstream in his argument.

Although he never spells out the case for holism quite so clearly, my sense is that Davidson believes it to be similar in form. If people's triangulations with objects were conditioned by an already existing conceptual scheme, perhaps they could fix the contents of their propositional attitudes one by one. Although each party to these triangulations would at any given moment be reacting to many different aspects of the environment that they share, perhaps the conceptual resources already at their disposal would enable them to coordinate their reactions to one of these aspects without coordinating their reactions to any others. But if the very idea of a conceptual scheme makes no sense, because it is ultimately people's reactions that have priority over their concepts, then it would seem impossible for people to coordinate their reactions to any one aspect of the environment without simultaneously coordinating their reactions to many others, and hence impossible that the content of any one of their propositional attitudes could avoid being dependent on the contents of many others. What people come to believe, in coming to believe one thing, will always be dependent on what they come to believe, in coming to believe other things.

Abstract—indeed, abstruse—though they are, I find these arguments quite convincing. But of course I recognize that a great many others do not. As we saw in Chapter 1, the fiercest critics are undoubtedly those who doubt that pro-attitudes and beliefs actually have contents of the sort Davidson assumes—that is to say, of the sort that requires their bearers to be in possession of the concept of objectivity and related meta-cognitive capacities. And it certainly is true that the success of Davidson's arguments depends on a stringent understanding of the kind of content we are trying to explain. My purpose in reiterating this point is not that I intend to entertain further challenges to that understanding in the case of descriptive beliefs. On the contrary, I shall assume throughout the remainder of this book that the triangulation argument goes through on that front as Davidson says it does. My aim in the chapters that follow will be to consider how the argument fares in its application to pro-attitudes and normative beliefs. But the first worry to be addressed there is whether pro-attitudes and normative beliefs have the sort of content that might need explaining via the triangulation argument.

We have already noted the fact that many people have views about the nature of pro-attitudes, and—we might add—about their relations to normative beliefs, which make it very difficult to see how any argument could possibly establish that the publicness and holism conditions are both true of them. In particular, anyone who holds that normative beliefs are simply expressions of pro-attitudes, and that pro-attitudes, in turn, are simply dispositions to act on descriptive beliefs, is likely to wonder why triangulation would be necessary to fix the contents of these dispositions and why these contents would necessarily be holistic. The descriptive beliefs on which people are disposed to act might necessarily have their contents fixed via triangulation, but if people's dispositions themselves needn't follow suit, then there will be no proof here either that normative properties exist or that people's pro-attitudes have to be largely in line with them. People could have pro-attitudes radically different from ours, a fact we could discover by first assigning them roughly the descriptive beliefs we take to be correct, then simply looking to see which sorts of outcomes they are disposed to try to promote and which sorts of outcomes they are not.[27]

If the triangulation argument is going to apply to pro-attitudes and normative beliefs, this familiar, neo-Humean account of their nature must be shown to be false. Rather than regarding people's normative beliefs as mere expressions of their pro-attitudes, we must show people's pro-attitudes to be responses to their normative beliefs.[28] People's pro-attitudes can still be regarded as dispositions to act on their beliefs, but normative as well as descriptive beliefs must be included in the mix. We will consider in due course what this view might come to, and what sorts of arguments Davidson has to offer in its defense. The point for now is just that there is unlikely to be any need for the triangulation argument in the case of pro-attitudes and normative beliefs unless people's normative beliefs turn out to be prior to and independent of their pro-attitudes in something like the manner being gestured towards here. Only then might it prove difficult to answer questions about how people's particular pro-attitudes and normative beliefs come to have the particular contents they do, forcing us to entertain the possibility that this is a consequence of their triangulations with one another and normative properties extant in their environment.

Of course, even if there is a need in the case of pro-attitudes and normative beliefs for an explanation of the sort that the triangulation argument is supposed to offer, it might be wondered whether this explanation is actually intelligible, given that it would require the environment that people share to possess normative properties upon which they could literally triangulate. Indeed, given that skepticism about normative properties tends to differ from skepticism about descriptive properties in precisely this respect, focusing more on ontological worries than on epistemological ones, many readers will have been wondering for some time how an argument like Davidson's could possibly be of any help, since it appears not to address the ontological worries at all. If someone doubts that the very idea of a normative property can be made intelligible, they are not going to be much impressed by Davidson's claim that we need to suppose such properties exist in order to explain how pro-attitudes and normative beliefs acquire content, for of course if the idea cannot be made intelligible then neither can the explanation. Thus our second order of business must be to consider what resources Davidson has to respond to the most familiar of the ontological worries about the intelligibility of normative properties. As I mentioned earlier, at the beginning of this chapter, some of the concerns here are bound up with the assumption that normative properties would have to involve normative laws. But the deeper worries, I believe, have to do with the assumption that normative properties, if they were to exist, would have to enjoy some impossible relation to people's motivations. So we shall have to spend some time considering how the relation between normative properties and people's motivations should be understood and whether Davidson can make good sense of it. My claim will be that he can if he is right in thinking, as I just suggested, that people's pro-attitudes are in an important sense responses to their normative beliefs. As we shall see, worries about the intelligibility of normative properties become much easier to resolve once we start working with more plausible accounts of the nature of people's motivations.

But now, even if it is perfectly intelligible to suppose that it is through their triangulations on normative properties that the contents of people's pro-attitudes and normative beliefs are fixed, this supposition could still turn out to be quite implausible, since it could prove very difficult to square with many other things that we believe about people's reasons for action. In particular, beliefs about the diversity of people's reasons for action might seem very difficult to square with this supposition, for wouldn't these normative properties be the same for everybody? Different people could still have different pro-attitudes and normative beliefs, since their normative beliefs could sometimes fail to be correct and their pro-attitudes could sometimes fail to accord with them. But if normative properties were the sorts of things on which people could literally triangulate, wouldn't normative truths be, at bottom, the same for everybody, directing everybody to promote certain outcomes and to avert others, or to perform certain actions and to refrain from others? And yet who actually believes that people's reasons for action are as monolithic as that? Our third order of business must therefore be to consider whether and to what extent Davidson's realism about normative truths can allow for serious diversity among people's reasons for action. As we shall see, Davidson does not himself have very much to say about this. He does remind us on one occasion (1995b, 40) that normative realism is perfectly compatible with relativism. But this general point, while true, is not enough to quiet the particular worries that arise when one tries to think this through within the context of his triangulation argument. So we shall have to spend some time considering what Davidson's version of normative realism might look like and how much diversity among people's reasons for action it could allow. Looking ahead, my claim will be that it does make room for agent-relative reasons, but without going so far as to deny that agent-neutral reasons exist as well. Indeed, far from being a source of concern about Davidson's triangulation argument, I shall maintain that its substantive implications for people's reasons for action actually count in its favor.

Broadly speaking, therefore, there are three sorts of doubts that one might have about the idea that skepticism about normative properties could be addressed through Davidson's argument. One might doubt that there is any need for Davidson's argument, on the ground that pro-attitudes and normative beliefs are nothing more than the neo-Humeans say they are. One might doubt that Davidson's argument is actually intelligible, on the ground that it makes very little sense to suppose that reasons for action could be real properties of things upon which people could literally triangulate. And one might doubt that Davidson's argument is particularly plausible, on the ground that it would seem to make people's reasons for action out to be much less diverse than most of us think they are. As I shall argue throughout the remainder of this book, however, I think these doubts are in each case much less serious than Davidson's critics have claimed. In Chapter 6, I shall argue that Davidson gives us good grounds for thinking that pro-attitudes and normative beliefs are very different than the neo-Humeans say they are. In Chapter 7, I shall argue that, once we leave the neo-Humean view behind, the basic intelligibility of normative realism becomes much easier to defend than opponents, such as John Mackie and Gilbert Harman, have claimed.[29] And finally, in Chapter 8, I shall argue that the sort of normative realism to which Davidson is committed is compatible with the diversity that most of us believe to exist among people's reasons for action.

Though I say "finally", I shall in fact conclude Chapter 8 with some more speculative remarks about the implications of Davidson's sort of normative realism for moral theory. This might seem odd, given the fact, as I remarked earlier in this chapter, that Davidson himself says little about the content or authority of specifically moral reasons. In recent years, however, worries about its implications for the content and authority of specifically moral reasons have emerged as perhaps the most important of the many challenges that have been raised to normative realism.[30] Constructivists, in particular, have been wont to argue that normative realists are confronted with a kind of dilemma, and as a result cannot give plausible accounts of both the content and the authority of moral reasons. On the one hand, they might hold that normative properties are all agent-neutral, and, because of this, that everyone's reasons for action are at bottom the same. This would make it easy for them to defend strong claims about morality's authority, but, as we have noted, could saddle them with implausible views about its content. On the other hand, they might allow that normative properties are sometimes agent-neutral but often agent-relative, which would put them in a position to disavow the more implausible of those views about morality's content. But then, it is argued, it would be difficult for them to defend strong claims about morality's authority, and they might find that even its content is difficult to pin down in a sufficiently determinate way.

Although Thomas Scanlon advocates a version of normative realism that is in some respects less robust than Davidson's, his (1998) version of contractualism is very much the sort of position towards which I think Davidson's arguments lead. Scanlon thinks there are truths about what people have reason to do, but truths that often put people in serious conflict with one another. He thinks this gives everyone some reason to agree on moral principles—not simply because this will contribute to the satisfaction of their first-order reasons, but also because second-order reasons exist for everyone to interact in this fashion. The challenge that Scanlon faces, however, is to show that these principles have sufficiently determinate content and that people's reasons to comply with them are sufficiently authoritative. Is there really some one set of moral principles on which every person has most reason to agree? And even if there is, does everyone always have most reason to comply with that set of principles? By setting moral reasons, which he regards as constructions of a sort, in opposition to more basic reasons, which he takes to be primitive, Scanlon can certainly seem to have painted himself into a corner here. As we shall see, this has led many philosophers in recent years to argue that constructivism cannot be restricted to moral reasons but must apply to all reasons. As they see things, it is only if even the most basic of reasons are constructed that moral reasons will prove to be sufficiently determinate and sufficiently authoritative.

Like most normative realists, I find this suggestion very difficult to understand. I can see how some reasons could be constructed out of others, but not how a reason could be constructed where none existed before. Instead of belaboring this familiar point, however, I will conclude Chapter 8 on a more positive note, explaining why I think normative realists are in a stronger position here than constructivists give them credit for. Continuing to use Scanlon's version of contractualism as an example of the sort of approach that normative realists such as Davidson should take towards questions about moral reasons, I shall argue that the sort of cooperation it calls for just is a largely determinate way of acting that people have extremely powerful reasons to engage in. While cooperators' shared reasons can in some respects be regarded as constructions, since they are sensitive to the individual reasons that each cooperator has, they still possess a determinate structure that is not subject to negotiation. My parting suggestion, in other words, will be that normative realists should respond to constructivists by doubling down, as it were, on their realism, applying it at the second order no less than at the first. If Scanlon seems vulnerable on this front, that is because his commitment to realism is not robust enough to allow him to take full advantage of its promise. Since he need not be so reticent, Davidson is on much firmer ground here than the recent movement in moral philosophy towards constructivism might lead one to think.

Notes

1. Readers familiar only with Davidson's early work may wonder whether he really was a cognitivist, let alone a normative realist, and, even if he was, whether he actually took himself to be providing arguments in support of such metaethical positions. Davidson 1995b, however, very explicitly argues for normative realism, so I take doubts of these sorts to be baseless. The interesting question is not whether Davidson advocated normative realism but how he thought his various arguments support that position.
2. Cf. Smith 1994, 96. As Smith notes, the distinction is sometimes said to be between "justifying" and "explanatory" reasons.
3. As we shall see in Chapter 7, there are exceptions. Two recent examples would be Enoch 2011 and Scanlon 2014.
4. This is already at least strongly implied in Davidson 1969. It is stated more explicitly at Davidson 1995b, 41.
5. Davidson 1969, 38. As I explain in Chapter 7, he would have done better to describe them as pro tanto.
6. Given this different emphasis, my presentation of the arguments will differ in some respects from Verheggen's presentation in Chapter 1. But we are in agreement on all the important points, and indeed my reading of Davidson owes much to hers.
7. The following eight paragraphs are taken almost verbatim from Myers 2004, 108–114.
8. For his views concerning first-person authority, see Davidson 1987b.
9. See his 1993a, especially page 81, for some confirmation of this reading.
10. This is clearly the suggestion in Fodor and Lepore 1993.
11. Fodor and Lepore raise this objection in 1992, Chapter 3.
12. For an explicit denial that it is, see Davidson 1993a, 80.
13. As Davidson himself has often stressed, this terminology is unfortunate because it might suggest that this step is somehow optional—as if we should find others largely in agreement with us just because that is the decent thing to do.

14. This will be no simple matter, as it will require us to develop a theory of meaning for our subjects. We cannot get clear about the contents of people's pro-attitudes and beliefs without getting clear about their meanings as well.
15. There is admittedly not much temptation to read the assumption about beliefs this way. As we shall see, however, this reading of the assumption about pro-attitudes can seem tempting.
16. To be more precise, the full story minus the truth about the contents of our beliefs and other attitudes (for otherwise the omniscient interpreter would not need to interpret us).
17. So the correct complaint to make against the omniscient interpreter argument is not that it begs the question but that it is largely superfluous. Davidson concedes as much in 1999c.
18. For a recent example, see Glüer 2011, 143.
19. As we might say, interpreters must be externalists, and externalists cannot avoid being charitable in their interpretations of one another.
20. See Stroud 1999, and Verheggen's discussion in Chapter 4.
21. As we shall see below, and again in Chapter 6, Humean accounts of pro-attitudes pose a special challenge to Davidson.
22. Now that we have Verheggen's account of the argument before us, this is no longer as true as it once was. I briefly recapitulate her account here for the benefit of readers who are focusing on Part Two of this book.
23. See Chapter 1 above, Section 2.2, for Verheggen's very much more rigorous exposition of this point.
24. A more rigorous exposition of these points can be found in Chapter 1 above, Section 3.2.
25. Recall the objection to the omniscient interpreter argument that we briefly considered earlier in this chapter.
26. This is of course not to say that they would be fully understandable to one another.
27. Discerning what these dispositions in fact are might actually not be quite as easy as this suggests. But since I will be rejecting this view of pro-attitudes, I won't pursue this question here.
28. As we shall see in the next chapter, Davidson needn't deny that some pro-attitudes can be as the neo-Humeans describe. He need only claim that this is not how pro-attitudes typically are.
29. The canonical sources here are Mackie 1976a and Harman 1977.
30. Hurley 2009 gives a particularly clear statement of this worry.

6 Pro-Attitudes and Normative Beliefs

As we saw in Chapter 5, Davidson's argument for normative realism is unlikely to get off the ground if normative beliefs are nothing more than expressions of pro-attitudes and pro-attitudes are nothing more than dispositions to act on descriptive beliefs.[1] In that case, the contents of people's pro-attitudes and normative beliefs can probably be specified without introducing any truly normative concepts, and so without raising the question of whether they could have acquired those concepts without triangulating on normative properties.

Ironically, this neo-Humean conception of pro-attitudes and their relation to normative beliefs is frequently attributed to Davidson himself. In this chapter, I shall argue that this is a mistake that comes of conflating two importantly different Humean theses. Davidson accepts what is called the Humean theory of motivation, but rejects what I shall call the Humean theory of pro-attitudes. And the theory of pro-attitudes that he accepts in its place is one that is quite congenial to normative realism.

1. The Humean Theoy of Motivation

As I understand it, the Humean theory of motivation revolves around the largely negative claim that beliefs alone are not sufficient to motivate actions. Non-cognitive states are necessary as well. So the questions for us are, why should we accept this claim? And does Davidson actually accept it?

Davidson clearly holds (1963, 3) that descriptive beliefs are insufficient for motivation and that pro-attitudes are also required. He would deny, for example, that my belief that arsenic poisons could suffice to motivate me.[2] He would maintain that some pro-attitude is necessary, such as a pro-attitude toward seeing you dead, before I could be motivated to do anything, such as lacing your morning coffee with arsenic. This is not enough, however, to establish that Davidson accepts the Humean theory of motivation, for it does not tell us what Davidson is accepting in accepting that pro-attitudes are necessary. In fact, as G. F. Schueler notes (2003, 24), Davidson seems to count people's normative beliefs among their pro-attitudes, which suggests that he may not be on board here with the Humeans after all.[3] For of course the Humeans are not simply denying that descriptive beliefs are sufficient for motivation. They would say the same of any set of beliefs, even one that included normative beliefs. So we need to get clearer about why the Humeans are so adamant on this score, and about whether Davidson's view of these matters is ultimately in accord with theirs, or not.

According to Michael Smith (1994, Chapter 4), the Humeans' thought here is that motivation requires possession of a goal, and that possession of a belief, even a normative belief, cannot constitute possession of a goal. Returning to our example, I may believe I have good reason to kill you, but that, in itself, does not make it the case that killing you is a goal of mine. What makes this the case, if indeed it is the case, is the fact that I am disposed to do various things that I believe will increase my chances of killing you. As we shall see in the next section, there are several ways to characterize such dispositions, and a lot turns in the end on what the right way to characterize them is. The point for now is simply that the Humeans hold both that motivation cannot exist until some such disposition is in place and that beliefs alone cannot constitute dispositions of this sort. So the questions for us, once again, are why we should accept these two Humean claims, and whether Davidson, in holding that pro-attitudes are necessary for motivation, means to be accepting them.

Davidson clearly does share the view that motivation requires possession of a goal. This is fundamental to the distinction he draws (see 1963, 5) between mere behavior and actual action. He counts behavior as action only if it is caused by the agent's aiming to achieve something and believing she could achieve it by behaving in that way. This strikes some critics as being a mistake because they take it to rule out the possibility that actions can be performed with no further goal in mind. Yet can't I keep my promise, for example, just because I believe keeping it is the right thing to do and so without aiming to achieve anything further? What Davidson is claiming, however, is not that I must have some further goal in mind but that I must really be *aiming* to keep my promise. (See 1963, 6.) That is to say, I must be disposed to adjust my behavior if I come to believe it does not in fact constitute the keeping of my promise. The disposition is crucial; without it, I am not acting even if my behavior is caused by beliefs of mine and I end up doing what I promised. It is not enough, for example, that I give you the five dollars I promised because I believe the object in my hand is a five-dollar bill. If that is not to be just an odd yet fortuitously well-timed reflex, my belief must cause my behavior because it is appropriately connected to my aim.

So the question is not whether Davidson thinks motivation requires possession of a goal; the question is what he thinks possession of a goal requires in its turn. Would he allow that I could possess the goal of keeping my promise simply by virtue of believing keeping my promise is what I have reason to do? It might seem obvious that he would, given passages of the sort Schueler cites, in which he seems to count people's normative beliefs among the pro-attitudes motivating their actions. I suspect, however, that in passages like these he is simply speaking loosely, counting people's normative beliefs among their pro-attitudes because he thinks they *shape* their pro-attitudes. And in fact, in a subsequent passage (1984c, 25), Davidson is careful to make it clear that he thinks it would be a distortion to identify normative beliefs and pro-attitudes. And presumably his reason for thinking this is precisely the reason Smith gives (1994, 120) for denying that possession of a normative belief ever literally constitutes possession of a goal—namely, that if normative beliefs are actual beliefs, and not merely expressions of pro-attitudes, then it must be possible to have them without being disposed to act accordingly.[4] If one can have a normative belief without having any disposition to act accordingly, and if a pro-attitude is a disposition to perform actions of a certain kind, then it is hard to see how normative beliefs could actually be identical to pro-attitudes, no matter how closely related states of these sorts may in other respects be.[5]

Of course, as followers of this debate will know, not everyone is persuaded by Smith on this point. Some insist that, if a belief has normative content, one will always be disposed to act on it, even if that disposition is sometimes hard to discern because one is also disposed to do other things. Others insist that normative beliefs can sometimes constitute motivating dispositions even if they do not always do so. For example, it is often argued that normative beliefs constitute motivating dispositions in people who are fully rational, even if they are prevented from enjoying that status in people who are not so perfect as that. I don't find either of these rebuttals at all plausible, however, for reasons I suspect Davidson shares. I don't think the content of an attitude can influence its nature in the ways being proposed here, and I certainly don't think it is in the nature of even descriptive beliefs to constitute motivating dispositions. Rather than arguing for these claims, however, I am simply going to assume them and move on. I do this in part because I don't have anything important to add to the arguments Smith offers (1994, Chapter 4), but also because I think this is the wrong place for Smith's opponents to be making their stand. It's the Humean theory of pro-attitudes that should be attracting their ire, not the Humean theory of motivation. As I shall be arguing in the next section, we can agree that pro-attitudes are necessary for motivation, and agree that they cannot be constituted by beliefs, yet still disagree about what, more precisely, they are. And this disagreement could be resolved in a way that is congenial to the prospects of normative realism; for people's normative beliefs needn't literally constitute their pro-attitudes in order to be deeply implicated in their pro-attitudes, and that would be sufficient to block the neo-Humean conclusion that they are merely expressions of those pro-attitudes.

Now it might be wondered whether it is actually necessary to reject even the Humean theory of pro-attitudes. If our hope is to block the conclusion that people's normative beliefs are merely expressions of their pro-attitudes, why isn't it enough to argue that people's pro-attitudes are at least sometimes caused by their normative beliefs? And isn't this something we could argue without taking a stand on questions about what, exactly, pro-attitudes are? As we shall see in due course, however, matters are far from being as simple as this, for if a belief really has normative content it must also have some rational bearing on one's motivations. Yet it is hard to see how it can if motivating states are nothing more than Humean pro-attitudes. As we shall see, Smith tries (1994, Chapter 5) to argue otherwise, but in a way that just reinforces the worry, for his argument has no chance of going through unless he fudges his commitment to the Humean view. If we hope to steer through these shoals, therefore, there is only one course we can take. If we cannot disown the Humean theory of motivation, but still want to avoid the neo-Humean conclusion that people's normative beliefs are merely expressions of their pro-attitudes, we need a non-Humean account of what pro-attitudes are. My claim throughout the remainder of this chapter will be that this is precisely what Davidson gives us. This will undoubtedly come as a surprise to some, and indeed Davidson doesn't say much about how we should characterize the dispositions that he thinks pro-attitudes are, but he does drop a clear and important hint when he says (1995a, 13) the holism of the mental applies among pro-attitudes and not just between pro-attitudes and beliefs. He calls this 'intra-attitudinal' as opposed to 'inter-attitudinal' holism, and my claim throughout the remainder of this chapter will be that we can learn a lot by trying to figure out what it could possibly be.

2. A Non-Humean Theory of Pro-Attitudes

Before trying to figure out what a non-Humean theory of pro-attitudes might be, however, let us be sure we are clear about what the Humean theory says.

A simple statement of it might go something like this: A pro-attitude towards Ψ-ing is a disposition to do whatever one believes will increase one's chances of Ψ-ing.[6] Hume himself, of course, talked of passions rather than pro-attitudes, and he identified passions with feelings of various sorts, rather than with dispositions to act in various ways. As Hume saw things, one may become disposed to act in various ways as a result of experiencing feelings of various sorts, but one can have the feelings without necessarily acquiring the dispositions, and it is with the feelings that one's passions are identified. Hume's modern-day followers, however, take the opposite view. They happily allow that one's pro-attitudes may also involve dispositions to experience thoughts or feelings of various sorts, but they don't think this is in any way necessary, and in any case they think it is with one's dispositions to act that one's pro-attitudes are identified. Further dispositions to experience thoughts or feelings of various sorts may be required for pro-attitudes to count as being of particular kinds, but dispositions to act in various ways are all the Humeans require for states to count as being pro-attitudes to begin with.

For our purposes, the striking feature of this Humean theory of pro-attitudes is not the fact that it identifies one's pro-attitudes with dispositions to act in various ways; it is the purely functional manner in which it characterizes one's pro-attitude towards Ψ-ing as a disposition to do *whatever* one believes will increase one's chances of Ψ-ing. The idea of one's Ψ-ing serves as a kind of template, and one seeks to bring one's behavior into conformity with it. One's beliefs about one's reasons for Ψ-ing are beside the point, and indeed it becomes unclear what their status could possibly be. If, as I intimated earlier, normative beliefs must have some rational bearing on motivations, it becomes difficult to see how this account of pro-attitudes leaves room for them, since possession of these purely functional states does not require that one be aiming in any sense to get normative matters right or to act on normative truths. It should not come as a surprise, therefore, that advocates of the Humean theory of pro-attitudes so often end up taking what I have been calling the neo-Humean view that normative judgments are not really beliefs at all but simply expressions of pro-attitudes.[7]

Now, pretty clearly, if this Humean account of pro-attitudes is correct, they will not be as holistic as Davidson says they are. They will be holistic in what he calls the inter-attitudinal sense, since their contents will depend on the contents of one's beliefs. But, crucially, they will not be holistic in what he calls the intra-attitudinal sense, since each one will have its content independently of the contents of the others. What one's pro-attitude towards Ψ-ing disposes one to do will depend on what one believes about Ψ-ing but not on what other actions one is disposed to perform. And this, as we saw in Chapter 5, will prevent either Davidson's triangulation argument or his interpretation argument from applying to pro-attitudes. Because pro-attitudes will not be holistic in the requisite sense, their contents could not have been fixed through triangulations on normative properties. And people could be interpreted without assuming that their pro-attitudes are governed by charity. It might still prove necessary to assume that their beliefs are governed by charity, but once their beliefs have been interpreted it will be possible to solve for their pro-attitudes by finding out what sorts of things they are disposed to do.[8]

We can agree that these are good reasons for Davidson to have reservations about the Humean theory of pro-attitudes. But should we? I think we should, for the simple reason that so few of our pro-attitudes actually seem to accord with the Humean model. Consider, for instance, one of the rare examples discussed by Davidson (see 1990c, 89) in this connection. Suppose I want to win at chess—not just to play, but to win. Am I disposed to do whatever I believe will increase my chances of winning, as the Humean theory insists I must be? That does not seem terribly likely. I may believe I could increase my chances of winning by taking care to play only the weakest opponents I can find. But it seems unlikely that this is a course of action I am in fact even the least bit disposed to take. As Davidson says (1990c, 89), what I am disposed to do with a view to winning seems much more likely to be conditioned by the other pro-attitudes that I have. In all but the most atypical of cases, our pro-attitudes just do not seem to be independent of one another in the way Humeans claim they must be.

In response, the Humeans will complain that this seems telling only because we are under-specifying the content of my pro-attitude. If I am not in fact even the least bit disposed to play only the weakest opponents I can find, that must be because my desire is not just to win at chess but rather to win against credible opponents. But suppose we grant, for the sake of the argument, that this actually is a better description of my desire. The question then is whether I am disposed to do whatever I believe will increase my chances of doing that. And of course the worry is that it will again be all too easy to show that I am not. What if I believe I can increase my chances of winning against credible opponents by unnerving them in various ways? Are we really to suppose that I must therefore be disposed to do what I can to unnerve them?

The Humeans will insist that we are, unless the content of my pro-attitude is still being under-specified in some fashion. Obviously enough, if my desire is actually to win at chess against opponents who are credible and firing on all cylinders, then the Humeans will expect my disposition likewise to be more narrowly focused on that more tightly specified result. Their claim is simply that my pro-attitude, once accurately described, will turn out to conform to their purely functional model. I will in fact be disposed to do whatever I believe will increase my chances of achieving the designated result. It seems to me, however, that this is true, if it is ever true, only in highly unusual cases. Typically, no matter how tightly specified the designated result is, it is quite easy to imagine ways of achieving it that the agent recognizes to be ways of achieving it but that she is not at all disposed to pursue.

The Humeans might try to contest this by arguing that in cases of this sort one disposition is simply being eclipsed by another. They might acknowledge, in other words, that even if my pro-attitude is accurately described as a desire to win at chess against credible opponents, and I believe my best chance of winning against such opponents is to unnerve them, I may not give the appearance of being at all disposed to take such steps. But that, they would quickly say, is only because I may have some other pro-attitude, such as, for example, a concern to maintain a reputation for fair and honorable play, more strongly disposing me to avoid unnerving my opponents in any way, even when I believe doing so would increase my chances of winning, because I believe taking such steps would pose an unacceptable risk to my chances of securing this other result that I desire more strongly. In this way, the Humeans might argue that we cannot draw any conclusions from the fact that I may not give the appearance of being disposed to unnerve my opponents. The reality is what matters, and according to them the reality is that I must be so disposed given our assumptions about the contents of my pro-attitude and related beliefs.

But why should we accept this? Is it really true that I could give the appearance of not being disposed to unnerve my opponents only if I had some other pro-attitude and believed I needed to avoid such behavior in order to safeguard my chances of satisfying it? That seems just false to me. I think it is perfectly possible that I may actually not be disposed to unnerve my opponents because I see no way at all in which defeating my opponents by unnerving them would respond to the reasons I believe I have for wanting to win at chess against credible opponents in the first place. For example, I may believe it is a good thing to develop skills of the sort required to win at chess against credible opponents, and it may be true of me that I wouldn't have any desire to play chess at all if I didn't have this belief. If such is indeed the case, and I believe defeating my opponents by unnerving them would not require skills of the sort that I believe I have reason to develop, then why would I be even the least bit disposed to try to unnerve them, even if I did believe that doing so would increase my chances of defeating them?

Considerations such as these lead me to conclude that the Humean theory of pro-attitudes should be rejected in favor of a theory more like the one Thomas Scanlon proposes, according to which pro-attitudes are typically not the purely functional states described by the Humeans but rather states in important respects sensitive to one's judgments about one's reasons for action.[9] Scanlon himself is not always clear about the fact that these states are existences distinct from the normative beliefs to which they are sensitive, but I think he agrees that the beliefs can exist without the pro-attitudes and that it is the pro-attitudes that constitute one's motivating dispositions. Be that as it may, my claim is that a pro-attitude towards Ψ-ing is typically not a simple disposition to do whatever one believes will increase one's chances of Ψ-ing but rather a considerably more complex disposition to act in ways one believes will respond to the reasons one believes one has for trying to Ψ in the first place. One might believe one has good reasons to try to Ψ without having this disposition and so without being at all motivated to Ψ. But if one has the disposition, its content will typically be sensitive to the beliefs one has about one's reasons for trying to Ψ.

Now this account of pro-attitudes will undoubtedly raise some eyebrows, even among those who share my reservations about the Humean idea that pro-attitudes are always and only purely functional states, for it does make pro-attitudes highly dependent on normative beliefs, and it might be wondered whether this is really the only or the best way to avoid the Humean view. Indeed, Davidson himself might be enlisted in support of this worry, for when he discusses cases like one's desire to win at chess, his suggestion is that the content of the pro-attitude is probably conditioned not by one's normative beliefs but by other pro-attitudes that one has.[10] Far from making one's pro-attitudes dependent on one's normative beliefs, the suggestion seems to be that one's normative beliefs could still turn out to be mere expressions of one's pro-attitudes; it's just that the relation between the two would have to be considerably more complex than the simple one-to-one relation that neo-Humeans often seem to have in mind. So I need to explain why I am not pursuing this suggestion, and why I think, despite what he says, Davidson is not either. As we shall see, the answer in my case is quite simple. The harder point to establish is that Davidson actually agrees with it.

I am not pursuing this suggestion because I see no plausible way to develop it, or anyway no plausible way to develop it that would actually have the effect of safeguarding it against the sorts of worries I have been raising about the Humean theory. How might the contents of one's pro-attitudes be conditioned by other pro-attitudes that one has? The best answer I can think of is this:[11] A pro-attitude towards Ψ-ing might be not a disposition to do just anything one believes will increase one's chances of Ψ-ing but rather a disposition to act in ways one believes will enhance one's chances of Ψ-ing without unduly jeopardizing one's chances of doing other things that one wants to do. So my desire to win at chess against credible opponents might not dispose me to try to unnerve them even though I believe that would increase my chances of winning because I might also desire to maintain a reputation for fair and honorable play and believe that trying to unnerve my opponents would unduly jeopardize my chances of accomplishing that. But, again, why should we think my failure to be disposed to take such steps depends in this way on the fact that I possess some other, and conflicting, desire? Isn't it much more likely that I simply don't believe trying to unnerve my opponents would speak to the reasons I believe I have for wanting to win at chess?

It must be acknowledged that Davidson's insistence on intra-attitudinal as well as inter-attitudinal holism and his suggestion that the contents of one's pro-attitudes are typically conditioned by other pro-attitudes that one has would seem to indicate that he favors an account of pro-attitudes along something like these lines over the more Scanlonian sort of account that I am recommending. On the other hand, if it is true that an account along anything like these lines would have the consequence that normative beliefs are nothing more than expressions of pro-attitudes, then this would raise the problem of explaining how Davidson could endorse an account like this and still believe his triangulation argument has some application to pro-attitudes and normative beliefs. Moreover, we have already found ourselves having to conclude that Davidson is not always as careful about the distinction between normative beliefs and pro-attitudes as he strictly should be. He often seems to count people's normative beliefs among the pro-attitudes disposing them to act, even though, on other occasions, he seems to acknowledge that they are actually distinct existences. My suggestion, therefore, is that he is making the opposite mistake when he asserts that the contents of one's pro-attitudes are typically conditioned by other pro-attitudes that one has. What he should say is that their contents are typically conditioned by one's normative beliefs, and that the appearance of intra-attitudinal holism is just a reflection of this underlying reality.

So, if I desire to win at chess against credible opponents but also to maintain a reputation for fair and honorable play, it may look as if the content of the first pro-attitude is conditioned in important ways by the presence of the second, and that Davidson's insistence on the possibility of intra-attitudinal holism has thus been vindicated, when in fact its content is conditioned by some normative belief that I have, such as my belief in the importance of treating people with dignity and respect, which also shapes my desire to maintain a reputation for fair and honorable play. And this is why my desire to win at chess against credible opponents would very likely continue to be conditioned by my normative beliefs even in the absence of conflicting desires such as my desire to maintain a reputation for fair and honorable play. If I desire to win at chess against credible opponents in part because I believe it would be good for me to develop the skills that that requires, that belief will typically shape the content of my disposition even if for some reason it is not reflected in any of the other pro-attitudes that I have.

As I read him, Davidson understands all this, but is not always as careful as he should be to state it correctly. Precisely because he thinks people's normative beliefs typically shape their pro-attitudes, he often attributes to the one properties belonging to the other. Sometimes this ends up making him look considerably less Humean than he really is, as when he seems to attribute to normative beliefs the capacity to motivate actions. Sometimes this ends up making him look considerably more Humean than he really is, as when he discusses the holism of pro-attitudes without making mention of normative beliefs. But the truth of the matter is pretty clearly that he holds the sort of intermediate position I have been recommending here. He agrees with the Humeans that, strictly speaking, motivation requires non-cognitive attitudes over and above whatever descriptive and normative beliefs one has. But, contrary to the Humeans, he holds that these attitudes, although strictly speaking non-cognitive, are typically shaped by one's normative beliefs as well as by one's descriptive beliefs. In the final analysis, therefore, he is in absolutely no danger of succumbing to the neo-Humean argument that people's normative beliefs are merely expressions of their pro-attitudes.

Of course, even if I am correct in concluding that Davidson is on board with an account of pro-attitudes that makes them so highly dependent on normative beliefs, it might still be wondered whether any account of this sort could really be on firmer ground than the simpler Humean theory that we are seeking to replace. Are we really to suppose that, in all but atypical cases, the contents of people's pro-attitudes are shaped by their normative beliefs? As David Velleman has famously objected (1992, 3), on the face of it, people just do not seem as earnest or dutiful as that. They frequently act without believing they have reason to do what they are doing; they often act despite believing they lack reason to do what they are doing; they sometimes do things because they believe they have no reason to do them; they even do things because they believe they have reason not to do them. They can be playful and silly, self-aggrandizing and self-destructive. They very often act out of anger, envy, depression and despair. Are we really to suppose that all such cases are atypical? What could possibly even be meant by saying that they are?

As we shall see in the next section, this last question is especially pressing, for no very plausible answer to it has ever gained traction in the literature. Too often the assumption is that, if pro-attitudes are typically dependent on normative beliefs, this can only be because they are in some sense paradigmatically dependent on them. But, as Velleman so forcefully argues, it is difficult to believe that silly or angry or depressed actions are not paradigmatically actions. They may be less rational than actions shaped by normative beliefs, but surely they are not for that reason lesser as actions. So it begins to look as if we may have a circle to square. Once we have granted that pro-attitudes are often and paradigmatically indifferent to normative beliefs, what can we mean by saying that they are nonetheless typically dependent on them? As we shall see, however, this is not as paradoxical as it looks, for the claim that they are typically dependent on normative beliefs is true of pro-attitudes considered as a system or a whole, and it is perfectly compatible with the claim that individual pro-attitudes can be every bit as unruly and as perverse as Velleman contends.

3. The Idea of a Systemic Aim

Before developing this line of thought, however, we should return to the question of whether the case for normative realism really requires anything along these lines at all.

This question arose because we were wondering whether it is really necessary to reject the Humean theory of pro-attitudes in order to pursue Davidson's argument for normative realism. Davidson's argument assumes that people have at least some propositional attitudes with normative contents, and hence that something needs to be said about how these contents are fixed. But this could be true even if people's pro-attitudes are simply dispositions to act on their descriptive beliefs, so long as it is not also true that people's normative beliefs are simply expressions of those pro-attitudes. So instead of arguing for the controversial claim that people's pro-attitudes are typically dependent on their normative beliefs, why not settle for the much weaker claim that people's pro-attitudes are sometimes caused by their normative beliefs? I responded to this question earlier in this chapter by suggesting that a belief must have some rational bearing on people's motivations in order to count as normative, and that it is difficult to see how any belief could satisfy this condition if the Humean theory of motivation and the Humean theory of pro-attitudes are correct. We need now to spell this out more rigorously, beginning with what is often called the internalist requirement that a belief must have some rational bearing on people's motivations if it is to count as normative. Why should we suppose this internalist requirement is correct? And why should we think it tells against the Humean theory of pro-attitudes and in favor of something like the Scanlonian alternative that I have been proposing?

In saying that a normative belief must have some rational bearing on people's motivations, I am not saying that it must somehow guarantee that they actually are motivated. Davidson himself occasionally seems to be making the stronger claim, as when he tentatively suggests (1969, 26) that a normative belief "must be reflected in wants (or desires or motives)." As he quickly makes clear (1969, 27), however, he recognizes that this claim, if taken literally, is too strong. It is possible for a person to have a normative belief and not be motivated to act accordingly. This is why, as I argued earlier, he is best interpreted as accepting the Humean theory of motivation, even if, as I have also argued, he rejects the theory of pro-attitudes that normally goes with it. Davidson's considered view of the relation between normative beliefs and motivating states is thus best captured in his famous principle of continence (1969, 41), which might be put like this: Rationality requires people always to form motivating states in line with their normative beliefs, and so always to do what they believe they have most reason to do. Of course, people are not always, or completely, rational; so the principle of continence is not always obeyed. But, in Davidson's view, it does nonetheless always apply; it tells us what it takes to be rational. The thought I want to pursue is that it also tells us something important about what it takes for propositional attitudes to count on the one hand as normative beliefs and on the other as motivating states.

I say this even though I fear that, strictly speaking, Davidson's principle of continence may be too strong. Is it true that rationality requires people *always* to form motivating states in line with their normative beliefs? As has often been pointed out in this context, there certainly seems to be room for doubt here. Suppose I am of the view that I frequently misjudge how much I should be doing for others. Should I nonetheless strive to act on my own considered beliefs about such matters? Or would I do better to let someone else's beliefs serve as my guide? Now of course it might be argued that even in this case I should be striving to act on my considered beliefs about who that person should be. But what if I believe my unreliability about such matters extends even to identifying a more reliable guide? Should I nonetheless strive to act on my own considered beliefs about who the best guide would be? I don't think we need to pursue this example any further in order to appreciate that there are some good grounds to wonder whether Davidson's principle of continence can ultimately outrun all worries of this sort. Fortunately, however, I also don't think we need to answer this question in order to invoke Davidson's principle in our argument against the Humean theory of pro-attitudes; for even if Davidson's principle of continence does turn out to be too strong, I think we can agree that something very much like it must be correct.

I say this because I think we can agree that people's normative beliefs must have some rational bearing on their motivations even if we are not in every case certain what form that bearing should take.[12] The suggestion in the example above was certainly not that I should just ignore my own normative beliefs; on the contrary, the worry had rather to do with how I should proceed in view of them. This is important because it obliges us to confront the following deceptively simple question: What ultimately guarantees that people's normative beliefs have this rational bearing on their motivations? Obviously the normative nature of their content provides a significant part of the answer; but the point not to miss is that this cannot be the full story. If people's motivations as a system or a whole were not also aiming to get normative matters right, no belief could be guaranteed to have the rational bearing on their motivations that normative beliefs must have. So the question is whether advocates of the Humean theory of motivation and the Humean theory of pro-attitudes can maintain that people's motivations as a system or a whole are aiming to get normative matters right. If not, then they have no choice but to embrace the neo-Humean conclusion that people's so-called normative beliefs are in fact nothing more than expressions of their pro-attitudes. And those of us who hope to avoid that conclusion despite embracing the Humean theory of motivation must find some way to reject the Humean theory of pro-attitudes.

We can get a good sense of the Humean's plight here by briefly considering Michael Smith's take on these matters. Smith is an extremely influential advocate both of the Humean theory of motivation and of the Humean theory of pro-attitudes. But he also takes the view (1994, Chapter 5) that people's normative judgments are really beliefs and not merely expressions of their pro-attitudes. He notoriously regards them as beliefs about what one's "systematically justified" self would advise one's currently constituted self to do.[13] This is problematic in various ways, as we shall see in the next chapter, but the point to note here concerns not his account of the content of these beliefs but his explanation of why the internalist requirement is real. Smith gives it a different name, a name I'll later use for something else, but what he calls (1994, Chapter 3) the "practicality requirement" resembles our internalist requirement in holding that people's normative beliefs must have some rational bearing on their motivating states. Smith actually agrees with Davidson that rationality requires people always to form motivating states in line with their normative beliefs, but, be that as it may, my question is how any such requirement could obtain given Smith's thoroughgoing Humeanism. If motivation requires pro-attitudes, and pro-attitudes are purely functional states, how could normative beliefs have any rational bearing on them? If pro-attitudes do not aim to get normative matters right, of what concern could normative beliefs possibly be to them?

In his book, *The Moral Problem* (1994), questions of this sort are never really confronted as squarely as they should be. Smith explains why he thinks the practicality requirement is real, and why he embraces Humean theories of motivation and pro-attitudes; but these two explanations are offered independently of one another, leaving it quite unclear how they could both be correct. How could normative beliefs have any rational bearing on motivations, if motivation requires pro-attitudes and pro-attitudes are purely functional states? Only towards the end of the book does Smith give us an indication how he would answer this question. He suggests (pp. 179 ff.) that people's normative beliefs have a rational bearing on their motivations because their motivations have an inherent tendency to move towards or seek out the sort of coherence he identifies as the principal concern of their normative beliefs. If people's normative beliefs are beliefs about what their systematically justified selves would advise their currently constituted selves to do, and their motivations are pro-attitudes with an inherent tendency to move towards or seek out this sort of systematic justification, then it is not surprising that people's motivations typically will and rationally should exhibit some sensitivity to their normative beliefs. As I have said, there may still be some question about exactly what form this sensitivity does or should take. But it is enough for our purposes that something like Smith's practicality requirement or our internalist requirement will be vindicated.

The problem, however, is that people's pro-attitudes cannot have the inherent tendency Smith finds in them if the Humean theory of pro-attitudes is correct. If people's pro-attitudes tend to adjust in light of their normative beliefs, they cannot typically be simple dispositions to act on their descriptive beliefs.[14] They must typically be more complex dispositions of the sort that, as I read him, Davidson makes central to his non-Humean account of what pro-attitudes are. What we have here, therefore, is an important breaking point in Smith's thought and a clear fork in the road for the Humeans. Either they must go all the way with the neo-Humeans and argue that so-called normative beliefs are in fact nothing more than expressions of pro-attitudes, or they must lower their sights and allow that Humeanism extends only to the theory of motivation and not to the theory of pro-attitudes. There is no hope for a version of Humeanism that is thoroughgoing when it comes to pro-attitudes yet cognitivist when it comes to normative beliefs. In order for Humeans to be cognitivists with respect to normative beliefs, they must embrace something like the view I am attributing to Davidson.

Smith might try to appeal this verdict on the grounds that one's pro-attitudes as a group could exhibit an inherent tendency to move towards systematic justification, even if each pro-attitude considered individually is simply a disposition to do whatever one believes will increase one's chances of achieving the targeted result. Instead of assuming that a concern for systematic justification would typically have to figure in the contents of the dispositions with which one's pro-attitudes are identified, why not allow that it could instead be a purely systemic property that is attributable to the whole but not any of the parts? I'm not sure why any Humean would bother to fight this battle, however, since the purely functional account of pro-attitudes would already have been lost. Once we allow that one's normative beliefs are implicated in one's pro-attitudes, it hardly matters whether this happens only systemically or often also individually. The spirit, if not every letter, of the Humean theory has been abandoned, so we might as well adopt a theory that makes this fact transparent. Such is the broadly Scanlonian theory I have been attributing to Davidson. So this is the theory I will continue to develop and defend.

Let us return now to Velleman's worries about theories of this sort. Are such theories really undermined by the counter-examples he cites? Does the fact that people's pro-attitudes are often unruly or even perverse show that they are not typically dependent on or conditioned by their normative beliefs? In saying that people's pro-attitudes are typically conditioned by their normative beliefs, I am certainly not claiming that they are necessarily conditioned by them. So the mere fact that unruly and even perverse pro-attitudes are possible poses no threat to the Scanlonian account of pro-attitudes I am developing and defending. The threat, if there is one, comes rather from the fact that unruly and even perverse pro-attitudes seem so typically and indeed paradigmatically human. For this fact may not seem to leave any room for the claim that people's pro-attitudes are typically dependent on or conditioned by their normative beliefs. This will seem especially true so long as the case for my Scanlonian claims about pro-attitudes rests entirely on appeals to phenomenology and commonsense; for such appeals would seem at best to support claims of precisely the numerical or statistical sort that Velleman's counter-examples are designed to undermine.

However, our discussion of the internalist requirement shows that the case against the Humean theory of pro-attitudes is not merely phenomenological and commonsensical. It's not simply that we don't seem to be disposed to do everything we would have to be disposed to do if that theory were correct. It's also that the Humean theory of pro-attitudes is flatly at odds with our deepest convictions about what would make any beliefs truly normative. Truly normative beliefs would have to have some rational bearing on people's motivations, which would require that people's motivations be striving to get normative matters right. We can agree that Smith is correct about this while remaining agnostic for the moment about whether normative matters are matters of systematic justification. (I am already on record as saying that I don't think they are, but the case for that verdict will be made in the next chapter.) The question for us here is whether the sense in which it is required that people's motivations strive to get normative matters right is at odds with the sense in which counter-examples of the sort Velleman cites might reveal people's pro-attitudes to be paradigmatically unruly or even perverse.

Obviously a lot is going to depend here on how we understand Smith's idea that people's pro-attitudes must possess an inherent tendency to seek out or move towards normative truth. Strikingly, Velleman (1992, 17 ff.) describes claims of this sort as claims about the constitutive aims of pro-attitudes, and seems to understand them as making claims about the essential nature of individual pro-attitudes. On this reading, Smith's claim would be that no disposition to act could count as a pro-attitude if it was not suitably sensitive to its bearer's beliefs about normative matters; and of course this claim would be undermined by the counter-examples Velleman cites. However, this is pretty clearly not how Smith intends his claim to be understood. He is not insisting that a person's each and every pro-attitude must display a tendency to fall into line with her beliefs about normative matters as they evolve over time.[15] His claim is directed at her pro-attitudes considered rather as a system or a whole. And indeed it is difficult to see why anything more than this should be required. Surely a person's normative beliefs can have a rational bearing on some pro-attitude of hers even if that pro-attitude of hers is not itself aiming to get normative matters right, provided it is part of a system of pro-attitudes that has this as its aim, for in that case the system will have failed in producing or countenancing the pro-attitude. Smith's claim that people's motivations must be striving to get normative matters right is thus best understood as a claim about the systemic aims possessed by pro-attitudes as a group, not as a claim about the constitutive aims possessed by individual pro-attitudes on their own, as Velleman seems to assume when he offers unruly and perverse pro-attitudes as counter-examples. And once it is taken in this way, I don't see how it is threatened by the fact that people's pro-attitudes are often and even paradigmatically unruly or even perverse. Clearly people's pro-attitudes can have it as their systemic aim to get normative matters right, even if various sorts of failings in the system are perfectly predictable and paradigmatically human.

In response, Velleman would undoubtedly take issue with the idea that there is this one systemic aim that every person must have in order to have any truly normative beliefs. He would of course not deny that people have higher-order desires of various sorts, and that one of them might often be a desire to get normative matters right. Nor indeed would he deny that the more unruly of people's pro-attitudes would often count as failings relative to any such higher-order desire to get normative matters right. What he would deny, however, is that everyone must have this higher-order desire, and that, when they have it, it must be the strongest such desire they have. As he sees things, it is perfectly conceivable that a person's strongest higher-order desire might sometimes even be to get normative matters very often and very badly *wrong*. As he remarks at one point (1992, 18 ff.), when Milton's Satan vows to make evil his good, is it not obvious that this is the sort of thing he has in mind? But my claim that people's systemic aim is necessarily to get normative matters right is not meant to imply that their strongest higher-order desire must always take this form. Even if the strongest of his higher-order desires is often starkly opposed to it, I would still maintain that Satan's systemic aim must be to get normative matters right; for I know of no other way to make any real sense of the fact that his normative beliefs are guaranteed always to have some rational bearing on his motivations. And I know of no other way to explain what distinguishes normative beliefs from others, except to say that they are guaranteed always to have this bearing on people's motivations. The hellish nature of Satan's predicament consists precisely in the fact that he cannot escape the pull of reasons even as he rages perfectly sincerely and perfectly understandably against them. He may wish that he were less attracted to reasons than he in fact is, but possessing that one higher-order desire does little to make that wish come true.

I submit, therefore, that the account of pro-attitudes I am attributing to Davidson is nuanced and flexible enough to accommodate all the alleged counter-examples Velleman cites. Once we appreciate the fact that the claims it makes are systemic in character, we can see how they are compatible with any number of individually discordant pro-attitudes. Indeed, even granting that it is the systemic aim of people's pro-attitudes to get normative matters right, few of their pro-attitudes are likely to be properly responsive to the full range of their normative beliefs. Velleman's alleged counter-examples focus our attention on cases where people fall very far short of the mark, seemingly ignoring their normative beliefs altogether and in some cases even yearning to act in opposition to them. But most of a person's pro-attitudes, while not being nearly so discordant as that, will inevitably fall short of the mark in some respect and to some degree. People typically have many normative beliefs bearing on the choices they have to make, and their pro-attitudes will rarely succeed in being properly responsive to all of them. Once again, however, there is nothing in any of this that is not perfectly compatible with the claim that the systemic aim of people's pro-attitudes as a whole is always to get normative matters right. And that claim is all we need in order to conclude that people's normative judgments are not mere expressions of their pro-attitudes but rather full-fledged beliefs to which their pro-attitudes are more or less responsive.

There is, however, one final objection that we should address before moving on, and that concerns the implications of this non-Humean account of pro-attitudes for young children. It would appear that children start acquiring pro-attitudes before they start acquiring normative beliefs. But in that case how can their pro-attitudes aim to get normative matters right? Yet if getting normative matters right is not the systemic aim of people's pro-attitudes when they are young, is it really possible that it could somehow become the systemic aim of their pro-attitudes as they mature?[16] Now of course one way to respond to this objection would be to argue that children in fact start acquiring normative beliefs much earlier than they seem to and no later than they start acquiring pro-attitudes. But I think a more promising response is to acknowledge that the systemic aim of people's pro-attitudes may indeed be slightly broader than we have been saying. What we should probably have been saying all along is that the systemic aim of people's pro-attitudes is to be aligned with whatever truths there happen to be. So if it is the case that children start acquiring descriptive beliefs before they start acquiring normative ones, then there will be a period during which their pro-attitudes are pretty much as the Humeans portray them. But once that period is over and they start acquiring beliefs about what they have reason to do, their pro-attitudes as a group will be aiming to get not just descriptive but also normative matters right.

This reformulation would have the added advantage of highlighting a further problem for the Humean theory of pro-attitudes; namely, that it does not get even the relation between people's pro-attitudes and their descriptive beliefs exactly right. In fact, it is not only people's normative beliefs that have a rational bearing on their pro-attitudes; people's pro-attitudes should also be aligned with their beliefs about what is possible and about what is likely. As a moment's reflection reveals, however, people do not always avoid such mistakes. A distraught parent might yearn to speak to a child she knows is dead. An undisciplined investor might pursue a strategy she regards as less likely to succeed.[17] Avoiding such mistakes is not a given; quite the contrary, it is an achievement. And the fact that it is an achievement again tells us something important about the nature of pro-attitudes; namely, that they have it as part of their systemic aim to get matters of this sort right. In the final analysis, therefore, I think it must be said that the Humean theory of pro-attitudes does not provide a satisfactory account even of the very basic pro-attitudes that are its bread and butter. So I suggest the time has come for us to set that theory aside, and with it the worry that people's propositional attitudes lack any truly normative contents. People's normative judgments are full-fledged beliefs in which truly normative concepts are applied; so we need some explanation of how it is that those concepts are acquired.

Now of course the explanation proposed by Davidson is that in the first instance people acquire normative concepts by triangulating with one another and with situations or outcomes in their shared environment that have normative properties. The question we should therefore take up next is whether it makes any real sense to suppose that situations or outcomes in their shared environment actually could have normative properties on which people could triangulate. For that would seem to require that normative properties have a role to play in the causal explanation of people's reactions to the situations or outcomes in question; yet the very idea that normative properties could play a role in causal explanations might seem for one reason or another just too ludicrous to be taken seriously. One familiar set of worries here, often associated with the work of John Mackie (1976a, Chapter 1), revolves around the thought that causal properties must be primary, secondary or tertiary and that normative properties could be neither of these. A different set of worries, often associated with the work of Gilbert Harman (1977, Chapter 1), focuses more on the thought that causal explanations of people's reactions to situations and outcomes can always be given in purely descriptive terms. As we shall see in the next chapter, Davidson's responses to these worries are not always worked out as fully or as rigorously as one might have wished. What I think we shall also see, however, is that he has good reason to be as confident of ultimate victory on these fronts as he is.

Notes

1. If normative 'beliefs' are nothing more than expressions of pro-attitudes, are they really beliefs at all? Strictly speaking, I don't think so; but I won't take time to make that case here. Whether they are denying that people have any normative beliefs or insisting that people's normative beliefs are merely expressions of their pro-attitudes, the arguments that follow show neo-Humeans to be wrong.
2. Perhaps actively embracing this belief could suffice to motivate me, but simply possessing it could not. And Davidson would insist that actively embracing it involves adopting some sort of pro-attitude towards it.
3. The reference is to Davidson 1963, 4, where favorable evaluative judgments are counted as pro-attitudes (which should already make one wonder whether Davidson is not being misled by his unfortunate terminology).
4. Notice that the point here is not simply that one can form an "all things considered" judgment without forming the corresponding "all out" judgment. Smith's thought, as I understand it, is that even an "all out" judgment can fail to issue in the disposition that motivation necessarily requires. Davidson again does not always put this as carefully as he should; in fact, he originally (1969) identified people's "all out" judgments with their intentions. But he eventually (1978) comes to the conclusion that intentions are pro-attitudes resulting from one's (not always particularly successful) endeavors to get normative matters right.
5. It is important to recognize that the question is whether normative beliefs can literally constitute goals, not simply whether they are capable of giving rise to pro-attitudes that will in turn constitute them. Are pro-attitudes ever merely "logical consequences" (Nagel 1970, 30) of goals that are strictly speaking constituted by normative beliefs, or is the truth of the matter always that the goal is constituted by the pro-attitude? One might wonder how anything of importance could turn on a point as fine as this; but we shall see in just a moment that a lot is actually at stake here.
6. Compare Smith 1994, 113.
7. As we shall see, Smith is an exception. He thinks the Humean theory of pro-attitudes is compatible with a form of constructivism about reasons.
8. As I allowed in Chapter 5, matters might be a little more complicated than this suggests. But such details need not detain us here.
9. See Scanlon 1998, Chapter 1.
10. In fact, when Davidson discusses this particular case, he does not mention normative beliefs at all!
11. We are left to speculate here because Davidson gives us absolutely no direction on this score.
12. This might seem to give externalists short shrift. But in fact, as Christine Korsgaard has remarked (1986, 9), it is not clear that there actually are many externalists here for us to contend with. Just as no one seriously denies that normative truths are considerations that count in favor of actions, so too no one seriously denies that people's normative beliefs have some rational bearing on their motivations. Many philosophers of course deny that there are normative truths or that people have normative beliefs; but no one seriously denies that these claims would be true of them if there were any.
13. He allows, therefore, that people's normative beliefs target truths that are in some sense constructions of their pro-attitudes. But this is not to say that they merely express those pro-attitudes.
14. Sharon Street stresses this point in her 2012. She recognizes that her Humean constructivism depends on a theory of pro-attitudes that is in crucial respects quite different than the standard Humean account.

15. They should do so, but that's another matter.
16. Velleman presses such worries in 1992, 7.
17. Humeans might try arguing that the distraught parent merely wishes she could speak to her child and that the undisciplined investor is acting on something other than her desire to make money. Surely, however, such maneuvers would be no more persuasive than their earlier attempts to show that people are always disposed to do whatever they believe will promote the ends they desire. Humeans might thus do better to try denying that such pro-attitudes are in any sense mistakes. But that once again strikes me as being a remarkably large bullet to have to bite. Thus the Humeans' best bet is probably to abandon their theory of pro-attitudes and embrace constructivism. But having allowed that truly normative concepts exist, can they keep Davidson's triangulation argument from succeeding?

7 Normative Properties and Explanation

If people's normative judgments are typically not mere expressions of their pro-attitudes, but rather full-fledged beliefs to which their pro-attitudes are typically sensitive, then the question arises, how are the contents of these beliefs fixed, and the possibility emerges that Davidson's triangulation argument might provide the answer. But Davidson's argument commits him to a kind of realism about reasons, and in many critics' eyes this rules it out from the start. They think realism about reasons is, if not perhaps quite literally unintelligible, then at any rate too implausible to be taken at all seriously.

As I have mentioned, the most familiar worries to this effect are undoubtedly those associated with the work of John Mackie and Gilbert Harman. Before turning to them, however, we should consider an importantly different set of worries that have more recently been pressed by Christine Korsgaard. As we shall see, Korsgaard's worries cut deeper than Mackie's or Harman's, in the sense that they are even more antithetical to normative realism. Understanding how Davidson could have replied to Korsgaard's worries might therefore help us to understand how he should have replied to Mackie's and Harman's.

1. Korsgaard's Worries about Normative Authority

Korsgaard's worries concern what I shall call the practicality requirement. (She herself refers to it (1986, 11) as the internalism requirement, but I think that way of putting it is misleading; it conflates the requirement with one strategy for meeting it, thereby making it difficult to keep other strategies in view.)[1] Because reasons for actions must count in favor of actions, there must be some sense of 'should' in which people should perform the actions they have most reason to perform. But what sense is this? As Korsgaard views the matter, the 'should' here can only be the 'should' of rationality. It must be that people should do what they have most reason to do because rationality requires that of them. So the question, Korsgaard thinks, is whether realists can guarantee that rationality always requires people to act on their reasons. And of course her worry is that they are prevented from guaranteeing this by the essentially internal focus of rationality.[2] Given this essentially internal focus, if we want to guarantee that rationality always requires people to act on their reasons, we need to equate people's reasons with the conclusions they would reach if they deliberated rationally about what to do. And that, in broad outline, is Korsgaard's verdict—that only constructivist accounts of reasons can guarantee them the requisite authority. Normative realism is a non-starter because it cannot guarantee that people's reasons for action will have any authority over them.

As I mentioned in Chapter 5, Davidson allows that people's reasons might always be accessible to them via rational deliberation, but only because he insists that nobody's normative beliefs could fail to be at least roughly as they should be. And like any realist, he understands this 'should' in terms of the notion of truth, not the notion of rationality. Normative reasons count in favor of actions or attitudes because they are the truths agents are trying to get right. So, for Davidson, people should perform the actions or acquire the attitudes they have most reason to perform or acquire not because that is rational (since it might not be) but because it is required to achieve their systemic aim. As Davidson likes to say, truth is the primitive concept. It cannot usefully be analyzed in terms of other concepts, such as the concepts of warranted assertion or rational belief, but must rather be assumed in our accounts of them. It plays the fundamental role in the theory of meaning. And being in accord with it is our systemic aim. As possessors of propositional attitudes and performers of intentional actions, we aim to believe what's true and desire what's right.[3] Small wonder, therefore, that Davidson does not regard the practicality requirement as posing any special problem for normative realism. Because he does not share Korsgaard's conception of normative authority, he does not share her concerns about normative realism either.

In defense of her conception of normative authority, Korsgaard argues that realists cannot account for even basic requirements of rationality. In particular, she argues (2009, Chapter 4) that they cannot account for the instrumental principle, according to which rationality requires people to adopt the means that they believe will most effectively promote the ends that they believe they have most reason to pursue. Now, again, as with Davidson's principle of continence, we might wonder whether Korsgaard's instrumental principle is in fact too strong. If I believe I am an unreliable assessor of ends or means, am I necessarily required by rationality to adopt the means that I believe will most effectively promote the ends that I believe I have most reason to pursue? As with the principle of continence, however, it is very difficult to deny that some instrumental principle is true. And this is all Korsgaard needs to press her case against realism, for her worry is that realists will seek to establish that instrumental beliefs have this rational import by reminding people of their aim to get normative matters right. Yet this, in her view, is hopelessly circular, since it assumes that instrumental beliefs have the very import in question. If someone needs persuading that she should comply with the instrumental principle, why should she be moved by the thought that complying with the instrumental principle might be an effective way of promoting her aim to get normative matters right?

But this misunderstands the intentions of the realists. They are not seeking to persuade people that they should be rational. Their hope is simply to explain what being rational requires of people, and their claim is that people are rational to the extent that they form beliefs and desires with a view to believing what's true and desiring what's right. What this in turn requires can be unclear, as their existing beliefs and desires can point them in conflicting directions. We have noted puzzles that arise when people doubt their own reliability, and there are of course countless other cases in which it can be difficult to say what rational people would conclude from the beliefs and desires they possess. All that matters for us here, however, is that the realists do not regard these as truly normative questions. On the contrary, they regard these questions as being evaluative in character, as questions about how people would form their beliefs and desires if they were aiming to believe what's true and desire what's right and they were deliberating well.[4] They are not arguing in circles, therefore, when they invoke this aim in their argument for the instrumental principle, for they are invoking this aim not to persuade people that they should comply with the instrumental principle but rather to explain why complying with the instrumental principle is in fact something people will do when they are deliberating well.

Now of course the suggestion that rational requirements are not truly normative is bound to strike Korsgaard as being absurd. As she understands it, the normative question is precisely a question about how we should form our beliefs and desires. When faced with decisions about what to believe or desire, by what principles or directives should our deliberations be guided? In Korsgaard's own view, our answers to this question must somehow be extracted from the bare idea of autonomous activity.[5] Constructivists of a less Kantian sort might instead say that we should be aiming to achieve a kind of coherence. They might endorse Michael Smith's claim that we should be aiming to form beliefs and desires that are systematically justified.[6] Either way, however, rationality becomes the truly normative notion and the realists' appeal to truth becomes at best misleading. Truths are nothing but conclusions we would draw about what we should believe and desire if we were perfectly rational, not independent standards in light of which our manner of deliberating and the products of our deliberations can be evaluated. We can still say, if we like, that people's systemic aim is to believe what's true and desire what's right. But all this can come to is that people typically aim to form beliefs and desires that are perfectly rational. Substantive conceptions of truth are incapable of gaining any purchase on people's deliberations about what they should believe and desire.

This is a seductive argument, but its understanding of the normative question is one no good realist would ever embrace. For realists, the question is not how we would form our beliefs and desires if we were deliberating

Normative Properties and Explanation 161

perfectly rationally; it is what our beliefs and desires would be if we actually succeeded in getting descriptive and normative matters right. Our systemic aim, as I have been calling it, is not to deliberate rationally but rather to get things right. Of course, given that this is our systemic aim, some forms of deliberation will be rational and others will not. In fact, it could turn out that rationality requires us to deliberate in precisely the ways that some constructivists recommend. Perhaps forming our beliefs and desires in ways that will increase what Smith calls their systematic justification is precisely what it makes sense for us to do given that our systemic aim is to get descriptive and normative matters right, in which case it would obviously be tempting to describe the demands of systematic justification as being normative in nature.[7] According to the realists, however, this would, strictly speaking, be incorrect. Only the demands of truth are actually normative. Substantive conceptions of truth are not required to gain a purchase on our deliberations—they have it from the beginning; for we cannot ask ourselves what to believe and desire without asking ourselves what is true and what is right.

I conclude, therefore, that Korsgaard's worries about normative authority do not pose a significant threat to Davidson's normative realism. And I think it is important to add that this negative assessment of her argument is widespread even among constructivists. As Korsgaard bravely acknowledges (2008, 28), her understanding of the normative question creates difficulties for empirical realism and not just normative realism. But very few constructivists follow her in equating empirical truths with the products of theoretical deliberations that are perfectly rational.[8] On the contrary, constructivists are much more likely to adopt empirical realism and to limit and qualify their position accordingly, by equating normative truths with the products of practical deliberations that are not just perfectly rational but also empirically informed.[9] It follows, of course, that these constructivists must be rejecting normative realism on the basis of arguments different from Korsgaard's. Their worries must have less to do with realism and more to do with its application to reasons for action. But now why, exactly, does the application of realism to reasons for action strike them as being so terribly problematic? If rationality does not always have priority over truth, why should it be assumed to have priority in this case? More often than not, the worries raised here depend on accounts of what motivation involves that Davidson has already dismissed. So it should not come as any great surprise that he does not spend very much time responding to them.

If motivation required desires and desires were purely functional states, as is suggested by Humean accounts of motivation and desires, then constructivists would of course be right in thinking that normative realism confronts an obstacle that empirical realism does not; for it is indeed difficult to see how normative truths could exist and count in favor of people's actions if people's motivations considered as a system or a whole were in no way aiming to get normative matters right.[10] But this argument, if it were any good, would rule out normative constructivism every bit as much as normative realism. Constructed normative truths are after all still truths, so if normative truths are ruled out, normative constructivism is ruled out. What the constructivists need, therefore, is an argument that in some respects walks an even finer line than Davidson's. As we noted in Chapter 6, Davidson endorses the Humean theory of motivation but dismisses the Humean theory of desire; he claims the desires are typically not purely functional states but share the systemic aim of getting normative matters right. It would seem that constructivists need an argument that would entitle them to embrace this but add a further qualification, to the effect that the normative matters that desires aim to get right have to do only with internal coherence, and not at all with the correspondence to external truths that normative realists make central to their account of things.

But what might this argument be? What might it be about desires that would encourage constructivists to add this qualification? My strong suspicion is that many constructivists are moved here by a residual attachment to the Humean account of desire. Much like Michael Smith, they hold with the Humeans that desires considered individually are nothing more than purely functional states, but then depart from the Humeans by maintaining that desires considered systemically share the aim of getting normative matters right. As I noted in Chapter 6, one might understandably wonder whether these two claims are ultimately compatible with one another, since sharing the aim of getting normative matters right would seem to indicate that desires are not purely functional states. But leave that aside. The more important question is whether the claim that desires considered individually are purely functional states should be regarded as having any bearing on the issue of what it is that desires considered systemically aim at. In other words, would it follow, if it in fact were true that desires considered individually are purely functional states, that desires considered systemically could aim at nothing over and above the sort of internal coherence that normative constructivists champion? My suspicion, once again, is that many constructivists think this would follow and thus think normative realism is a non-starter. It cannot account for normative authority because it is incompatible with the truth about what motivation and especially desire involves.

A purely functional desire to Ψ is a disposition to do whatever one believes will increase one's chances of Ψ-ing. A person who has such a desire might therefore be described as aiming to achieve a kind of coherence. She is aiming to perform an action that will cohere with her desire in light of her evolving instrumental beliefs. Of course, as constructivists themselves have often pointed out, this sort of aiming would not involve any normative guidance. Normative guidance enters the picture only when a person's desires as a system are aiming to get normative matters right.[11] However, it might be thought that this primitive connection between desires and coherence carries over to the normative realm. If it is literally in the nature of desires, considered individually, to aim at achieving a kind of local coherence, should we not conclude that the aim of desires, considered systemically, must be to achieve a kind of global coherence? Although it is rarely put as bluntly as this, I suspect many constructivists are moved by something like this argument. Bernard Williams, for example, constructs his account of "a sound deliberative route" by adding nuance to the "sub-Humean" model (1980, 102 ff.), but without ever calling into question its basic assumption that the aim of practical deliberation is to increase coherence. So too Michael Smith; the possibility that practical deliberation might aim at uncovering external truths is never on his radar.[12]

My own view, as I explained in Chapter 6, is that desires, considered individually, are typically *not* purely functional states, but rather dispositions to act in ways one believes will respond to the reasons for action one believes one has, in which case their main concern, from the beginning, is that one's actions accord with the truth about one's reasons.[13] Even if I am wrong about this, however, and there really is a primitive connection between desires and coherence, this surely is a remarkably flimsy basis on which to build a case for normative constructivism and against normative realism, especially considering how different the sort of coherence sought here is from the sort of coherence championed by normative constructivists. Suppose, by way of comparison, that realists were to assert that there is a primitive connection between desires and correspondence, on the perfectly analogous grounds that a person with a purely functional desire to Ψ may be described as aiming to perform actions that will correspond to the evolving facts about what will most effectively promote her chances of Ψ-ing. This claim, I take it, would not be regarded as tipping the scales very decisively in favor of normative realism, for the obvious reason that this kind of correspondence is so different from the kind that normative realists insist on. I submit that the only reasonable conclusion to draw here is that neither of these arguments can carry much weight.

Now of course advocates of normative constructivism will likely object, against this, that the difference between correspondence to descriptive facts and correspondence to normative facts is greater than the difference between coherence with one desire and coherence among multiple desires, and in consequence that the argument contemplated here for normative constructivism is stronger than the parallel argument for normative realism. In order to make an objection along these lines stick, however, they would have to establish that there is some independent problem with the realists' suggestion that there are normative facts with which people's actions can accord or not, in which case one would suppose our focus should be on that alleged problem and not on this abstruse objection. And this is precisely the conclusion I think we should draw from this section—that no terribly persuasive argument against normative realism can be built on claims about the nature of normative authority and the relation between reasons and desires.[14] If there are grounds for concluding that realism about reasons is a non-starter, they must be of another sort. They must have more to do with the metaphysics of normative reasons themselves. This is of course precisely the sort of worry about normative realism that John Mackie and Gilbert Harman try in their rather different ways to articulate. So let us turn now to the question of whether they manage to fare any better here than Korsgaard does.

2. Mackie's Worries about Metaphysical Queerness

Mackie raises two broad sorts of worries about normative realism, which he famously describes (1976a, 36–42) as the argument from queerness and the argument from relativity. We'll be taking up worries about relativity in Chapter 8, so my focus in this section will be exclusively on the argument from queerness. More precisely, my focus here will be on worries about metaphysical queerness. Mackie also argues that normative realism should be rejected on epistemological grounds. That is, he worries that a faculty of intuition would provide our only way of knowing about normative properties if they were to exist, a scenario that in his view would be sufficiently queer to suggest that properties of this variety do not in fact exist after all. But I take it that Davidson would have a promising response to this worry if his triangulation argument were otherwise to pass muster, for he could then say that the contents of people's normative beliefs are fixed in ways that ensure they are by and large correct, which might in turn be held to underwrite a coherentist normative epistemology, perhaps along the lines of John Rawls's method of wide reflective equilibrium. Although important details would obviously remain to be filled in, I think it is at least reasonably clear how the story here would go. The greater challenge to Davidson comes from Mackie's metaphysical worries, for they threaten to keep the triangulation argument from even getting off the ground.

What's so queer about the suggestion that reasons for action are real properties of some situations or outcomes? Why couldn't it be the case that some situations or outcomes are really to be promoted and others really to be averted? Mackie's assumption is that such properties would have to be or involve powers to generate the corresponding motivations, and his worry is that the universe simply does not contain any powers of the very special sort that would be required. Consider, for example, Gilbert Harman's (1977, 4) case of the boys who are about to set fire to a cat. Mackie's idea is that, for this situation to be objectively bad, it would have to possess a remarkable and hence unlikely power—the power to generate, in everyone who recognizes it for what it is, some motivation to stop it. And his conclusion is that, as a matter of empirical fact, the universe simply does not contain any powers of this sort.

But is Mackie right in thinking "objectively prescriptive" properties would have to be "intrinsically motivating" in this way? Realists will certainly want to say that, if the situation Harman describes is objectively bad, everyone *should* want it to be stopped.[15] Although not everyone could be

Normative Properties and Explanation 165

expected to recognize this, this is the desire that would get matters right. But this does not on the face of it commit realists to any further claim about who would actually acquire this desire. On the contrary, one of the marks of realism is surely the insistence that error is always possible—that even the best informed and most rational of observers could fail to acquire the desires that are correct to the situation. So it is tempting to conclude that Mackie's argument from (metaphysical) queerness is directed at a straw person—at a view of normative properties that is not required of any realist and that few if any realists have ever held.

This would be too quick, however, for it would not get at the root of Mackie's concern. Even if realists aren't committed to saying that the objective badness of what Harman's boys are doing is a power to generate, in every person who recognizes what they are up to, at least some desire that they be stopped, Mackie would still insist that they are committed to saying that it is or involves a power of some sort or other. But what sort of power could this possibly be? Surely not the sort involved in so-called tertiary qualities. Inasmuch as normative properties are claimed to influence purely material events, it is surely via influence they exercise over people's mental states. So it seems safe to conclude that normative properties would have to be either primary or secondary qualities. And Mackie's worry is that it is very difficult to make sense of objectively prescriptive properties on either of these two models.

On Mackie's Lockean account of what secondary qualities are, to say that the objective badness of what Harman's boys are doing is a secondary quality is to say that it is "nothing but" a power to generate certain (somehow adverse) sorts of desires in certain (affectively normal, etc.) sorts of people in certain (affectively favorable) sorts of circumstances, in much the same way as the blueness of the boys' jeans is "nothing but" a power to generate certain (of-blue) sorts of experiences in certain (normally sighted, etc.) sorts of people in certain (perceptually favorable) sorts of circumstances.[16] However, if this is all there is to its badness, in what sense should people desire that the boys be stopped? Mackie's worry is that the normative authority of badness goes missing on this account of what it is. There are descriptive facts about the powers that situations actually have, but no normative facts about the desires that people should acquire.

Mackie's tacit assumption, as I read him, is thus that, for reasons like these, it simply makes no sense to suggest that normative properties could be secondary qualities. If normative properties are somehow to make demands on the desires people should have, they must be something more than mere powers to affect the desires people do have. What this means, according to Mackie, is that they must be not secondary but primary qualities—properties that can be specified independently of the responses that they do or even could generate, but that even so are such as to make demands on what people's responses should be, if only in the sense that people's responses can succeed or fail at "resembling" those properties. Unlike many of Locke's modern-day critics, Mackie himself sees nothing wrong with the general idea that independently specifiable properties and intrinsically mental states can resemble one another.[17] The challenge, on his view of things, is rather to make good on the particular suggestion that the relation between normative properties and desires is of this sort. What, precisely, are we to imagine? That prompting people to act is actually an intrinsic property of many situations, and that desires resemble these properties when they incline people to go along? Mackie's claim, as I understand him, is that such intrinsically motivating properties are the best normative realists can offer, and that, because there clearly are no such properties, their theory is mistaken.

As I read him, therefore, Mackie is not simply attacking a straw person—on the contrary, he is following his account of things to its logical conclusion. If primary and secondary qualities are the sorts of things Mackie thinks they are, reasons fit under neither heading and so are not properties of situations at all.[18] There might still be something to the idea that reasons should be regarded as secondary qualities, and that Mackie goes wrong because he instead pursues the possibility that they are primary qualities—but only if secondary qualities can be understood as something other than Mackie says they are, as something more than mere powers to generate certain responses in certain people in certain circumstances. Without going so far as to suppose that secondary qualities could be specified entirely independently of the responses that they would generate in those people in those circumstances, we would need to find a way to make of them something more than mere powers so that the designated responses could be regarded as getting something right. Without supposing that the objective badness of what Harman's boys are doing could be specified entirely independently of the fact that it would generate certain desires in certain people in certain circumstances, we would need a way to make of it something more than this so that failures to acquire those desires could be regarded as failures to register a truth about the situation.

Such is John McDowell's (1985) response to Mackie, and one might expect Davidson's response to be similar. In his sole discussion of Mackie's argument, however, Davidson appears to miss the point entirely. Whereas McDowell takes pains to defend an alternative, non-Lockean account of what secondary qualities are, one which would create space for the possibility that secondary qualities make demands on people's responses, Davidson mentions Mackie only in order to take him to task for worrying about where normative properties would be located in the world of physical objects and events. He points out (1995b, 44) that properties, being abstract entities, are not located anywhere at all, as if this is all it takes to put an end to the matter! But when Mackie worries about whether normative properties are "part of the fabric" of the world, he is not worrying about the location of those properties so much as about their nature. He wants to know whether any properties are really capable of making demands on people's motivations, or whether the claim that objectively prescriptive properties exist should be rejected as a mere fiction. This would seem to be a perfectly reasonable question to ask, and would seem to call for exactly the sort of answer that McDowell is hoping to give—either an account of secondary qualities that would show them to have normative authority, or an account of primary qualities that would apply to normative properties after all.

My suspicion, however, is that, when he admonishes Mackie for worrying about where normative properties would be located, Davidson actually means to raise an objection at least something like McDowell's. McDowell accuses Mackie of drawing the distinction between primary and secondary qualities in the wrong way, and I do not think there can be any doubt at all that Davidson would agree. He certainly would agree that the distinction is not between those properties that are and those properties that are not resembled by the responses they generate in people. McDowell traces this mistake to the fact that Mackie conflates experiences with mere sensations, states that cannot get anything about a situation right except perhaps by resembling it. As McDowell argues (1985, 139), however, and Davidson agrees (1983, 144), experiences typically involve judgments that are truth-assessable; so they get things right when, and to the extent that, those judgments get things right. Unlike Mackie, therefore, neither McDowell nor Davidson draws the distinction between primary and secondary qualities by saying that only experiences of primary qualities are capable of getting something right about them. When blue things look blue to me, I do get something right about them, just as I get something right about squares when they look square to me. The trick, of course, is to say what I get right in each case; that is where the real distinction between primary and secondary qualities will be found.

So when Davidson admonishes Mackie for worrying about where normative properties would be located in the world of physical objects and events, I interpret him as admonishing Mackie for worrying about what features of that world people's motivations could resemble. His complaint, like McDowell's, is that Mackie is being misled by an inadequate conception of the distinction between primary and secondary qualities, and that a better understanding of this distinction would reveal that it poses no threat to normative properties. However, whereas McDowell develops this idea by considering how normative properties are to be understood on the model of secondary qualities, Davidson would seem to be in a position to think of them on the model of primary qualities. Since this would yield a much more robust form of realism, it is worth pausing to consider how the argument might go. The premise to build on is once again going to be Davidson's non-Humean account of what desires are.

McDowell famously rejects the Humean theory of motivation, arguing (e.g., in 1979) that normative beliefs can constitute motivating dispositions in people who are sufficiently virtuous. His explanation of how they do this is complex, and not all the complexities need concern us here. The point for us to focus on is the way in which he models his explanation on an account of perceptual experience. According to McDowell, the ability to see objects as blue requires both a suitable sensibility and proper training. Untutored children may well have the appropriate sensations, but they learn to see objects as blue only as they develop color judgment. McDowell argues that the ability to act on reasons likewise requires both a suitable sensibility and proper training. Untutored children may well share our most basic responses to things, but they cannot act on reasons until they develop normative judgment. According to McDowell, normative beliefs can constitute motivating dispositions because they ultimately are just trained capacities for response.

I have already explained (in Chapter 6) why I think it is a mistake to suppose that normative beliefs can ever constitute motivating dispositions. So even if McDowell were right in holding that normative judgment gets developed as basic responses get trained, I still think it would be one thing to form a normative belief and another thing to become disposed to act accordingly. But the worry I want to press here has more to do with McDowell's understanding of normative properties, for the analogy to secondary qualities would seem to suggest that he is prepared to countenance a very unsettling sort of relativism. After all, if different forms of sensibility are possible, then different secondary qualities must be possible as well. This may not be troubling in the case of perceptual properties, but it is highly problematic in the case of normative properties; for it makes it extremely difficult to see how morality could mediate differences among people's reasons for action.

The worry here is not that McDowell allows considerations to count in favor of actions for some people but not for others. As we shall see more clearly in Chapter 8, that much is true of many reasons for action.[19] The fact that someone is my old friend but not yours gives me reasons to act that it does not give you. As I understand it, however, this is a truth that we are all equally capable of appreciating. McDowell's account, by contrast, allows that one group of people might have reasons for action that other groups are incapable of appreciating, very much as one group of people might experience perceptual properties that other groups are incapable of experiencing. This may not be troubling in the case of perceptual properties because there is no need to mediate such differences among people. But we do expect morality to reveal how people have reason to mediate differences among their other reasons.

Imagine, indeed, that there exist Martians whose affective sensibility and consequent training differ significantly from ours, enabling them to register normative properties of a sort significantly different from those we can register. Let us say that, whereas humans are capable of registering and acting on Type H reasons for action, the Martians are capable of registering and acting on Type M reasons for action. And now suppose that, whereas we find Type H reasons to try to stop Harman's boys, they find Type M reasons to promote behavior of just that sort. How are we to interact given the fact of such differences among our reasons? One might have thought that this is precisely where morality should enter the picture. And, indeed, normative realists commonly do regard morality as a set of constraints that people have strong second-order reasons to abide by because their first-order reasons put them at loggerheads.[20] The problem, however, as we shall again see more clearly in Chapter 8, is that such accounts of morality require that people at least be capable of appreciating one another's reasons. If the Martians and we are actually not capable of appreciating each other's reasons, we can hardly share second-order reasons to interact on terms of mutual respect! Thus McDowell's analogy to secondary qualities threatens to put his understanding of normative properties at odds with the best account of morality's function that normative realists can offer.

McDowell is of course perfectly aware that these worries exist about his understanding of normative properties. So why does he insist on taking secondary qualities as his model rather than primary qualities? His reasons are complex, but the basic idea is that he thinks the primary quality model is ruled out by the facts about the nature of desire and its role in motivation.[21] Much as he holds that mere sensations are not to be conflated with experiences, because they do not involve the element of judgment that full-blown experience requires, so too McDowell holds that mere desires are not to be conflated with motivations, because they do not involve the element of judgment that full-blown motivation requires. His account of desires remains a Humean one, even though his account of motivation does not; and this prevents his overall view from being as anti-Humean as it might otherwise have been. As we have seen, while he allows that normative beliefs are capable of constituting motivating dispositions, he thinks they can do this only because they are manifestations of sensibilities originating with desires. This goes well beyond the neo-Humean claim that normative judgments can only express desires, and makes it possible to understand normative properties on the model of secondary qualities. But if we would rather understand normative properties on the model of primary qualities, we need to make a bigger break from the Humeans than McDowell has contemplated.

What we need to do is exactly what I have been arguing Davidson does—reject not the Humean account of motivation but rather the Humean account of desires. By firmly refusing to allow that normative beliefs are capable of constituting motivating dispositions, we avoid any need to regard them as manifestations of sensibilities originating with desires. And by regarding desires, even purely functional desires, as states aiming to get various matters right, we in any event make it very implausible to treat them as being analogous to sensations. The accounts of motivation and of desires that I have been attributing to Davidson thus set us up perfectly to understand normative properties on the model of primary rather than secondary qualities. So far as I know, this is not an opportunity Davidson actually seizes himself. He never does make it terribly clear what he understands normative properties to be. Nonetheless, given that it promises to deliver more of what we want, and that it seems a better fit with his account of what desires are, I think Davidson should be interpreted as understanding normative properties on the model of primary qualities, but of course as rejecting Mackie's inference that they would then have to be intrinsically motivating. That inference may have made sense to Mackie, given his account of what primary qualities are, but once we move beyond his Lockean premises, there is nothing to recommend it at all.

To deny that these normative properties would have to be intrinsically motivating is not to deny that they would have to have some ability to influence people's desires. It is simply to say that their success in influencing a person's desires could depend on the person's exercise of judgment and not just on the properties themselves.[22] And indeed it is plausible to suppose that, no matter how perfect a person's circumstances are, and no matter how well trained she is, she might fail to act as she should. What is intrinsic to the situation Harman describes, for example, is a reason, not a desire—the fact that people should desire that it be stopped, not the fact that they will. But still, while judgment is always necessary, realists like Davidson insist that normative properties can also have an important part to play in causal explanations of people's desires. This possibility is especially important for Davidson, for people could not triangulate on normative properties if the presence of those properties never had any actual effects on them. Although he occasionally (e.g., 1995b, 44) obscures this point by describing the worries here as epistemological rather than ontological, he elsewhere (e.g., 1995b, 47) states explicitly that values or reasons are "attitude-causing properties" of situations and outcomes. So the next question for us to consider is how he should respond to Harman's claim that normative properties can never be involved in truly causal explanations of people's attitudes or actions.

3. Harman's Worries about Explanatory Role

Harman's idea (1977, Chapter 1) is that the wrongness of what the boys are doing cannot be an attitude-causing property of the situation he describes because it would never be necessary to postulate the existence of such a property in order to explain people's normative reactions to such a situation. All such explanations ever require, in his estimation, are postulations about the descriptive properties in play and the prior training the observers have received—for example, that the boys are setting fire to a live cat, and that the observers have been trained to disapprove of such activity. By contrast, Harman thinks the fact that it involves a live cat is a causal property of the situation because it typically would not be possible to explain why observers come to the conclusion that the cat is alive without postulating that the cat is in fact alive. It would of course also be necessary to postulate that the situation has further descriptive properties providing evidence of the state of the cat, and that the prior training of the observers has made them capable of recognizing the state of cats on the basis of such evidence.

But Harman's idea is that these postulations typically would not undermine the necessity of postulating that the cat is in fact alive, whereas he thinks postulations about the descriptive properties of the situation and the prior training of the observers would invariably undermine the necessity of postulating normative properties.

Now, as Harman would be the first to acknowledge, this statement of his idea cannot be quite right. It may never be necessary to postulate that the cat is alive in order to explain why observers judge that it is, since it could always be argued that they are making a mistake or being misled in some way. In view of this, Harman's idea must be recast in terms of what would typically be necessary for good or reasonable explanations. On the one hand, therefore, his claim would have to be that a good or reasonable explanation of why observers judged the cat to be alive might very well require the postulation that the cat is in fact alive. On the other hand, by contrast, his claim would have to be that a good or reasonable explanation of why observers disapproved of the boys' treatment of the cat would never require the postulation that it is in fact wrong.

This might seem at first like a minor adjustment, but in fact it complicates matters for Harman considerably. We can agree that it is always possible to explain people's normative reactions to situations without postulating the existence of normative properties, without agreeing that it is always possible for good or reasonable explanations of their reactions to do this. How can Harman be so certain that explanations eschewing normative properties will always turn out to be better than explanations invoking them? It's true that they invoke properties of fewer sorts, but it's not obvious why that should be dispositive. Perhaps the resulting explanations are less good than they could be, precisely because they attempt to do so much with so little! That would certainly be Davidson's view. He would insist that Harman's loose talk of training is clearly inadequate, because we need to postulate the existence of normative properties in order to explain how the contents of normative beliefs get fixed.

Of course, Harman would take issue with this, arguing that other accounts of content determination are preferable. His own preference is to view the contents of normative judgments as being fixed through processes of mutual adjustment and implicit bargaining (Harman 1975). He would urge us not to regard people as triangulating with one another on independently existing normative properties, but rather as bargaining with and adjusting to one another in ways that are unchecked by the presence of anything so mysterious. But of course we already knew that the application of Davidson's triangulation argument to normative judgments is controversial. The question is whether it can be rejected out of hand, on the grounds of being somehow too implausible to take seriously, or whether it must be regarded as a serious contender to be accepted or rejected on its merits. And so far we have not found anything in Harman's argument to suggest that Davidson's approach can be rejected out of hand.

As we have seen on so many other occasions, a lot turns here on one's account of motivation. If one is assuming, with the Humeans, both that desires are necessary for motivation and that they are purely functional in nature, then it makes sense to view normative training as a matter of focusing people's desires on particular outcomes, and there will indeed be no good grounds to think this must involve triangulating with them on independently existing normative properties. This may be how Harman is viewing the matter, but Davidson, as we know, takes a different approach. So the question we need to take up next is whether there are any better grounds to think reasons cannot be causes. Assuming, with Davidson, that people's desires are typically sensitive to their judgments about the reasons existing for actions, are there any good grounds to think normative properties could never figure as causes in the best available explanations of those judgments?

Davidson is of course famous for defending (in 1963) the view that reasons can be causes. The view he actually defends is that motivating reasons can be causes of actions, whereas our question here is whether normative reasons can be causes of motivating reasons. But it is clear that he thinks similar arguments apply to the two cases. In particular, he thinks causal explanations are possible in both cases even though nomological explanations are not, at least not so long as we persist in describing the cases in these terms. Although Davidson introduces and defends his anomalous monism (in 1970) as a position in the philosophy of mind, he clearly intends to adopt something like it as a position within metaethics as well. So the idea would be that the event (or events) we describe as the boys' wrongly setting fire to the cat could also be described in other terms, as could the event (or events) we describe as observers concluding that there are reasons to try to stop the boys and desiring to try to stop them, and that it would be only at one of those other levels of description that we should expect to find a strictly nomological explanation of the latter in terms of the former. For Davidson, causality is a relation between events, however described, whereas explanation is dependent on description. Explanations are causal when they reveal events to be of kinds that are often causally related.

One common criticism of anomalous monism is that it makes mental properties merely epiphenomenal. If motivating reasons can cause actions only because they are describable in non-mental terms, aren't the non-mental properties of motivating reasons the ones doing all the causal work? And won't normative properties be equally suspect, if anomalous monism is true of them? On Davidson's account of events, properties and causality, however, worries of this sort are misplaced.[23] Because causality is a relation between events, however described, properties never really do any causal work. It's not because they are ultimately describable in non-mental terms that motivating reasons can cause actions; it's just that only descriptions in non-mental terms will reveal the strict regularities that causality involves. Descriptions in mental terms will reveal quite different regularities that are considerably less strict, but in part for that very reason are often of much greater use to us. Knowledge that I want to win at chess is often easy to come by and enables people to make simple predictions about my behavior that are fairly accurate. By contrast, knowledge of how my desire to win at chess is to be described in non-mental terms is almost impossible to come by, and extremely difficult to put to good use. In principle, one could use it, together with other information equally hard to come by, to predict my behavior with a remarkable degree of accuracy—but good luck with that in practice!

Crispin Wright (1996) raises a different worry about the application of anomalous monism to metaethics. He allows that there is a sense in which normative reasons can be said to exist and to play a part in causal explanations of people's motivating reasons, but then insists that more is needed to establish that normative realism is true. What worries Wright is the fact that normative properties do not seem to play a part in causal explanations of anything other than people's motivating reasons or their propositional attitudes more generally, whereas one might have supposed that real properties of situations or outcomes should also be playing an important part in causal explanations of developments that do not depend on observers at all. For example, it's not just in order to explain why observers believe the boys are setting fire to a cat that we need to assume they actually are; we also need to assume this in order to explain why the poor cat is suddenly howling as it is and why it will probably soon be dead. By contrast, it seems obvious to Wright that good explanations of this sort would never require us to assume that what the boys are doing to the cat is actually objectively wrong. And this leads him to worry that wrongness may not be a fully objective property but simply an artifact of whatever processes lead observers to react to such situations in such ways.

But if Davidson's triangulation argument is sound, there is no room for worry here, for among the processes leading observers to react to such situations in such ways are the processes fixing the contents of their normative beliefs in the first place, and if Davidson's triangulation argument is sound, these involve their triangulating on normative properties. Triangulation is a matter of focusing and coordinating our reactions to properties that are already there, not a matter of inventing or constructing ways of "reacting" to "properties" that we merely imagine.[24] It may be true that descriptive properties play a wider cosmological role than normative properties do, but it's not at all clear to me why that should make them any more real. Descriptive properties, after all, underwrite claims about what is the case; it's only to be expected that they will have an influence on what will be the case. Normative properties, by contrast, underwrite claims about what should be done; so one might expect their influence to be limited to creatures actually capable of acting on reasons. Insisting that they play a wider cosmological role is simply to beg the question against them by requiring them to be something entirely different from what they are obviously intended to be. Realists should only be required to establish that normative properties have some cosmological role to play, and even

Wright acknowledges that they will have if anything like the triangulation argument is correct.

At this point, however, we should acknowledge that there are many normative realists who think even this requirement is too strong. In their view, it is not reasonable to expect real normative properties to play a role in any causal explanations at all. That is an expectation that it is reasonable to have of merely descriptive properties, but truly normative properties, as David Enoch has put it (2011, 4), would be "just too different" to be involved in explanations of the same type. Thomas Scanlon takes a similar line, insisting (2014, lecture 2) that the normative domain is separate from the scientific domain and governed by distinct requirements. The scientific domain is concerned precisely with causal explanation, so of course its requirements for realism will be formulated in those terms. But the normative domain is concerned with justification, not explanation, so its requirements for realism will be different. To think otherwise is to succumb to what Scanlon rather precipitately describes as the "hegemony" of the scientific.

But why should we think normative properties would be so different? And why should we think reality comprises more than one domain? As we have just seen, Davidson does not require normative properties to play the same wide cosmological role that descriptive properties do. As hegemonies go, therefore, this seems pretty benign. Normative properties are hardly being identified with descriptive properties. They are simply being required to supervene on them, and to play a part in explaining normative judgments. Especially considering that these requirements were weak enough to raise doubts in Wright's mind about whether normative properties could actually be real, it would be helpful to hear more from Enoch and Scanlon about why they think they demand too much of normative properties. So far as I can tell, however, neither of them offers us a good account of this. We are simply supposed to take it as given that normative facts could not possibly have descriptive consequences.

Moreover, because they refuse to allow even that normative properties could have a role to play in explanations of normative judgments, both Enoch and Scanlon encounter serious difficulties when it comes time to explain how knowledge of normative truths could ever be possible. Scanlon tries to overcome these difficulties by building his normative epistemology on Rawls's method of wide reflective equilibrium. He vehemently denies that this requires any independent assurance that people's normative judgments are in their nature veridical, arguing instead that people's judgments about normative matters can be satisfactorily disciplined by considerations that are internal to those judgments themselves.[25] But if there really were no limits to the differences that could in principle separate different people's initial judgments about normative matters, what assurance could we have that their more considered judgments would begin to converge on shared normative truths? Scanlon admittedly does not go into much detail here, but the prospects certainly do not look very good.

Presumably Scanlon's idea is that people's initial judgments about normative matters couldn't differ very much while actually being judgments about normative matters. This would obviously be an idea very much to Davidson's liking; but in Scanlon's case, what would the argument for it be? Davidson argues for it by considering how it is that these judgments come to be about normative matters. It is because he thinks this results from triangulation that he thinks these judgments couldn't differ very much. Since Scanlon is not willing to allow that normative properties could be involved in causal explanations of how propositional contents get fixed, he would need to provide us with a different argument here, if indeed this is the line he means to take. But just as I am unclear about why Scanlon is so reluctant to follow Davidson on this point, so too am I unclear about what he thinks an alternative to Davidson's argument might actually look like.

Things are a bit clearer in Enoch's case, but so too are the challenges he confronts. Like Davidson, he attempts to provide some assurance that normative judgments are in their nature veridical. Unlike Davidson, however, he does not attempt to do this by arguing that normative properties play a role in causal explanations of the processes generating normative judgments and determining their contents. His claim (2011, 168 ff.) is rather that these processes are themselves good, and that because they are good they are likely to result in normative judgments that are true. He appeals to normative properties only in the assessment of these processes, not in their explanation, in keeping with his view that they could not possibly be causal. As he recognizes, this leaves one question unanswered: How trustworthy are our assessments of these processes? Why, exactly, should we think the processes generating normative judgments and determining their contents are good? Enoch answers this by noting that these processes must presumably have contributed to human reproductive success, and suggests that, in view of this fact, they can safely be said to be good. And I think we must grant him that this claim is difficult to deny, and consequently that the reliability of our other normative judgments could conceivably be established if they could be linked to this judgment in the right sort of way.[26] But I also find it difficult to see how this link could be secured.

If nothing but human reproductive success was good, one could see how Enoch's argument might work. But suppose we have reasons to do things that are actually detrimental to human reproductive success. In that case, processes leading us to form false beliefs to the effect that we don't have such reasons could be the ones likely to contribute the most to human reproductive success. Anticipating worries of this sort, Enoch suggests (2011, 170) that, even then, such processes would still generate enough true beliefs to make the method of reflective equilibrium viable as an epistemology. But surely that would depend on the extent of the differences separating actions promoting human reproductive success and the other sorts of things we have reason to do. Enoch assumes these differences will be small enough to give his argument some chance of working, but so far as I can see, the basis for this optimism is never made clear. Especially considering how adamant he is in maintaining that normative properties need to be metaphysically robust, it seems odd for him to be denying that they might be substantively robust as well. Once again, therefore, as with Scanlon, I find it extremely difficult to see how our epistemology can avoid giving normative properties roles in explanations that are causal—and even more difficult to see why this is something it should be avoiding, since I don't find anything puzzling in the thought that such explanations are possible.

Of course, this is because I think anomalous monism is a perfectly plausible view—and I have obviously not addressed every worry critics have had on that score. However, I do hope to have said enough to indicate that normative realism is not the completely unintelligible or hopelessly implausible view that many claim it is. I agree that it would be hopelessly implausible if Korsgaard were right about the practicality requirement, or if Mackie were right about primary qualities, or if Harman were right about normative training. But I think Davidson gives us powerful arguments with which to repel each of these assaults. As I have repeatedly insisted, his accounts of motivation and (especially) desire are particularly important here. Even when critics target some other consideration, they often prove to be relying on the tacit assumption that motivation requires desire and that desires are purely functional states. And once we reject that assumption, allowing that motivation indeed requires desire but holding that desires are typically conditioned by normative beliefs, their worries become much less troubling. Perhaps this explains why Davidson gives such very short shrift to most critics of normative realism. Because he does not accept the Humean assumptions about desire lurking behind many of their worries, he cannot be bothered to address them even in the cursory manner I have done here. Indeed, he sometimes talks as if there are no worries here to be addressed!

Such remarks are undoubtedly exaggerations, indeed provocations, but they point to an important truth. Once it is acknowledged that normative beliefs are never actually sufficient to motivate actions, even though they typically influence people's actions by influencing the contents of their desires, it becomes difficult to deny that normative realism is at least a possible view. For now it becomes clear that normative properties could be intrinsically authoritative without being intrinsically rational, without being intrinsically motivating, and without settling for the status of something other than primary qualities. So the only question is whether there is any explanatory role for such properties to play, and of course that is precisely the question Davidson hopes to answer with his triangulation argument. I trust enough has already been said to demonstrate how promising this answer is. But one might still wonder how well it squares with other things we believe. In particular, one might wonder how normative properties could be primary qualities and still exhibit the sort of agent-relativity most people believe reasons for action to exhibit. And then, depending on the details of the answer to this question, one might also wonder how well normative realism squares with our beliefs about the content or the authority of morality. These are large questions about which Davidson himself has little to say; but we need some reassurance on these points if we are going to take his normative realism at all seriously.

Notes

1. So I use the term 'practicality requirement' where Korsgaard uses 'internalism requirement', and I use the term 'internalism requirement' where Smith uses 'practicality requirement'! But the rational import of normative beliefs obviously is an internal matter, whereas the practical import of normative truths may possibly not be.
2. By this I mean simply that assessments of the rationality of people's actions are always made relative to their beliefs and other propositional attitudes.
3. Hence his memorable claim (1970, 222) that we must endeavor to interpret each person as being a "believer of truths and a lover of the good".
4. I should acknowledge that I am painting with a broad brush here. See Davidson 1985 and Kolodny 2005 for more discussion of these issues.
5. Korsgaard 2008 provides a useful overview. I will have more to say about exactly how she intends this argument to work in Chapter 8.
6. As Smith insists (1994, Chapter 5), this could conceivably still yield conclusions that are non-relative. But it seems more likely to yield a Humean version of constructivism.
7. Given that he thinks people's desires must be by and large correct, Davidson could be expected to have considerable sympathy for suggestions like this. Given his views about the dependence of desires on normative beliefs, however, his account of rationality would be better couched in those terms.
8. To be fair, Korsgaard also declines to draw this conclusion, insisting instead (2008, 28) that empirical *concepts* may be constructed but that empirical *contents* are not. But even if we could make sense of this dualism, it still concedes more ground to empirical anti-realism than most constructivists would like to.
9. This is how "internal reasons" were characterized in Bernard Williams's seminal article (1980). There was certainly no suggestion that empirical truths might also be "internal".
10. As I put the point in Myers 2012, how could reasons for action exist if people were not even capable of acting for reasons?
11. See, for example, Williams 1980, 104, where he makes the point that simple means/ends deliberation is not an instance of truly practical reasoning.
12. The importance of uncovering non-relative truths is very much on his radar, but again he regards that as something purely internal reasoning could accomplish.
13. This does not rule out the possibility that normative truth is a matter of internal coherence, but it certainly does not require it either.
14. As I shall explain below, in Chapter 8, I think Korsgaard's stronger arguments against normative realism concern the normative authority of specifically *moral* reasons. If Kantian constructivism makes better sense of our convictions about morality's authority, that will indeed give it a significant leg up over Davidson's realism.
15. As we shall we in due course, this would strictly speaking be true only if the reason in question was agent-neutral in character. But that is certainly what most realists would say about this case; so for now that is the assumption I will be proceeding on.

16. For Mackie's views about secondary qualities, see his 1976b, especially Chapter 1.
17. For discussion of this point, see again his 1976b, especially Chapter 2.
18. This assumes that, in order to be a property of a situation, a reason for action must involve a causal power of some sort. As we shall see, Davidson is indeed prepared to assume this; but various other normative realists do not follow him on this point.
19. The point here is again just that many reasons for action are agent-relative in character.
20. To be sure, some realists insist that basic reasons for action are always agent-neutral in character and so embrace a form of consequentialism. But those realists who allow that agent-relative reasons exist alongside agent-neutral ones commonly do abandon consequentialism for either contractarianism or contractualism.
21. I assume that this is what he means to be getting at when he says (1985, 143) that normative properties cannot be specified independently of responses. They cannot be specified independently of the training in responses that is needed in order for one to appreciate them for what they are.
22. So they are causes, but not of the outlandish sort that Mackie is concerned to criticize.
23. Davidson's account of properties and their role in explanation is obviously controversial. Although I will not take time to try to defend it here, I want to stress that I do believe it is largely sound. Stoutland 2011 provides an overview that I find more helpful than most.
24. We of course invent words with which to refer to these properties, and different people sometimes end up reacting to them in different ways, but that sort of merely lexical or semantic relativism is perfectly innocuous, and perfectly compatible with the sort of normative realism Davidson is espousing.
25. See Scanlon 2014, especially Chapter 4. As I go on to say, I cannot see what the argument for this claim is supposed to be. As Scanlon's own talk of "reasons fundamentalism" might be thought to suggest, the appeal here seems to be more to faith than to argument.
26. I am in fact not fully persuaded that Enoch's argument establishes the presumptive truth of our normative beliefs and not just their presumptive value, notwithstanding his claims on pages 169 ff., but I am willing to grant that it might for the purposes of our discussion here.

8 Normative Realism and Morality

Even if normative realism is a perfectly coherent and otherwise plausible view, it can seem very hard to square with other things we believe. Perhaps most obviously, it can seem hard to square with the belief that people's ultimate reasons for action are partly agent-relative in character. However, as constructivists have argued, it can also seem hard to square with common beliefs about the content and the authority of morality. And many of the constructivists' worries about morality can seem to retain their force even after the worries about agent-relativity have been addressed.

Although Davidson always expressed considerable interest in ethics and often taught it early in his career, he said very little about it in print. So we can only speculate about what he could and should have said in response to worries of the sort the constructivists have raised. My suggestion in this final chapter will be that he should have defended a version of contractualism not unlike the version Thomas Scanlon advocates, though one which at several points leans much more heavily on the underlying realism about normative properties than Scanlon himself seems prepared to do.

1. Agent-Relativity

The worries about agent-relativity I have in mind here are different from the worries about relativity John Mackie raises (1976a, 36–8). Mackie is mainly concerned about the extent and the nature of the disagreements that we find among people's normative beliefs. It seems to him that these disagreements are too frequent and too persistent to be plausibly explained in realist terms. In response, however, realists can argue that normative disagreements are actually not as frequent and persistent as Mackie suggests, and that, inasmuch as they are, this fact is not nearly as difficult to explain as he contends. After all, when there are multiple factors to be considered, it is easy to lose sight of some of them; and when they bear on one another in complex ways, it is easy to go wrong when weighing them together. There are often also powerful psychological and social forces making it difficult to get a clear view of normative matters. Normative mistakes tend to become deeply entrenched, and normative progress is not always welcomed by those in positions of power. Of course, if it had turned out that normative properties could never figure in good explanations of people's normative judgments, then they would also be unhelpful in explaining normative disagreement. But once we have put such general worries behind us, it is difficult to see why the actual facts about normative disagreement should cause any special problems for normative realists.

In any event, the worries about agent-relativity I have in mind to discuss here are not worries about disagreement. On the contrary, I assume most people would agree that ultimate reasons for action are partly agent-relative in character. Most would agree, for example, that while everyone may have some reason to promote the well-being of everyone else, each person has additional reasons to promote her own well-being and the well-being of her relatives and friends. Most would agree that similarly special reasons also exist to promote the well-being of one's own colleagues and neighbors, and indeed that further agent-relative reasons exist having to do with matters other than the promotion of well-being.[1] The worry about agent-relativity is that realists might not be able to acknowledge that any such reasons are ultimate. If reasons for action are properties of situations or outcomes, must they not be at bottom the same for everyone? No doubt each person's derived or proximate reasons for action will be relative to facts about her circumstances and capabilities, since facts of those sorts will determine what she can do to meet any goal that is set for her. But there is ultimately only one world that people inhabit, so if its properties determine what their goals should be, it might be thought that their ultimate or distal reasons for action must always be in every respect the same.[2]

Now of course realists might try to bite this bullet, arguing that if most people possess beliefs to the contrary, that is not because those beliefs are in fact true, but is rather because possessing those beliefs can be useful. And as we know from consequentialist discussions of such matters, there are many arguments they could offer in this vein. For example, it might be argued that most people will prove to be more effective promoters of agent-neutral value if they can sometimes be brought to believe that their ultimate reasons for action are actually agent-relative in character, in which case it should not be surprising that so many people are in the thrall of such mistaken beliefs.[3] Or again, it might be argued that the agent-neutral value to be realized in relationships often depends even more directly on the fact that the parties involved believe themselves ultimately to have some special importance for one another, in which case we should once again not conclude that widespread agreement in such beliefs is indicative of their truth.[4] But of course, as we also know from consequentialist discussions, none of these arguments are terribly convincing in the end. Even if we overlook the "just so" element in these stories about how agent-neutral value is most effectively promoted, it is very hard to accept that our beliefs about agent-relative reasons are to be explained away like this.

Given that "unmasking" explanations of these sorts are so unconvincing, I think realists are better advised to search for ways to embrace the claim that people's ultimate or distal reasons for action in fact are partly agent-relative in character. And I think it is also at least reasonably clear that this is the line Davidson meant to take himself. He admittedly does say at one point (1995b, 47) that normative properties "are not defined or understood in terms of a relation." But I take him to be referring there only to agent-neutral reasons and precisely not to agent-relative ones. And among the examples he gives of reasons for action, many are certainly most naturally read as being agent-relative. For instance, in saying (1969, 33) that pleasure is to be pursued, or (1995b, 41) that the lives of children are to be saved, he obviously means that each person has special reasons to promote her own happiness and to protect her own children, over and above whatever reasons there may be for people to promote happiness or to protect children quite generally. So the question for us is how Davidson can embrace such claims regarding the agent-relativity of reasons for action. How can he hold that reasons for action are to be understood as properties of the world we all share, without maintaining that they are ultimately all agent-neutral in character and that agent-relative reasons can only be derived?

It might be suggested that Davidson's only hope of answering this question is to find a credible way of modeling the distinction between agent-neutral and agent-relative reasons on the more familiar distinction between primary and secondary qualities.[5] That would give him a way of allowing that agent-neutral reasons are more basic than agent-relative ones, in the sense that they are involved in the explanation of why people's agent-relative reasons are as they are, whereas people's agent-relative reasons are not involved in explanations of why things have the agent-neutral importance they do, while still maintaining that people's agent-relative reasons are ultimate properties of the world they inhabit and not mere derivations. It might then be argued, however, that this strategy has no serious chance of succeeding because special sensibilities are not required for the appreciation of agent-relative reasons in the way they are for the experience of secondary qualities. And it does seem difficult to deny that agent-relative reasons differ from secondary qualities in this absolutely fundamental way. Whereas the color of an object can be experienced as such only by people who share the requisite sensibility, the special importance that a child has for her parents is a property of the situation that everybody can appreciate.[6] But if agent-relative reasons do not resemble secondary qualities, perhaps they must be understood as mere derivations after all.

I think there is something that this argument gets right, but also—and more importantly—something that it gets wrong. What it gets right, I think, is the fact that normative realists must regard agent-relative reasons as needing explanation. Could it really be a basic fact about the world that people have special reasons to protect their own children? Surely not. It might well be a basic fact about the world that children in general are to be protected. After all, explanations must come to an end somewhere, so some reasons for action will have to be basic. But surely any special reasons for particular people to protect particular children will stand in need of some further explanation.[7] However, while that much seems exactly right to me, I think these further explanations could take radically different forms. Why must we assume that explanations of agent-relative reasons would be anything even remotely like explanations of secondary qualities? Surely what happens is that agent-relative reasons simply grow out of agent-neutral ones as special relationships are forged. There are agent-neutral reasons to protect children in general, and because protecting any child has this agent-neutral importance, special agent-relative reasons can emerge for parents to protect their own children as they develop special relationships with them. The fact that these agent-relative reasons will not be explanatorily basic does not mean that they are merely derived.[8]

To be sure, this requires that normative properties supervene not merely on intrinsic properties of the relevant situations or outcomes but also on the relation of those situations or outcomes to the agent whose reasons for action are at issue. But I see no reason why this should be thought to pose a problem for realist accounts of agent-relativity.[9] In fact, it seems plausible to suppose that all reasons for action have a place for this sort of relativity—given the prevailing conditions, C, a fact, F, gives a person, P, a reason, R, to perform some action, A, in view of P's history with the components of F.[10] But of course sometimes there is no history to consider. In consequence, we all share the same default reasons to protect children with whom we do not have special ties, but we each possess our own additional reasons to protect those particular children with whom we have developed special relationships. These special relationships will typically involve our coming to believe that these particular children have a special importance for us. However, whereas the consequentialists were obliged to regard the acquisition of such beliefs as a common—because useful—mistake, the suggestion now is that they are in fact more often than not both accurate reflections of priorities that have so far emerged and important elements in the developing history that might make those priorities even greater down the road.

Of course, if this is correct, the special reasons some parents have to protect their own children may be minimal, since they may only have developed minimal relationships with them. Other parents may have developed relationships that are unusually strong, in which case their special reasons to protect their own children could turn out to be unusually strong as well. But this seems right to me, for I think agent-relative reasons do vary in just these sorts of ways. All parents have special reasons to protect their own children, but the reasons they have are not all the same. Analogous claims can be made about agent-relative reasons to promote the well-being of relatives, and friends, and neighbors. But what of the special reasons people have to pursue their own pleasures or to promote their own well-being? Are they also to be explained in this realist fashion, as resulting from special relationships people forge with themselves? At first sight, that admittedly may sound a bit contrived, but I think it again holds up well under scrutiny.

People who grow up in more communal settings arguably do have less reason than others to favor their own interests; those heavily invested in their individual projects arguably have more. The claim made above seems to hold here as well: All people have special reasons to promote their own interests, but the reasons they have are not all the same.

Obviously there are other issues that could be raised about how agent-relative reasons develop out of agent-neutral ones. A book on Davidson is hardly the place for that, however, given his silence on substantive questions about reasons. Let us therefore turn our attention to a different sort of worry about realist accounts of agent-relative reasons. The worry this time is not that realists have no way of acknowledging the existence of ultimate agent-relative reasons. It is rather that their way of acknowledging them wreaks havoc with some of our most important beliefs about morality, for it allows them to grow out of agent-neutral reasons without subjecting either sort of reason to any restrictions. It would seem that, for realists, restrictions on what people are permitted to do must be introduced in other ways—for example, by demonstrating that they provide mutually agreeable constraints on how people may act on the reasons they have. Because their agent-relative reasons often put people at loggerheads, everybody stands to gain if suitable constraints are widely respected. The worry, however, is that by construing morality's restrictions as constraints on how people may act on their reasons, we open the door to various intractable questions about the content of those restrictions and people's reasons for respecting them. Thus the suggestion is that the realists' account of reasons must be wrong because it does not get morality right.

This is, to my mind, a more daunting challenge to realism than any of the metaphysical worries we have discussed. I associate it with Kantian constructivists, even though, as we saw in Chapter 7, they typically highlight a different objection—that realism is a non-starter because it cannot explain how a consideration could count in favor of an action.[11] That objection, as I argued, is one realists can overcome by insisting on the primacy and irreducibility of truth. There is nothing in the idea of a reason for action requiring it to be the result of rational deliberation. But there could be something to the suggestion that only constructivism can account for the content and authority of morality. Kantian constructivists, in particular, seem well placed to argue that moral restrictions are not external constraints on reasons for action, but reasons for action in their own right that emerge along with the reasons we have been discussing so far whenever people set about constructing their reasons for action out of the bare ideas of rational and autonomous activity.[12] By contrast, advocates of contractarian approaches, even those who acknowledge that reasons for action are frequently other-regarding in character, may seem to dig themselves an inescapably deep hole by refusing to include moral restrictions among people's ultimate reasons and insisting instead that they be justified as mutually agreeable to people in light of whatever reasons are ultimate.

Although Davidson's own approach to these issues is hardly obvious, he does make his antipathy towards Kantian approaches abundantly clear. He simply assumes (1995b, 41) that principles generating reasons for action will yield only what he refers to as prima facie reasons—though he would have done better to call them pro tanto reasons, since his point is more metaphysical than epistemological. In any event, whatever the words, his claim is that principles generating reasons for action are always subject to exceptions, in the sense that they could always conceivably be overridden by other principles that in the circumstances generate stronger reasons. He rejects out of hand the idea that there might be a single master principle governing interactions among all others. Because he is not as careful as he should be to distinguish traditional Kantian approaches from Kantian versions of constructivism, what he presumably has in mind here is the idea of a principle from which all others could be deduced, and not the allegedly much less troubling idea of a procedure in light of which all principles could be constructed. But it cannot seriously be supposed that Davidson would have looked on the constructivists' idea with any greater favor. However, before we speculate any further about what exactly his objections to constructivist accounts of morality might have been, let us first take some time to consider what approach to morality he might himself have been tempted to embrace.

As I mentioned in the closing paragraphs of Chapter 5, I think Davidson would have been well advised to abandon contractarian approaches to morality in favor of something like the sort of contractualism Thomas Scanlon has long been advocating. I say this, in part, simply because I think Scanlon's contractualism (see especially his 1998) provides the best account of morality currently on offer, and, as we shall see, it is certainly compatible with Davidson's more robust sort of realism about reasons for action. But the more important point I want to make is that Davidson's realism can be of great help to contractualists, both in combatting worries about their account of morality's content and in combatting worries about their account of morality's authority. These are large topics to be taking up for the first time as we approach the end of the book, but I think enough can still be said to indicate that beliefs about the content and the authority of morality, far from posing insuperable obstacles to Davidson's account of reasons, could actually prove to be strong points in its favor. The fact that Scanlon's account of morality is so widely known should also help us get quickly to the point. Before turning to Scanlon, however, let us briefly review some of the long-standing worries about contractarian accounts of morality. We need to be clear about what Scanlon is trying to avoid in order to see where Davidson might help.

2. The Promise of Contractualism

Contractarian theories can take several forms, but what they share is the claim that people have only instrumental reasons to make and keep agreements. At one extreme, radically Hobbesian theories hold that what people have reason to do depends on how they can most effectively satisfy their desires, and that people have reason to make and keep agreements only insofar as that will lead over time to greater satisfaction of their desires. Any agreement will have its costs, since its existence will make it harder for one to satisfy certain of the desires that one has, but of course the familiar hope is that those costs will be more than offset by the fact that others will be similarly constrained. The equally familiar fear, however, is that the constraints Hobbesian people have reason to agree on may lack features we associate with morality. For one thing, it looks like they may not include any significant requirement to promote the well-being of people who are too poor, since wealthier people who happen not to care about their fellows may have little or nothing to gain from agreements that incorporate such demands.[13] And, however this is resolved, it looks like people may often have little reason to comply with whatever agreement they finally do make, since it may often not be necessary for them to do so in order to continue to reap the benefits of other people's compliance.

In response, it might be argued that this overestimates the importance of beneficence within the correct moral theory, while at the same time underestimating the reasons that even wealthy people have to insurance themselves against the possibility of a fall. Likewise, it might be argued that it overestimates the importance of people's reasons to respect morality's verdicts, while at the same time underestimating the chances that free riders will be caught out and the penalties that they could suffer.[14] Another option for contractarians, however, is to jettison the Hobbesian assumption that people's desires determine their reasons, in favor of the realists' claim that reasons for action are properties of situations or outcomes to which people's desires are answerable. Since that would be Davidson's recommendation, there is no need for us to dwell further on the Hobbesians. Let us therefore turn our attention immediately to the question of what an injection of normative realism can do for contractarianism.

Pretty clearly, it can help a lot to address worries about the importance of beneficence within moral theory, since the governing assumption will now be that people's ultimate reasons for action are both agent-neutral and agent-relative in character.[15] So whereas Hobbesians needed to justify beneficence as a constraint on people's endeavors to satisfy their own desires, it will now be more accurate to say that beneficent actions are among the ones moral restrictions are precisely intended to constrain. After all, it will not only be people's agent-relative reasons that are often putting them at loggerheads; people will often be at loggerheads because some are responding to agent-neutral reasons while others are responding to agent-relative ones. So if the aim is to agree on principles that will enable one to better address one's reasons, people will have reason to favor principles that constrain action on agent-neutral reasons as much as action on agent-relative ones.

But could different people seriously be expected to agree on the scope and the strength of these restrictions? This is far from being clear, given the obvious fact that different restrictions would threaten to impact different people in different ways. For example, the wealthy might have reason to fear that everyone's agent-neutral reasons would speak in favor of taxation and redistribution policies that would make it considerably more difficult for them to act on their own agent-relative reasons. The poor, by contrast, might have reason to hope that they would end up benefitting from such policies, and so might be reluctant to accept the broader and stronger restrictions on such policies that the wealthy would no doubt seek. So while the existence of agent-neutral reasons does help explain the importance of beneficence within moral theory, it still leaves us with some very difficult questions about how the content of moral restrictions can be both universal and determinate.

Nor is it obvious how the existence of agent-neutral reasons would help with worries about morality's authority. So long as we are working with the contractarians' defining assumption that people's reasons to make and keep agreements are merely instrumental, it looks like people may often have little reason to comply with whatever agreement they finally do make, since it may often not be necessary for them to do so in order to reap the benefits of other people's compliance. If anything, the existence of agent-neutral reasons threatens to make this worry worse than it was before, since the existence of such reasons will give people another range of incentives to sometimes ignore whatever restrictions have been agreed upon. But of course the adoption of normative realism also introduces the possibility of objective yet agent-relative reasons, which now makes it possible to argue that people's reasons to make and keep agreements are perhaps not merely instrumental after all.

This is the possibility contractualists seize upon. Central to their approach is the claim that every person has reasons to make and keep agreements that are not merely instrumental. Different accounts of these reasons are possible, but the hope shared by all contractualists is that the nature of these reasons will help answer our questions about morality. As they see things, therefore, we should be looking to the content of these reasons for answers to our questions about how the content of morality's restrictions are to be determined, and we should be looking to the importance of these reasons for answers to our questions about how morality's restrictions can be guaranteed to have whatever authority they are guaranteed to have. For example, in Thomas Scanlon's influential formulation, the idea is that every person has ultimate agent-relative reasons to interact with other people on terms of mutual respect, which is in his view to say, in accord with principles that no one who was seeking to interact with other people on such terms could reasonably reject.[16] For Scanlon, therefore, we determine the content of morality by considering what principles people have reason to agree to given that their interest in agreement takes this particular agent-relative form, and we determine the authority of morality by considering how important these reasons to live together on terms of mutual respect are in comparison to the other reasons for action people have.

It has to be said, however, that Scanlon does not take full advantage of the possibilities afforded to him by the fact that he embraces normative realism; for he declines to embrace agent-neutrality, continuing to agree with the Hobbesians about the ultimate agent-relativity of reasons for action even as he insists upon their reality. As a result, he does not fare much better than the Hobbesians with worries about beneficence, since it is far from clear why interacting with other people on terms of mutual respect would necessarily call for one to take part in efforts to promote their well-being even when one stands in no special relation to them and they are under no immediate threat. Unlike, for example, a principle of rescue, which might call for people to come to the assistance of anyone in their immediate vicinity who is under immediate threat, principles of beneficence, with their broader scope, would seem to be at odds with the underlying assumption that ultimate reasons for action are exclusively agent-relative in character.[17] To be sure, the idea of respecting others could in theory be understood in such a manner that it required one to promote everyone's well-being in a perfectly agent-neutral fashion. But that is not how Scanlon understands it, and surely people would not have strong agent-relative reasons to act as if reasons were agent-neutral if in fact they were not.

Nor is this the end of it. By failing to embrace agent-neutral reasons, Scanlon also puts himself at a disadvantage when responding to worries about morality's authority. If agent-neutral reasons do not exist, then agent-relative reasons must be basic, and there cannot be much to say about why some are stronger than others. Again, explanations have to end somewhere, so Scanlon can claim that they end here in the fact that agent-relative reasons to interact on terms of mutual respect are just very strong.[18] But are they always equally strong? Is it not again going to be much more plausible to suppose that these reasons will be stronger for some people than they are for others? By allowing that agent-neutral reasons exist, Davidsonian contractualists make their task easier here, for they can explain why people always have some special reasons to act morally, and why these reasons are stronger for some people than they are for others, by holding that these agent-relative reasons grow out of underlying agent-neutral ones. Their basic claim, in other words, will be that everyone has agent-neutral reasons to try to increase the extent to which people interact with one another on terms of mutual respect, since that is a good thing, and that corresponding agent-relative reasons emerge in differing degrees for different people depending on how important the enjoyment of that good becomes to their lives.

In these two critical ways, therefore, contractualists would do well to follow Davidson in holding that ultimate reasons for action are both agent-neutral and agent-relative. It might still be objected, however, that the existence of agent-neutral reasons does nothing to address what is surely a much more troubling worry about contractualism—namely, that contractualists end up begging the question by building into their understanding of 'reasonable rejection' or 'mutual respect' the very conclusions regarding morality's content that they are meant to be establishing. Suppose, again, that we are trying to determine whether morality includes only the minimal restrictions on redistributive taxation that might favor the poor or the substantial restrictions that might favor the wealthy. Even allowing that everyone has reason to live together on terms of mutual respect, is it clear that one of these answers would be preferable to the other? That would seem to depend on how the notion of mutual respect is understood, but the worry is that very different understandings might prove to be equally defensible. Trivially, we might all agree that mutual respect requires each of us to accept some restrictions on actions that interfere with other people's freedom to act on their own agent-relative reasons. But, again, given that different restrictions would inevitably end up impacting different people to different degrees, this may not move us much closer to a universal and determinate account of morality's content.

But the fact that different understandings of mutual respect are possible is not really to the point if normative realism is correct. What matters is rather the substantive issue of how people actually have reason to interact with one another, given that they have both agent-neutral and agent-relative reasons and that these reasons put them at loggerheads in various ways. Contractualists are not seeking to construct the truth about morality out of the bare concept of mutual respect. They are claiming to find strong second-order reasons for people to deal with these first-order conflicts in a particular fashion. Talk of mutual respect is just one way of describing the salient features of this form of interaction. Thus more detailed questions about morality's content are not to be answered by staring more intently at the concept of mutual respect. They are to be answered by looking more closely at the particular form of interaction contractualists are touting.

Talk of mutual respect may in fact not be the best way to describe the particular form of interaction contractualists are touting, at least not once contractualists are understood as acknowledging that both agent-neutral and agent-relative reasons exist. While it nicely highlights the importance of giving one another adequate room to maneuver in pursuit of our differing agent-relative reasons, it arguably does not put enough emphasis on the fact that many of our reasons are agent-neutral. Elsewhere (Myers 1999b, Chapter 2), I have suggested that we talk instead of our reasons to cooperate with one another in the promotion of the good, the thought being that this involves addressing shared agent-neutral reasons together while still respecting agent-relative differences. People who are cooperating in the pursuit of some end do not expect one another to give themselves over entirely to it; they recognize that they each have various other ends and look for fair ways to accommodate that fact.

No matter how we describe it, however, the contractualists' claim is that our first-order reasons put us at loggerheads, and that this fact in turn generates important second-order reasons for us to interact in particular ways. We are to avoid interfering with one another in various respects, and to make good on various kinds of commitments and expectations, so that each of us has some stable space within which to address our own agent-relative reasons. We have discovered over time that it is a good thing for people to interact with one another on terms of this sort, and hence that we have strong agent-neutral reasons to promote such interaction among people whenever we can; but it also tends to become very important for us as individuals that we interact with others on terms of this sort, leading us each to develop special agent-relative reasons always to interact with others on such terms ourselves.

It might be objected that this account of contractualism leaves very little work for the notion of reasonable agreement to do, and consequently puts much more distance between contractualism and contractarianism than contractualists like Scanlon intend there to be. How much work can the talk of reasonable rejection be doing if the reasonableness of someone's rejection of a putative moral principle depends on independent truths about the terms on which people have most reason to interact with one another? In fact, it might be suggested that the account of contractualism being recommended here looks more like a version of virtue ethics, a version according to which the principal moral virtues are the virtues of respecting others and being cooperative—the idea being that people well trained in these virtues will be well placed to discern what morality requires in particular cases, and that there is no need for the appeals to reasonable agreement so central to the contractarian tradition.

The first point to make in response to these objectors is that contractualist accounts of morality have always owed as much or more to virtue theories as they do to contractarian theories. After all, the claim, as Scanlon puts it (1998, Chapter 5), is that moral principles are ones that no one could reasonably reject who was seeking to interact with others on terms of mutual respect. Parties to reasonable bargaining over morality's content are assumed all to share the aim of identifying principles that could serve as the basis of such mutually respectful interactions because they would exhibit appropriate concern for the fact that people's first-order reasons for action very often put them at odds with one another in important ways. This reason for the parties to seek agreement does not itself result from any bargaining; it imposes limits on the sorts of agreements that parties to any bargaining would deem reasonable. Thus Scanlon is not denying that morality's content is partially fixed by considerations that limit bargaining; nor would he deny that virtue is necessary to discern what these limits on bargaining are. But—and this is the second point to make in response to these objectors—neither would he suppose that these limits on bargaining suffice to make it otiose. There is a lot of work for the notion of reasonable rejection to do even if the limits on reasonable agreement are themselves grounded in other considerations.

The simple reason for this is that the sort of mutually respectful interaction we have reason to engage in often requires us to settle our differences by bargaining or taking a vote. It will of course require that this bargaining or voting be conducted in mutually respectful ways, but it will not determine in advance what the results of these procedures must actually be. Thus the contractarians are right to insist that morality is, at least in part, a kind of construction, and that moral truths are often shaped by political realities. The worry is simply that they take this too far, letting political realities fill in all the content, and leaving moral truth with almost no work to do. Contractualists avoid this worry by insisting that there are limits not only on the contours of what can reasonably be agreed but also on the how the details can reasonably be filled in. But they certainly do not suppose that the virtuous person who appreciates what these limits are thereby knows everything there is to know about what morality requires of her in the circumstances. The principles that she could not reasonably reject will include many that have been agreed upon by her fellows via procedures to which she could not reasonably object. She would therefore need to know what these agreements actually are in order to know the full story about what morality calls for in any given case.

As I have acknowledged from the outset, it is impossible to be certain that Davidson would have endorsed precisely this combination of normative realism, contractualism and virtue theory. Given the esteem he felt for Aristotle, I suspect he would have looked favorably on the manner in which it makes essentially political virtues so central to morality. But that's just speculation. The more important point for our purposes is simply that Davidson certainly could have developed an account of morality along these lines in defense of his normative realism. Had he done so, I think he could have put to rest many of the worries people have about the implications of normative realism for the content and the authority of morality. In fact, once we take on board the idea that second-order reasons exist for everyone to manage their differences by interacting with each other in particular ways, worries about the content and the authority of morality can be treated less as negative pronouncements on the theory and more as positive guides to its further development. If the theory seems not to be getting morality's content quite right, that suggests that we have not gotten totally clear about the particular ways in which people have reason to interact; if the theory seems not to be guaranteeing morality's verdicts enough authority, that suggests that we have not fully appreciated how important are the reasons people have to interact in those ways.

This train of thought does, however, have one very clear and important limitation: It cannot plausibly deliver the result that morality's verdicts are always and necessarily overriding. After all, for a realist like Davidson, people's reasons to interact with one another in mutually respectful or properly cooperative ways are just some reasons among many others. They may have an importance that is inescapable, and that is very often sufficient to ensure that people have more reason to comply with morality's verdicts than not to comply with them. But of course many philosophers want much more; they want it always and necessarily to be the case that any action required by morality is one people have most reason to perform. Kantian constructivists have been particularly adamant on this score, treating it in many cases as a kind of desideratum that any acceptable account of normative truths must meet. Before closing the book on this debate, therefore, we should return to Davidson's misgivings about Kantianism and consider how he might have responded to the constructivists' arguments. Given that one of today's most influential constructivists, Christine Korsgaard, makes an appeal to the public and social character of language central to her argument for the overriding authority of morality's verdicts, this promises also to bring our speculations back around to their roots in Davidson's triangulation argument and to provide us an opportunity to take final stock of his case for normative realism.

3. Final Thoughts about Constructivism

As I mentioned earlier, Davidson thinks it is obvious that there is no single normative principle from which all normative truths can be derived. So he clearly would have denied that morality's verdicts are guaranteed always to be overriding because they are inevitably favored by some such principle. Kantian constructivists, however, are not proposing that the Categorical Imperative is the fundamental normative principle from which all normative truths can be derived. Their claim is that normative truths are not derived but rather constructed, and that the Categorical Imperative highlights important facets of the constructive procedure—facets that have the effect of ensuring that the reasons for action emerging from the constructive procedure will always be recognizably moral in character. The idea, therefore, is not that moral reasons are one kind of reason that turns out always to be victorious over other kinds, but rather that all reasons for action are conditioned by morality because they are constructed via a procedure that is structured by moral imperatives. In particular, Kantian constructivists hold that reasons for action must be constructed with a view to ensuring that dignity is accorded to all agents, and that all agents could accept the constructions as normative for them regardless of what their place within the unfolding situation happened to be. Thus Kant's Formulas of Humanity and Universal Law are recast, not as substantive principles, but as morally salient facets of the basic constructive procedure.

Why should we grant the Kantians that the constructive procedure must be structured by these two moral imperatives? Humean constructivists of course deny that we should, insisting instead that the only imperatives of construction are the imperatives of individual coherence. Reasons must be constructed by reasoning from one's desires and values to conclusions about what one should do, so they may end up not being recognizably moral if one's initial set of desires and values point in a different direction.[19] In response, however, Korsgaard objects that such reasoning is not guaranteed to yield actual reasons for action. It will undoubtedly yield considerations that seem to count in favor of action because they fit well with one's desires and values. But for considerations really to count in favor of action, Korsgaard thinks they must meet the Kantian imperatives. One must be according dignity to all agents and drawing conclusions that all agents could accept as normative for their own actions.

Korsgaard's worry about Humean constructivism is not that one's initial set of desires and values could be mistaken, and hence that the constructive procedure might end up yielding the wrong results because it might set off on the wrong foot. Such worries assume that there are independent normative truths, which is precisely the view Korsgaard wants to deny. What worries Korsgaard about Humean constructivism is rather the procedure with which it would have people construct the truth about their reasons. Given what she thinks reasons for action must be, she thinks they cannot be constructed as the Humeans say. The challenge for us, therefore, is to understand what it is about reasons for action that she thinks secures this result, and then of course to decide whether she is right in concluding that it vindicates her Kantian alternative. There are two lines of argument that we need to consider, though in the end they probably come to the same thing.

The first line of argument runs something like this (Korsgaard 1996, 100–25): Reasons for action must count in favor of action, so in trying to decide what one has reason to do, one is not trying to decide what should happen to one; one is trying to decide what one should *do*, what form of behavior one should actively engage in, and that requires one to think of oneself not simply as a means to others' ends but as an end-in-oneself. But then consistency would seem to require that one also think of other people as ends-in-themselves, and thus that one construct one's reasons for action in a manner that accords dignity, in this Kantian sense, to all agents. Hence reasoning to decisions that merely cohere with one's initial set of desires and values is not enough. If one's conclusions are really to count in favor of actions, they must always be in line with Kant's Formula of Humanity.

The second line of argument turns on the fact that actions typically, if not always, unfold over time (Korsgaard 2009, 73–80). So in trying to decide what one has reason to do, one typically is not constructing reasons just for one's present self; one is also constructing reasons for one's future selves, the selves who must complete whatever action one starts, and this requires one's decisions about one's reasons for action to be such that one's future selves could also find them normative. Since one's future selves could have desires and values other than the desires and values one currently has, this effectively requires one's decisions about one's current reasons for action to be such that all possible agents could find them normative. Again, reasoning to decisions that merely cohere with one's initial set of desires and values is not enough. If one's conclusions are really to count in favor of actions, they must always pass muster with Kant's Formula of Universal Law.

However, while these are mesmerizing arguments, neither one of them is ultimately convincing. It is the first step in the argument that is problematic in each case. Humeans will allow that, in trying to decide what I have reason to do, I am trying to decide what form of behavior I should actively engage in, and that this requires me to think of myself not just as a means to others' ends but also as a creature that possesses ends, and hence reasons, in its own right. But how does it follow from this that I should think of myself as an end-in-myself in the Kantian sense of a being to whom others should accord dignity? Korsgaard writes as if, in thinking of myself as a creature that possesses ends, I must be treating myself as a creature to whom dignity should be accorded, since I am acknowledging that I have reason to take my own ends seriously, and that consistency then requires me to treat other people in a similar manner. But Humeans will insist that trying to decide what I have reason to do is not the same as trying to decide how I have reason to treat the person I am. This, in their view, is to lose hold of the idea that is definitive of constructivism—that people's reasons for action are not independent truths but constructions of their desires and values.[20]

Humeans will find fault with Korsgaard's second line of argument at a similar point. Obviously they will agree that people's actions typically, if not always, unfold over time, and hence that the success of my actions typically depends on my future selves. But they will adamantly reject the conclusion that Korsgaard seeks to draw from this. They will agree that facts about my future desires and values can influence my current reasons, for they can influence my chances of succeeding at things I now set out to do. But it is still, in their view, my current desires and values that ground my reasons; my current reasons are not answerable to my future selves in the ways that Korsgaard claims. It is not that my conclusions about what I currently have reason to do must be ones that my future selves could regard as being normative for them; it is just that things will typically go smoother for me if they could, so this is a consideration that I typically have reason to take into account. But in many cases it will not be a terribly pressing consideration, as the chances that my desires and values will change significantly before my action is complete will be quite remote. And in any event it is manifestly the wrong sort of consideration to secure the deep and thoroughgoing moralization of reasons for action that Korsgaard and other Kantian constructivists are seeking.

I have little interest in defending Kantianism, so I am not going to take time here to discuss all the ways in which Korsgaard responds to such objections. It is interesting to note, however, that she often responds to objections of this Humean sort by invoking the public and social character of language and thought. (See 1996, 132–45; 2009, 188–97.) Her thought seems to be that Humean constructivism is based on a familiar kind of fantasy, the fantasy of the individual who exists just in the present moment and just for herself. Each person is to do the best she can by her own current desires and values, treating any other desires and values as just potential means or potential obstacles to her success. Korsgaard's thought seems to be that desires and values cannot be treated this way, because in recognizing them as desires and values we must take them more seriously. We must regard them much as we regard our own current desires and values, as the presumptively normative stuff out of which normative truths are to be constructed. Thus it is the public and social character of desires and values that ostensibly keeps constructivism from taking a form that leaves Kant's imperatives of humanity and universal law out of account. Because everyone's desires and values are in principle accessible to and presumptively normative for everyone else, reasons for action must accord dignity to everyone and be such that everyone could accept them.

Now I certainly share these worries about the Humean conception of desire and value. But I doubt very much that Korsgaard is in a position to invoke them. As we have maintained throughout this book, Davidson's case for the public and social character of language and thought is premised on perceptual externalism and a concomitant realism. It does indeed wreak havoc with Humean constructivism, but not in the way that Korsgaard suggests. While Davidson might agree with Korsgaard that desires and values are public and social in character, his idea would not be that everyone's desires and values are presumptively normative for everyone else, but rather that they are all shaped by and answerable to the same independent normative reality. So if Korsgaard's hope is that considerations regarding the public and social character of language and thought will lead away from Humean constructivism and toward her Kantian alternative, she is going to have to defend an understanding of those considerations that is very different from Davidson's via arguments that are likewise very different from his. Nothing that we have argued in this book proves that such arguments could not be provided, but I think it is fair to say that Korsgaard has so far not provided them. Towards the end of *The Sources of Normativity* (1996), then again near the end of *Self-Constitution* (2009), considerations regarding the public and social character of language and thought are invoked but not defended. Like the *deus ex machina* of Greek theater, they rescue Kantian constructivists from their Humean opponents, but not in a way that makes much sense or that stands up to serious scrutiny.

My conclusion, therefore, is that our Davidsonian amalgam of realism and contractualism is safe from worries about the authority of morality. If Korsgaard's Kantian constructivism had really been able to guarantee that morality's verdicts are always and necessarily overriding, that might have given us good reason to wonder whether Davidson's realist approach to reasons is the one we should be taking. But if it is true that Korsgaard's Kantian argument needs a premise anti-realists are not entitled to, then the threat from that quarter vanishes and it is in fact our Davidsonian position that emerges as the champion of morality; for even though it is incapable of accommodating the view that morality's verdicts are always and necessarily overriding, our Davidsonian position can make sense of the conviction that people always have at least some fairly strong reason to act morally. And that would appear to be another important point in favor of Davidson's underlying realism about normative properties.

Now this last remark might lead Humean constructivists to object that their account of morality's authority is actually better than realist accounts. After all, they might remind us, when Scanlon himself first introduced his contractualist approach to moral theory (1982), his idea was that being capable of justifying their actions to one another is something for which people commonly have strong desires. If that struck him then as a satisfactory basis on which to account for the authority of morality, how much of an advantage can our Davidsonian amalgam of realism and contractualism have over an amalgam of contractualism and Humean constructivism? And since an amalgam of contractualism and Humean constructivism could manage this without having to postulate normative properties, would this not suggest that it in fact has the advantage and that Davidson's normative realism should be rejected as a mistake? Normative realism may be an option, but is it not an option we should avoid if we can?

In response, it can be tempting to argue that Davidson's realism makes possible a much stronger inescapability claim than Humean constructivism does. Strong desires to be capable of justifying their actions to one another may indeed be common among people, but it is always going to be possible that people could exist who would have little or no concern for such niceties. By contrast, one might hope to establish that agent-neutral reasons to promote mutual respect are always present, and that actually interacting with others on such terms is something that comes to have significant agent-relative importance for every person.[21] It must be acknowledged, however, that the second of these claims could prove vulnerable to counter-arguments, since interacting with others on such terms might acquire only limited agent-relative importance for people having only limited experience of it. So it could turn out that Davidson's realism does not enjoy such a great advantage here after all.

If this response were the best we could muster, therefore, we might find that Davidson's realist position is in real trouble. Humeans might grant that realism makes possible a somewhat stronger conclusion about morality's authority than they can provide, but insist that it does so at a much higher metaphysical and epistemological cost than it makes sense for anyone to pay. We might reply in turn by working once again through arguments of the sort advanced in Chapter 7, in hopes of convincing them that the metaphysical and epistemological costs involved in postulating the existence of normative properties are perfectly affordable. But no matter how successful those arguments ultimately are, they will presumably never reduce the costs to nothing, and so the Humeans could continue to complain that a small increase in the inescapability of moral reasons is not worth it. Davidson's case for normative realism could be in real trouble if it actually were hanging on this thread.

It is therefore of the utmost importance to emphasize that Davidson's case for normative realism does not depend on establishing that its account of morality's authority is superior to Humean accounts. The argument against constructivism, whether Humean or Kantian, is in the first instance that it presupposes an unsatisfactory view of how the contents of normative beliefs and desires come to be fixed. Davidson's fundamental claim is that this requires people to be triangulating on normative properties, and that the benefits of this claim outweigh the costs of embracing normative realism. Issues about the authority of morality enter the picture only when Kantian constructivists suggest that they can make sense of a stronger account of it than realists can. That might well have given us some reason to reconsider Davidson's realism had it proven true, since the Kantians were promising a much stronger account of morality's authority than Davidson can deliver. But Humean constructivists are not promising an account of morality's authority so very different from Davidson's, so they need to provide us alternative grounds on which to reconsider his commitment to realism. Their complaint cannot be that Davidson's commitment to realism, while in many ways compelling, fails to deliver a significantly stronger account of morality's authority than their approach does. It must rather be that, no matter how compelling Davidson's commitment to realism is, it falls short on some other score that should disqualify it from further consideration.

What Humean constructivists often maintain at this point is that appeals to realism such as Davidson's should be disqualified from further consideration because they are clearly and fatally contradicted by evolutionary biology. Sharon Street, for example, maintains (2006) that we know from evolutionary biology that individual desires are little more than functional states linking descriptive beliefs to agential responses in ways that enhance reproductive success. Any account according to which desires track normative truths must be abandoned, she argues, because a general ability to track such truths would not contribute to reproductive success. Nor, she adds, would it explain why the particular desires people end up with contribute as much and as reliably to reproductive success as they so obviously do. By contrast, Street insists, a general ability to track at least a certain range of descriptive truths would obviously contribute to reproductive success, and particular descriptive beliefs pose no parallel puzzle. The particular descriptive beliefs people end up with contribute as much and as reliably to reproductive success as they do only because they tend, within the favored range, to be true. But one would suppose that the particular desires people end up with would contribute as much and as reliably to reproductive success even if they were not correct. Thus Street concludes that appeals to realism such as Davidson's must be rejected because they have been supplanted by the best science of human nature that we have.

As I mentioned earlier, when discussing David Enoch's views, I suspect that people's desires very often do not contribute as much and as reliably to their reproductive success as Street is supposing. Moreover, I agree with

Enoch that, because human reproductive success is actually a good thing, actions that contribute significantly and reliably to it have a lot to be said for them. Sometimes, of course, there is even more to be said against such actions, but those tend to be cases where people's desires are often ambivalent as well. When I look at the particular desires that people end up with, therefore, it is far from obvious to me that realists have anything to worry about. Street is no doubt correct in thinking that people's basic instincts and urges are the fairly direct result of natural selection and best understood along the lines of her "adaptive link" account. But this is perfectly compatible with concluding that people's desires as a whole are better understood according to the sort of "tracking" account that I have been claiming to find in Davidson.[22] As Street says, this requires us to suppose that a reproductive advantage is conferred on people by their ability to track not just descriptive but also normative truths. But this is not as implausible as she seems to think; on the contrary, what seems remarkably implausible is her assumption that these different abilities are fundamentally distinct.

This is perhaps the overarching lesson for ethics that we should take from Davidson's triangulation argument. People must be capable of triangulating in order to fix the contents of their descriptive beliefs, so they already have what it takes to triangulate on normative properties should any actually exist. There is no need for a distinct argument showing that this capacity contributes to reproductive success. The question is simply how the contents of normative beliefs and desires are fixed. Are they fixed in the first instance through the formation of Street's adaptive links, and after that via exclusively "internal" reasoning of the sort favored by Humean constructivists? Or are they primarily fixed through triangulation and reasoning of a more "external" sort? Once it is agreed that Street's constructivist explanation is no more scientific than Davidson's realist one, I think it becomes very difficult to understand why her account should be preferred over his. Even most anti-realists acknowledge that normative realism appears to offer a better account of things; they just think we know on other grounds that this appearance must in fact be illusory. By now, however, I think we are in a position to conclude that we know no such thing and that these alleged grounds for doubt are spurious. There is no good reason to assume that Davidson's normative realism must be false, and every reason to maintain that it, or something very like it, is true.

Notes

1. For example, in addition to the special reasons I have to promote the well-being of my friends, I may also have special reasons to perform actions of other sorts that are called for by friendship.
2. Such worries are clearly at work in Hurley 2009. Hurley stipulates that agent-relative reasons can be ultimate, and largely on that basis concludes that constructivist accounts of reasons are to be preferred over realist ones.

198   *Desires, Reasons and Morality*

3. Railton 1984 offers an influential argument of this kind.
4. Pettit 1997 offers a nice example of this approach.
5. This is not an uncommon way of thinking about the relation between agent-relative and agent-neutral reasons, notwithstanding the worry that I go on to mention. See, for example, Thomas Nagel's seminal discussion in his 1986.
6. This is just to say that the worries I raised in Chapter 7 about the analogy to secondary qualities hold for agent-relative reasons every bit as much as they do for agent-neutral ones.
7. Interestingly, Scanlon does not seem to share this conviction; he seems to regard all reasons as agent-relative. (That is certainly his position in 1998, anyway; his position in 2014 is not quite so clear.) I assume this is connected to the fact that he does not regard reasons as properties of situations, but rather as principles that are applied to situations in order to make what he calls (2014, 37 ff.) "mixed" claims.
8. This might not seem all that different from the consequentialists' claim that agent-relative reasons can be contingent on facts about what patterns of behavior will promote the overall good without being derived from those facts. (See, e.g., Railton 1984, 141 ff.) But in saying that particular agent-relative reasons grow out of corresponding agent-neutral ones I do not mean to suggest that they are somehow contingent on facts about what will promote the overall good.
9. It does mean that historical information about their subjects is something radical interpreters must be assumed to have. But as we have already seen in Chapter 3, this is only to be expected in any case.
10. Scanlon (2014, 31 ff.) defends a very similar account of reasons, but without tying agent-relativity so closely to history, and so without making it so clear how or even whether agent-neutral reasons are also possible.
11. This is certainly true of Korsgaard, at any rate. It is clear, however, that she also thinks realism is untenable because it cannot provide a satisfactory account of the content and the authority of morality.
12. As we shall see, calling them reasons for action in their own right is actually not quite correct. For Kantian constructivists, moral considerations are not separate reasons but something more like conditions all reasons must meet.
13. I focus here on the poor and the wealthy, but obviously the point is more general than that.
14. For a more detailed, but still ultimately dismissive, discussion of Hobbesian contractarianism, see Myers 1999b, 33 ff.
15. As I have mentioned, some realists, like Scanlon, are reluctant to acknowledge the existence of agent-neutral reasons. However, since I regard that as a mistake, I assume that our realist contractarians are not making it.
16. See especially Scanlon 1998, Chapter 4. Scanlon talks not just of mutual respect but also of mutual recognition. For our purposes here, however, we can treat these two ideas as coming to the same thing.
17. Even principles of rescue are problematic for Scanlon, however, given how they allow the numbers to count. (See 1998, 229 ff.)
18. Although he does embroider it with some further considerations, this is the core of Scanlon's argument in his 1998 (see 160 ff.).
19. See in particular Street 2006. Bernard Williams could also be included in this camp, given his willingness to countenance the possibility that reasons for action might be relative.
20. I assume something like this is what Street is getting at when she complains (2012, 48 ff.) that Korsgaard's arguments reveal her still to be in the grip of normative realism.
21. For more on this, see Myers 1999a.
22. FitzPatrick 2015 comes to a similar conclusion.

Bibliography

Amoretti, Maria Cristina. 2007. "Triangulation and Rationality." *Epistemologia*, 30: 307–26.
Amoretti, Maria Cristina. 2011. "Triangulation Between Externalism and Internalism." In Amoretti and Preyer 2011.
Amoretti, Maria Cristina. 2013. "Concepts Within the Model of Triangulation." *Protosociology*, 30: 49–62.
Amoretti, Maria Cristina and Gerhard Preyer, eds. 2011. *Triangulation: From an Epistemological Point of View*. Frankfurt: Ontos Verlag.
Andrews, Kristin. 2012. *Do Apes Read Minds? Toward a New Folk Psychology*. Cambridge, MA: MIT Press.
Andrews, Kristin and Ljiljana Radenovic. 2006. "Speaking Without Interpreting: A Reply to Bouma on Autism and Davidsonian Interpretation." *Philosophical Psychology*, 19–5: 663–78.
Bar-On, Dorit and Matthew Priselac. 2011. "Triangulation and the Beasts." In Amoretti and Preyer 2011.
Baron-Cohen, Simon, Alan M. Leslie and Uta Frith. 1985. "Does the Autistic Child Have a 'Theory of Mind'?" *Cognition*, 21: 37–46.
Bernecker, Sven. 2013. "Triangular Externalism." In Lepore and Ludwig 2013.
Blackburn, Simon. 1984. "The Individual Strikes Back." In Miller and Wright 2002.
Boghossian, Paul. 1989. "The Rule-Following Considerations." In Miller and Wright 2002.
Boghossian, Paul. 2005. "Is Meaning Normative?" In A. Beckermann and C. Nimtz (eds.), *Philosophy—Science—Scientific Philosophy*. Paderborn: Mentis.
Bouma, Hanni K. 2006. "High-Functioning Autistic Speakers as Davidsonian Interpreters: A Reply to Andrews and Radenovic." *Philosophical Psychology*, 19–5: 679–90.
Bridges, Jason. 2006. "Davidson's Transcendental Externalism." *Philosophy and Phenomenological Research*, 73–2: 290–315.
Bridges, Jason. 2014. "Rule-Following Skepticism, Properly So Called." In James Conant and Andrea Kern (eds.), *Varieties of Scepticism*. Berlin: De Gruyter.
Brink, Ingar. 2004. "Joint Attention, Triangulation and Radical Interpretation: A Problem and Its Solution." *Dialectica*, 58–2: 179–206.
Briscoe, Robert Eamon. 2007. "Communication and Rational Responsiveness to the World." *Pacific Philosophical Quarterly*, 88: 135–59.
Brueckner, Anthony. 1991. "The Omniscient Interpreter Rides Again." *Analysis*, 51: 192–205.

Burge, Tyler. 1979. "Individualism and the Mental." *Midwest Studies in Philosophy*, 4: 73–121.
Burge, Tyler. 1982. "Other Bodies." In Woodfield 1982.
Burge, Tyler. 1986. "Cartesian Error and the Objectivity of Perception." In Pettit and McDowell 1986.
Burge, Tyler. 1992. "Philosophy of Language and Mind, 1950–1990." *The Philosophical Review*, 101: 3–51.
Burge, Tyler. 2003a. "Social Anti-Individualism, Objective Reference." *Philosophy and Phenomenological Research*, 67–3: 682–90.
Burge, Tyler. 2003b. "Reply to Hahn." In Hahn and Ramberg 2003.
Burge, Tyler. 2010. *Origins of Objectivity*. Oxford: Clarendon Press.
Campbell, John. 2011. "Review of *Origins of Objectivity*." *The Journal of Philosophy*, 108–5: 269–85.
Child, William. 1996. *Causality, Interpretation and the Mind*. Oxford: Oxford University Press.
Child, William. 2001. "Triangulation: Davidson, Realism and Natural Kinds." *Dialectica*, 55–1: 29–49.
Davidson, Donald. 1963. "Actions, Reasons, and Causes." In Davidson 1980.
Davidson, Donald. 1967. "Causal Relations." In Davidson 1980.
Davidson, Donald. 1969. "How Is Weakness of the Will Possible?" In Davidson 1980.
Davidson, Donald. 1970. "Mental Events." In Davidson 1980.
Davidson, Donald. 1973. "Radical Interpretation." In Davidson 1984a.
Davidson, Donald. 1974a. "Belief and the Basis of Meaning." In Davidson 1984a.
Davidson, Donald. 1974b. "On the Very Idea of a Conceptual Scheme." In Davidson 1984a.
Davidson, Donald. 1974c. "Replies to David Lewis and W.V. Quine." In Davidson 1984a.
Davidson, Donald. 1975. "Thought and Talk." In Davidson 1984a.
Davidson, Donald. 1976. "Reply to Foster." In Davidson 1984a.
Davidson, Donald. 1977. "Reality Without Reference." In Davidson 1984a.
Davidson, Donald. 1978. "Intending." In Davidson 1980.
Davidson, Donald. 1979. "The Inscrutability of Reference." In Davidson 1984a.
Davidson, Donald. 1980. *Essays on Actions and Events*. Oxford: Clarendon Press.
Davidson, Donald. 1982. "Rational Animals." In Davidson 2001a.
Davidson, Donald. 1983. "A Coherence Theory of Truth and Knowledge." In Davidson 2001a.
Davidson, Donald. 1984a. *Inquiries into Truth and Interpretation*. Oxford: Clarendon Press.
Davidson, Donald. 1984b. "Communication and Convention." In Davidson 1984a.
Davidson, Donald. 1984c. "Expressing Evaluations." In Davidson 2004.
Davidson, Donald. 1985. "Incoherence and Irrationality." In Davidson 2004.
Davidson, Donald. 1986. "A Nice Derangement of Epitaphs." In Davidson 2005.
Davidson, Donald. 1987a. "Afterthoughts." In Davidson 2001a.
Davidson, Donald. 1987b. "Knowing One's Own Mind." In Davidson 2001a.
Davidson, Donald. 1988a. "Epistemology and Truth." In Davidson 2001a.
Davidson, Donald. 1988b. "The Myth of the Subjective." In Davidson 2001a.
Davidson, Donald. 1989a. "What Is Present to the Mind." In Davidson 2001a.
Davidson, Donald. 1989b. "The Conditions of Thought." In J. Brandl and W.L. Gombocz (eds.), *The Mind of Donald Davidson*. Amsterdam and Atlanta, GA: Rodopi.

Davidson, Donald. 1990a. "The Structure and Content of Truth." *Journal of Philosophy*, 87–6: 279–329.
Davidson, Donald. 1990b. "Meaning, Truth, and Evidence." In Davidson 2005.
Davidson, Donald. 1990c. "Representation and Interpretation." In Davidson 2004.
Davidson, Donald. 1991a. "Epistemology Externalized." In Davidson 2001a.
Davidson, Donald. 1991b. "Three Varieties of Knowledge." In Davidson 2001a.
Davidson, Donald. 1992. "The Second Person." In Davidson 2001a.
Davidson, Donald. 1993a. "Reply to Jerry Fodor and Ernest Lepore." In Stoecker 1993.
Davidson, Donald. 1993b. "Reply to Akeel Bilgrami." In Stoecker 1993.
Davidson, Donald. 1994. "The Social Aspect of Language." In Davidson 2005.
Davidson, Donald. 1995a. "The Problem of Objectivity." In Davidson 2004.
Davidson, Donald. 1995b. "The Objectivity of Value." In Davidson 2004.
Davidson, Donald. 1997a. "Indeterminism and Antirealism." In Davidson 2001a.
Davidson, Donald. 1997b. "Seeing Through Language." In Davidson 2005.
Davidson, Donald. 1998. "The Irreducibility of the Concept of Self." In Davidson 2001a.
Davidson, Donald. 1999a. "The Emergence of Thought." In Davidson 2001a.
Davidson, Donald. 1999b. "Reply to Dagfinn Føllesdal." In Hahn 1999.
Davidson, Donald. 1999c. "Reply to A.C. Genova." In Hahn 1999.
Davidson, Donald. 1999d. "Interpretation: Hard in Theory, Easy in Practice." In Mario de Caro (ed.), *Interpretations and Causes: New Perspectives on Donald Davidson's Philosophy*. Kluwer Academic Publishers.
Davidson, Donald. 1999e. "Reply to Barry Stroud." In Hahn 1999.
Davidson, Donald. 1999f. "Reply to John McDowell." In Hahn 1999.
Davidson, Donald. 1999g. "Reply to Thomas Nagel." In Hahn 1999.
Davidson, Donald. 2001a. *Subjective, Intersubjective, Objective*. Oxford: Clarendon Press.
Davidson, Donald. 2001b. "Externalisms." In Kotatko et al. 2001.
Davidson, Donald. 2001c. "Comments on Karlovy Vary Papers." In Kotatko et al. 2001.
Davidson, Donald. 2001d. "What Thought Requires." In Davidson 2004.
Davidson, Donald. 2003. "Responses to Barry Stroud, John McDowell, and Tyler Burge." *Philosophy and Phenomenological Research*, 67–3: 691–9.
Davidson, Donald. 2004. *Problems of Rationality*. Oxford: Clarendon Press.
Davidson, Donald. 2005. *Truth, Language, and History*. Oxford: Clarendon Press.
Davidson, Donald. 2006. "The Perils and Pleasures of Interpretation." In Lepore and Smith 2006.
Dummett, Michael. 1974. "The Social Character of Meaning." In his *Truth and Other Enigmas*. Cambridge, MA: Harvard University Press, 1978.
Dummett, Michael. 1975. "What Is a Theory of Meaning?" In Samuel Guttenplan (ed.), *Mind and Language*. Oxford: Clarendon Press.
Dummett, Michael. 1993. "What Do I Know When I Know a Language?" In his *The Seas of Language*. Oxford: Clarendon Press.
Enoch, David. 2011. *Taking Morality Seriously*. Oxford: Oxford University Press.
Evans, Gareth. 1982. *The Varieties of Reference*, edited by John McDowell. Oxford: Oxford University Press.
FitzPatrick, William. 2015. "Debunking Evolutionary Debunking of Ethical Realism." *Philosophical Studies*, 172: 883–904.
Fodor, Jerry. 2015. "Burge on Perception." In Eric Margolis and Stephen Laurence (eds.), *The Conceptual Mind: New Directions in the Study of Concepts*. Cambridge, MA: MIT Press.

Fodor, Jerry and Ernest Lepore. 1992. *Holism: A Shopper's Guide*. Oxford: Blackwell.
Fodor, Jerry and Ernest Lepore. 1993. "Is Radical Interpretation Possible?" In Stoecker 1993.
Foley, Richard and Richard Fumerton. 1985. "Davidson's Theism?" *Philosophical Studies*, 48: 83–89.
Føllesdal, Dagfinn. 1999. "Triangulation." In Hahn 1999.
French, Peter, Theodore Uehling and Howard Wettstein, eds. 1992. *Midwest Studies in Philosophy, Volume XVII: The Wittgenstein Legacy*. Notre Dame: University of Notre Dame Press.
Genova, A.C. 1999. "The Very Idea of Massive Truth." In Hahn 1999.
Ginet, Carl. 1992. "The Dispositionalist Solution to Wittgenstein's Problem About Understanding a Rule: Answering Kripke's Objections." In French et al. 1992.
Ginsborg, Hannah. 2010. "Review of *Oughts and Thoughts: Rule-Following and the Normativity of Content*." *Mind*, 119: 1175–86.
Ginsborg, Hannah. 2011a. "Primitive Normativity and Skepticism about Rules." *The Journal of Philosophy*, 108: 227–54.
Ginsborg, Hannah. 2011b. "Inside and Outside Language: Stroud's Nonreductionism about Meaning." In Jason Bridges, Niko Kolodny and Wai-hung Wong (eds.), *The Possibility of Philosophical Understanding: Essays for Barry Stroud*. Oxford: Oxford University Press.
Ginsborg, Hannah. 2012. "Meaning, Understanding and Normativity." *Proceedings of the Aristotelian Society Supplementary Volume*, 86: 127–46.
Glock, Hans-Johann. 2003. "Donald Davidson, *Subjective, Intersubjective, Objective*." *Philosophical Investigations*, 26–4: 348–60.
Glock, Hans-Johann. 2005. "The Normativity of Meaning Made Simple." In A. Beckermann and C. Nimtz (eds.), *Philosophy Science—Scientific Philosophy*. Paderborn: Mentis.
Glüer, Kathrin. 2006. "Triangulation." In Lepore and Smith 2006.
Glüer, Kathrin. 2011. *Donald Davidson: A Short Introduction*. Oxford: Oxford University Press.
Glüer, Kathrin. 2013. "Convention and Meaning." In Lepore and Ludwig 2013.
Glüer, Kathrin and Peter Pagin. 2003. "Meaning Theory and Autistic Speakers." *Mind and Language*, 18–1: 23–51.
Glüer, Kathrin and Åsa Wikforss. 2009. "Against Content Normativity." *Mind*, 118: 31–70.
Glüer, Kathrin and Åsa Wikforss. 2015. "The Normativity of Meaning and Content." In Edward N. Zalta (ed.), *The Stanford Encyclopedia of Philosophy* (Summer 2015 Edition), URL = <http://plato.stanford.edu/archives/sum2015/entries/meaning-normativity/>.
Godfrey-Smith, Peter. 1989. "Misinformation." *Canadian Journal of Philosophy*, 19–4: 533–50.
Goldberg, Nathaniel. 2008. "Tension Within Triangulation." *The Southern Journal of Philosophy*, 46: 261–80.
Goldberg, Nathaniel. 2009. "Triangulation, Untranslatability, and Reconciliation." *Philosophia*, 37: 261–80.
Goldfarb, Warren. 1985. "Kripke on Wittgenstein on Rules." In Miller and Wright 2002.
Haddock, Adrian. 2012. "Meaning, Justification, and 'Primitive Normativity'." *Proceedings of the Aristotelian Society Supplementary Volume*, 86: 147–74.

Hahn, Lewis Edwin, ed. 1999. *The Philosophy of Donald Davidson*. Chicago and La Salle, IL: Open Court.
Hahn, Martin. 2003. "When Swampmen Get Arthritis: Externalism in Burge and Davidson." In Hahn and Ramberg 2003.
Hahn, Martin and Bjørn Ramberg, eds. 2003. *Reflections and Replies: Essays on the Philosophy of Tyler Burge*. Cambridge, MA: MIT Press.
Harman, Gilbert. 1975. "Moral Relativism Defended." *Philosophical Review*, 84–1: 3–22.
Harman, Gilbert. 1977. *The Nature of Morality*. New York: Oxford University Press.
Hattiangadi, Anandi. 2006. "Is Meaning Normative?" *Mind and Language*, 21: 220–40.
Hattiangadi, Anandi. 2007. *Oughts and Thoughts: Rule-Following and the Normativity of Content*. Oxford: Oxford University Press.
Heil, John. 1992. *The Nature of True Minds*. Cambridge: Cambridge University Press.
Horwich, Paul. 1998. *Meaning*. Oxford: Oxford University Press.
Hurley, Paul. 2009. *Beyond Consequentialism*. Oxford: Oxford University Press.
Hutto, Daniel D. and Erik Myin. 2013. *Radicalizing Enactivism: Basic Minds Without Content*. Cambridge, MA: MIT Press.
Klein, Peter D. 1986. "Radical Interpretation and Global Skepticism." In Lepore 1986.
Kolodny, Niko. 2005. "Why Be Rational?" *Mind*, 114–455: 509–63.
Korsgaard, Christine. 1986. "Skepticism About Practical Reason." *Journal of Philosophy*, 83–1: 5–25.
Korsgaard, Christine. 1996. *The Sources of Normativity*. Cambridge: Cambridge University Press.
Korsgaard, Chistine. 2008. "The Activity of Reason." *Proceedings and Addresses of the American Philosophical Association*, 83–2: 23–43.
Korsgaard, Christine. 2009. *Self-Constitution: Agency, Identity, and Integrity*. Oxford: Oxford University Press.
Kotatko, Petr, Peter Pagin and Gabriel Segal, eds. 2001. *Interpreting Davidson*. Stanford: CSLI.
Kriegel, Uriah. 2002. "Phenomenal Content." *Erkenntnis*, 57: 175–98.
Kripke, Saul. 1972. *Naming and Necessity*. Cambridge, MA: Harvard University Press.
Kripke, Saul. 1982. *Wittgenstein on Rules and Private Language*. Cambridge, MA: Harvard University Press.
Kusch, Martin. 2006. *A Sceptical Guide to Meaning and Rules: Defending Kripke's Wittgenstein*. Montreal & Kingston: McGill-Queen's University Press.
Lasonen, Maria and Tomas Marvan. 2004. "Davidson's Triangulation: Content-Endowing Causes and Circularity." *International Journal of Philosophical Studies*, 12–2: 177–95.
Lepore, Ernest, ed. 1986. *Truth and Interpretation: Perspectives on the Philosophy of Donald Davidson*. Oxford: Blackwell.
Lepore, Ernest and Kirk Ludwig. 2005. *Donald Davidson: Meaning, Truth, Language, and Reality*. Oxford: Clarendon Press.
Lepore, Ernest and Kirk Ludwig, eds. 2013. *A Companion to Donald Davidson*. Wiley Blackwell.
Lepore, Ernest and Barry Smith, eds. 2006. *The Oxford Handbook of Philosophy of Language*. Oxford: Clarendon Press.

Loar, Brian. 1982. "Conceptual Role and Truth-Conditions." *Notre Dame Journal of Symbolic Logic*, 23: 272–83.
Ludwig, Kirk. 1992. "Skepticism and Interpretation." *Philosophy and Phenomenological Research*, 55: 345–60.
Ludwig, Kirk. 2011. "Triangulation Triangulated." In Amoretti and Preyer 2011.
Luntley, Michael. 1991. "The Transcendental Grounds of Meaning and the Place of Silence." In K. Puhl (ed.), *Meaning Scepticism*. Berlin: de Gruyter.
Mackie, J.L. 1976a. *Ethics: Inventing Right and Wrong*. Harmondsworth: Penguin Books.
Mackie, J.L. 1976b. *Problems from Locke*. Oxford: Clarendon Press.
McDowell, John. 1977. "On the Sense and Reference of a Proper Name." *Mind*, 86: 159–85.
McDowell, John. 1979. "Virtue and Reason." In his *Mind, Value, and Reality*. Cambridge, MA: Harvard University Press, 1998.
McDowell, John. 1984. "Wittgenstein on Following a Rule." In Miller and Wright 2002.
McDowell, John. 1985. "Values and Secondary Qualities." In his *Mind, Value, and Reality*. Cambridge, MA: Harvard University Press, 1998.
McDowell, John. 1987. "In Defence of Modesty." In his *Meaning, Knowledge, and Reality*. Cambridge, MA: Harvard University Press, 1998.
McDowell, John. 1992. "Meaning and Intentionality in Wittgenstein's Later Philosophy." In French et al. 1992.
McDowell, John. 1994. *Mind and World*. Cambridge, MA: Harvard University Press.
McDowell, John. 2003. "Subjective, Intersubjective, Objective." *Philosophy and Phenomenological Research*, 67–3: 675–81.
McDowell, John. 2008. "Avoiding the Myth of the Given." In Jakob Lindgaard (ed.), *John McDowell: Experience, Norm and Nature*. Oxford: Blackwell.
McGinn, Colin. 1982. "The Structure of Content." In Woodfield 1982.
McGinn, Colin. 1984. *Wittgenstein on Meaning*. Oxford: Blackwell.
Millar, Alex. 2004. *Understanding People: Normativity and Rationalizing Explanation*. Oxford: Oxford University Press.
Miller, Alex and Crispin Wright, eds. 2002. *Rule-Following and Meaning*. Montreal and Kingston: McGill-Queen's University Press.
Millikan, Ruth. 1984. "Truth Rules, Hoverflies, and the Kripke-Wittgenstein Paradox." In Miller and Wright 2002.
Montminy, Martin. 2003. "Triangulation, Objectivity and the Ambiguity Problem." *Critica*, 35: 25–48.
Myers, Robert. 1999a. "The Inescapability of Moral Reasons." *Philosophy and Phenomenological Research*, 59–2: 281–307.
Myers, Robert. 1999b. *Self-Governance and Cooperation*. Oxford: Oxford University Press.
Myers, Robert. 2004. "Finding Value in Davidson." *Canadian Journal of Philosophy*, 34–1: 107–36.
Myers, Robert. 2012. "Desires and Normative Truths: A Holist's Response to the Sceptics." *Mind*, 121–482: 375–406.
Nagel, Thomas. 1970. *The Possibility of Altruism*. Oxford: Oxford University Press.
Nagel, Thomas. 1986. *The View from Nowhere*. Oxford: Oxford University Press.
Nagel, Thomas. 1999. "Davidson's New *Cogito*." In Hahn 1999.
Pagin, Peter. 2001. "Semantic Triangulation." In Kotatko et al. 2001.

Pagin, Peter. 2013. "Radical Interpretation and the Principle of Charity." In Lepore and Ludwig 2013.
Pettit, Phillip. 1997. "The Consequentialist Perspective." In M. Baron, P. Pettit and M. Slote, *Three Methods of Ethics*. Oxford: Blackwell.
Pettit, Phillip and John McDowell, eds. 1986. *Subject, Thought, and Context*. Oxford: Oxford University Press.
Pritchard, Duncan. 2013. "Davidson and Radical Skepticism." In Lepore and Ludwig 2013.
Pritchard, Duncan and Christopher Ranalli. 2013. "Rorty, Williams, and Davidson: Skepticism and Metaepistemology." *Humanities*, 2: 351–68.
Putnam, Hilary. 1975. "The Meaning of 'Meaning'." In his *Language, Mind and Reality*. Cambridge: Cambridge University Press.
Putnam, Hilary. 1981. *Reason, Truth and History*. Cambridge: Cambridge University Press.
Quine, W.V. 1960. *Word and Object*. Cambridge, MA: MIT Press.
Quine, W.V. 1996. "Progress on Two Fronts." *The Journal of Philosophy*, 93–4: 159–63.
Railton, Peter. 1984. "Alienation, Consequentialism, and the Demands of Morality." *Philosophy and Public Affairs*, 13–2: 134–71.
Ramberg, Bjørn. 2001. "What Davidson Said to the Skeptic Or: Anti-Representationalism, Triangulation and the Naturalization of the Subjective." In Kotatko et al. 2001.
Reboul, Anne. 2006. "HOT Theories of Meaning: The Link Between Language and Theory of Mind." *Mind and Language*, 21–5: 587–96.
Rescorla, Michael. 2013. "Rationality as Constitutive Ideal." In Lepore and Ludwig 2013.
Rorty, Richard. 1986. "Pragmatism, Davidson and Truth." In Lepore 1986.
Scanlon, T.M. 1982. "Contractualism and Utilitarianism." In A. Sen and B. Williams (eds.), *Utilitarianism and Beyond*. Cambridge: Cambridge University Press, 1982.
Scanlon, T.M. 1998. *What We Owe to Each Other*. Cambridge, MA: Harvard University Press.
Scanlon, T.M. 2014. *Being Realistic About Reasons*. Oxford: Oxford University Press.
Schueler, G.F. 2003. *Reasons and Purposes*. Oxford: Clarendon Press.
Sinclair, Robert. 2005. "The Philosophical Significance of Triangulation: Locating Davidson's Non-Reductive Naturalism." *Metaphilosophy*, 36–5: 708–28.
Smith, Michael. 1994. *The Moral Problem*. Oxford: Blackwell.
Sosa, Ernest. 2003. "Knowledge of Self, Others, and World." In K. Ludwig (ed.), *Donald Davidson*. Cambridge, MA: Cambridge University Press.
Sreenivasan, Gopal. 2001. "Understanding Alien Morals." *Philosophy and Phenomenological Research*, 62–1: 1–32.
Stoecker, Ralf, ed. 1993. *Reflecting Davidson*. Berlin and New York: Walter de Gruyter.
Stoutland, Frederick. 2006. "A Mistaken View of Davidson's Legacy." *International Journal of Philosophical Studies*, 14–4: 579–96.
Stoutland, Frederick. 2011. "Interpreting Davidson on Intentional Action." In J. Malpas (ed.), *Dialogues With Davidson: Acting, Interpreting, Understanding*. Cambridge, MA: MIT Press.

Street, Sharon. 2006. "A Darwinian Dilemma for Realist Theories of Value." *Philosophical Studies*, 127: 109–66.
Street, Sharon. 2012. "Coming to Terms With Contingency: Humean Constructivism About Practical Reason." In J. Lenman and Y. Shemmer (eds.), *Constructivism in Practical Philosophy*. Oxford: Oxford University Press.
Stroud, Barry. 1968. "Transcendental Arguments." *The Journal of Philosophy*, 65: 241–56.
Stroud, Barry. 1996. "Mind, Meaning, and Practice." In Stroud 2000.
Stroud, Barry. 1999. "Radical Interpretation and Philosophical Scepticism." In Hahn 1999.
Stroud, Barry. 2000. *Meaning, Understanding, and Practice*. New York: Oxford University Press.
Stroud, Barry. 2003. "Ostension and the Social Character of Thought." *Philosophy and Phenomenological Research*, 67–3: 667–81.
Stroud, Barry. 2012. "Meaning and Understanding." In Jonathan Ellis and Daniel Guevara (eds.), *Wittgenstein and the Philosophy of Mind*. Oxford: Oxford University Press.
Stroud, Barry. Forthcoming. "Davidson and Wittgenstein on Meaning and Understanding." In Verheggen forthcoming a.
Talmage, Catherine. 1997. "Meaning and Triangulation." *Linguistics and Philosophy*, 20: 139–45.
Thornton, Tim. 1998. *Wittgenstein on Language and Thought*. Edinburgh: Edinburgh University Press.
Velleman, David. 1992. "The Guise of the Good." *Nous*, 26–1: 3–26.
Verheggen, Claudine. 1997. "Davidson's Second Person." *The Philosophical Quarterly*, 47–188: 361–9.
Verheggen, Claudine. 2000. "The Meaningfulness of Meaning Questions." *Synthese*, 123: 195–216.
Verheggen, Claudine. 2003. "Wittgenstein's Rule-Following Paradox and the Objectivity of Meaning." *Philosophical Investigations*, 26: 285–310.
Verheggen, Claudine. 2005. "Stroud on Wittgenstein, Meaning, and Community." *Dialogue: Canadian Philosophical Review*, 54: 67–85.
Verheggen, Claudine. 2006. "How Social Must Language Be?" *Journal for the Theory of Social Behavior*, 36–2: 203–19.
Verheggen, Claudine. 2007. "Triangulating With Davidson." *The Philosophical Quarterly*, 57–226: 96–103.
Verheggen, Claudine. 2011a. "Triangulation and Philosophical Skepticism." In Amoretti and Preyer 2011.
Verheggen, Claudine. 2011b. "Semantic Normativity and Naturalism." *Logique et Analyse*, 216: 552–67.
Verheggen, Claudine. 2013. "Triangulation." In Lepore and Ludwig 2013.
Verheggen, Claudine. 2015. "Towards a New Kind of Semantic Normativity." *International Journal of Philosophical Studies*, 23–3: 410–24.
Verheggen, Claudine, ed. Forthcoming a. *Wittgenstein and Davidson on Language, Thought and Action*. Cambridge: Cambridge University Press.
Verheggen, Claudine. Forthcoming b. "Davidson's Treatment of Wittgenstein's Rule-Following Paradox." In Verheggen forthcoming a.
Whiting, Daniel. 2013. "What Is the Normativity of Meaning?" *Inquiry*, 56: 1–20.
Wikforss, Åsa. 2001. "Semantic Normativity." *Philosophical Studies*, 102: 203–26.

Williams, Bernard. 1980. "Internal and External Reasons." In his *Moral Luck*. Cambridge: Cambridge University Press, 1981.
Williams, Meredith. 1999. *Wittgenstein, Mind and Meaning*. London: Routledge.
Williams, Meredith. 2000. "Wittgenstein and Davidson on the Sociality of Language." *Journal for the Theory of Social Behaviour*, 30: 301–18.
Williams, Meredith. 2010. *Blind Obedience: Paradox and Learning in the Later Wittgenstein*. London: Routledge.
Williams, Michael. 1988. "Scepticism and Charity." *Ratio*, 1: 176–94.
Williamson, Timothy. 2004. "Philosophical 'Intuitions' and Scepticism About Judgment." *Dialectica*, 58: 109–53.
Wilson, George. 1994. "Kripke on Wittgenstein and Normativity." *Midwest Studies in Philosophy*, 19: 366–90.
Wilson, George. 1998. "Semantic Realism and Kripke's Wittgenstein." In Miller and Wright 2002.
Wittgenstein, Ludwig. 1958. *Philosophical Investigations*, translated by G.E.M. Anscombe. New York: Macmillan.
Woodfield, Andrew, ed. 1982. *Thought and Object*. Oxford: Oxford University Press.
Wright, Crispin. 1986. "Does *Philosophical Investigations* I 258–60 Suggest a Cogent Argument Against Private Language?" In McDowell and Pettit 1986.
Wright, Crispin. 1996. "Truth in Ethics." In B. Hooker (ed.), *Truth in Ethics*. Oxford: Blackwell.
Yalowitz, Steven. 1999. "Davidson's Social Externalism." *Philosophia*, 27: 99–136.
Zalabardo, José. 1997. "Kripke's Normativity Argument." In Miller and Wright 2002.
Zalabardo, José. 2003. "Wittgenstein on Accord." *Pacific Philosophical Quarterly*, 84: 311–29.

Index

abstract entities, 14, 19, 99, 130, 166
Amoretti, Maria Cristina, 91n1, 93n36, 112, 114n13
analytic-synthetic distinction, 79–80
Andrews, Kristin, 39n51, 39n53, 39n54
animals, nonlinguistic, 25–28, 38n43, 39n45, 39n47
anomalous monism, 6, 172–73, 176
anti-realism, 107, 177n8, 194, 197
a priori knowledge, 30–31, 114n12
argument from queerness, 6, 164–70
argument from relativity, 164, 179–80
Aristotle, 190
aspect problem, 18–22, 25–28, 37n23, 46, 48, 76, 89–90, 92n25, 130–32

Bar-On, Dorit, 40n60
Baron-Cohen, Simon, 39n52
beliefs
—attribution of, 5, 13–14, 30–32, 38n44, 72, 97–98, 100–104, 113nn6–7, 114n8, 119, 123, 128
—and motivation, see motivation; pro-attitudes
—veridicality of, 5, 96–97, 100–104, 106–107, 109, 111, 113n6, 119, 128, 132, 174–175
—see also content; meaning
Bernecker, Sven, 38n32, 76, 91n1, 91n2
Blackburn, Simon, 43, 63n13
Boghossian, Paul, 43, 59
Bouma, Hanni K., 39n54
Bridges, Jason, 25, 34, 37n22, 38n32, 38n37, 39n48, 64n15, 91n1
Brink, Ingar, 40n60
Briscoe, Robert Eamon, 39n48
Brueckner, Anthony, 113n2
Burge, Tyler, 25–28, 35n5, 38n41, 38n43, 39n46, 39n51, 77, 83, 91n1, 92n26, 93n27, 93n37

Campbell, John, 28
Categorical Imperative
—Davidson's rejection of, 184, 191
—Formula of Humanity, 191–192
—Formula of Universal Law, 191–192
causal explanations vs. causal relations, 120–21, 172–73
causes
—common, 17–8, 95, 99
—distal, 15, 17–19, 24–27, 89
—indeterminacy of, 17–18, 20–21, 34, 46–48, 52, 64n19
—proximal, 17–19, 25–27, 89
—typical, 16, 18–19, 56, 65–67, 102, 108, 112
charity, principle of, 2, 72–73, 97, 124–29, 137n13, 138n19, 143
Child, William, 39n48, 93n34, 93n35
circularity, 1, 3, 15, 20–21, 24, 33–35, 40n62, 50, 105
communitarian view, see externalism
conceptual schemes, 108, 132
consequentialism, 7, 178n20, 180, 182, 198n8
constitutive aims, 152
constructivism, 120, 122, 136–37, 156n7, 156nn13–14, 157n17, 158–64, 177n6, 177n8, 177n14, 179, 183–84, 191–97, 197n2, 198n12
content
—attribution of, 5, 13–14, 26, 30–32, 38n44, 91n7, 98, 113n7, 114n8, 123, 128
—conceptual, 12, 35n5, 109–110, 115n15
—constitution of, see meaning
—fixing of, see meaning
—intentional, 12, 51
—intuitional, 12, 115n15

—non-conceptual, 12, 25, 27, 35n5, 109
—perceptual, 12, 25, 35n5
—phenomenal, 35n5
—propositional, 1, 12–14, 20, 24–28, 30, 33, 38n43, 64n19, 97, 101, 129, 175
—representational, 12, 25–26, 28
continence, principle of, 149, 159
contractarianism, 178n20, 183–86, 189–90, 198nn14–15
contractualism, 121, 136–37, 178n20, 179, 184–91, 194–95
convention, 1, 4–5, 42, 44, 66, 83, 87, 91, 94n45

Descartes, René, 96–97, 103
desires, *see* pro-attitudes
disagreement, 24, 49, 84, 124, 127–28, 135n6, 179–180
dispositionalism, 49, 52–54, 56, 64n20
distance problem, 18, 25, 37n23
division of linguistic labor, 82, 93n38
Dummett, Michael, 55–57, 93n37

Enoch, David, 6, 137n3, 174–75, 178n26, 196–97
epiphenomenalism, 172
error
—concept of, 12, 23, 30, 38n33, 50
—*see also* objectivity
Evans, Gareth, 35n5
evolutionary biology, 175, 196–97
externalism, 19, 36n17, 39n50, 91nn1–2, 91n4, 102, 104, 112, 138n19
—historical, 4–5, 65, 67–70, 74, 77, 91, 198n9
—holistic, 4–5, 65, 71–74, 77, 91. *See also* holism.
—individual, 99–100
—perceptual, 4, 16–17, 19, 25, 36n17, 37n26, 37n27, 42, 45, 56, 62, 65–77, 90, 95, 99, 130–32, 194
—physical, 4, 65–66, 77–82, 92n26, 113n4
—social, 4, 42, 62, 65, 82–90, 129, 131–32
——communitarian, 1, 4, 44, 62n7, 66, 84–87, 90
——interpersonal, 4, 65–67, 83–91, 100, 130–31
extension, 62, 66, 77–83, 93n32
extensionality, 14, 24, 28, 56

first-person authority, 137n8
first-person point of view, 111
FitzPatrick, William, 198n22
Fodor, Jerry, 36n8, 39n46, 91n6, 123, 137nn10–11
Foley, Richard, 113n2
Føllesdal, Dagfinn, 34
Frith, Uta, 39n52
Fumerton, Richard, 113n2

Genova, A. C., 113n2, 114n12
Ginet, Carl, 64n20
Ginsborg, Hannah, 41–43, 49–58, 63n14, 64n15, 64nn16–19, 64n25
Glock, Hans-Johann, 39n48, 39n51, 62n5
Glüer, Kathrin, 29, 36n8, 37n23, 37n27, 38n32, 39n51, 39n55, 40n61, 60–62, 62n2, 70, 72–73, 91n2, 94n45, 138n18
goals, 140–41, 156n5, 180
Godfrey-Smith, Peter, 37n23
Goldberg, Nathaniel, 76, 91n2, 92nn14–16, 92n24
Goldfarb, Warren, 64n20

Haddock, Adrian, 64n18
Hahn, Martin, 91n2, 92n15
Harman, Gilbert, 6, 135, 138n29, 155, 158, 164–66, 168, 170–77
Hattiangadi, Anandi, 43, 63n8
Heil, John, 39n48
holding true, 13, 37, 66, 68, 72, 108, 114n13
holism
—of content and meaning, 4–5, 13–14, 24, 65, 71–74, 76–77, 79, 81, 91, 92nn17–19, 94n42
—of pro-attitudes, 6, 133, 142–48
—of the mental, 92nn17–20, 93n30, 123–33
—intra-attitudinal vs. inter-attitudinal, 142–43, 146–47
Horwich, Paul, 64n20
Hume, David, 142
Hurley, Paul, 138n30, 197n2
Hutto, Daniel D., 36n6

instrumental principle, 159–60
intensionality, 14–15, 20, 24–5, 28, 31, 34–35, 37n26, 38n44, 40n62, 56

internalism, semantic, 19, 92n26, 99–100
internalist requirement, 148–52, 156n12, 158
—vs. practicality requirement, 177n1
interpersonal externalism, *see* externalism
interpretation
—problem of, 47, 54, 57–58, 63nn11–12, 87–89
—radical, 2, 4–5, 36n8, 36n16, 37n27, 38n33, 55–56, 64n23, 65–78, 91n3, 91nn6–7, 92nn12–14, 92n20, 92n23, 95, 97–103, 105, 108, 113n7, 114n8, 138n19
—wide notion of, 55, 87, 91n8, 95
interpretationism, 36n8, 91n2

Kant, Immanuel, 97, 191–92, 194
Khalidi, Muhammad Ali, 93n35
Klein, Peter D., 113n2
Kolodny, Nico, 177n4
Korsgaard, Christine, 6, 120, 156n12, 158–64, 176, 177n1, 177n5, 177n8, 177n14, 191–94, 198n11, 198n20
Kriegel, Uriah, 35n5
Kripke, Saul, 50, 57, 62n7, 63nn11–12, 64n15, 66, 77, 88–91, 92n26, 94nn40–41, 94nn46–47, 94n50
Kusch, Martin, 63n8, 64n28, 94n47, 94n50

Lasonen, Maria, 38n32, 38n35, 40n62
Lepore, Ernest, 29–30, 36n8, 36n17, 37n22, 38nn31–32, 39n47, 69, 91n2, 91n6, 92n16, 123, 137nn10–11
Leslie, Alan M., 39n52
Loar, Brian, 92n26
Locke, John, 165
Ludwig, Kirk, 29–30, 36n17, 37n22, 38nn31–32, 39nn47–49, 69, 91n2, 92n16, 113n2
Luntley, Michael, 63n13

Mackie, J. L., 6, 135, 138n29, 155, 158, 164–170, 176, 178nn16–17, 178n22, 179
Marvan, Tomas, 38n32, 38n35, 40n62
McDowell, John, 35n5, 36n9, 55–7, 63n13, 85, 94n41, 94n48, 106, 108–111, 114n14, 115n15, 166–9, 178n21

Index 211

McGinn, Colin, 38n37, 62nn4–5, 92n26
meaning
—attribution of, 5, 13, 50, 72, 90, 91n7, 93n33, 98
—constitution of, 5–6, 13, 27, 30–31, 37n28, 41, 49–53, 59–61, 63nn11–12, 64n18, 67, 69, 72–74, 79–81, 91n7, 98, 113n7
—determinants of, 38n29, 46–54, 63n11, 67, 80, 82, 89–90, 99–100
—fixing of, 3, 11–12, 17–18, 20–21, 24–29, 38n40, 39n47, 39n58, 48, 74–75, 105, 110, 115n15, 173
—holism of, *see* holism
—normativity of, *see* normativity
mental pictures, 19, 46, 52, 88, 99
Millar, Alex, 62n5
Millikan, Ruth, 63n13
Montminy, Martin, 29
motivation
—Humean theory of, 6, 133–35, 139–142, 148–50, 156nn2–5, 161–63, 167–69, 172
—non-Humean theory of, 141–2, 167–69
Myers, Robert, 137n7, 177n10, 188, 198n14, 198n21
Myin, Erik, 36n6

Nagel, Thomas, 103, 108, 113n1, 114n13, 156n5, 198n5
non-reductionism, 2–3, 5, 34–35, 36n10, 36n12, 41–3, 49, 53–59, 62, 91, 105–107, 109–111
normative attitudes
—primitive, 50–51
—semantic, 3–4, 41, 43, 48–51, 58
normative properties
—explanatory role of, 6, 120–21, 155, 170–74, 178n23
—knowledge of, 6–7, 174–76, 178nn25–26
—nature of, 6, 134–35, 155, 164–70, 178n22
normative realism
—Davidson's commitment to, 5–7, 119–22, 137n1
—substantive vs. procedural, 120
—vs. normative constructivism, 120, 122, 158–64, 191–97

normativity
—meaning determining, 42, 50, 62, 66, 91
—meaning engendered, 4, 42–3, 50, 59–62, 64n26
—primitive, 49–53
—semantic attitudinal, 3–4, 41, 45–49, 59, 61–2
—trivial, 42–50, 59–62, 62n7, 63n8, 66, 88

objectivity
—concept of, 3–4, 11–12, 15, 20–24, 29–35, 35nn2–3, 38n33, 39n47, 39n58, 48–49, 73–76, 84, 130–31, 133
—and normative properties, 164–66, 173, 186
omniscient interpreter, 2, 98–99, 113n2, 125–26, 132, 138nn16–17, 138n25
ostension, 15, 76
ostensive definition, 18, 63, 73, 76, 78–79, 93n32, 130

Pagin, Peter, 29, 34, 36n17, 37n18, 38n32, 39n51, 39n55, 92n21
perceptual beliefs, 38n43, 107–110, 114n13
perceptual externalism, see externalism
Pettit, Phillip, 198n4
physical externalism, see externalism
practical reasoning, 177n11
practicality requirement, 150–51, 158–63, 176
—vs. internalism requirement, 177n1
primary qualities, 1, 7, 165–70, 176
Priselac, Matthew, 40n60
Pritchard, Duncan, 98, 103, 113, 114n12, 115n16
pro-attitudes
—Humean theory of, 6, 133–35, 138n21, 138n28, 139, 141–55, 156n1, 156n7, 161–63, 169, 172, 176, 196
—non-Humean theory of, 6, 142–55, 156n14, 167
propositional attitudes, see beliefs; pro-attitudes
publicness condition, 5, 37n27, 67, 99, 122–25, 128–33, 191, 193–94
Putnam, Hilary, 66, 77–83, 92n26, 93nn27–29, 93n32, 93nn34–35, 113n4, 114n12

Quine, W. V., 67–68, 91nn3–4
quietism, 2–3, 5–6, 35, 62, 64n21, 91, 105

radical interpretation, see interpretation
Radenovic, Ljiljana, 39n51, 39n54
Railton, Peter, 198n3, 198n8
Ramberg, Bjørn, 113n7, 114n9
Ranalli, Christopher, 114n12, 115n16
rationality, 73, 149–50, 158–61, 177n2, 177n7
Rawls, John, 164, 174
Reboul, Anne, 39n55, 39n57
realism, 93n34, 107
—see also normative realism
reasons
—agent-neutral, 7, 135–36, 177n15, 178n20, 180–89, 195, 198nn5–6, 198n8, 198n10, 198n15
—agent-relative, 135–136, 178nn19–20, 179–89, 195, 198nn5–8, 198n10
—moral, 7, 121–22, 136–37, 177n14, 179–198
—motivating/explanatory vs. normative/justifying, 119–20, 137n2
—primary, 119–120
reductionism, 1–3, 5–6, 34–35, 36n10, 38n29, 41, 48–53, 56, 64n20, 76, 104–105, 131
reflective equilibrium, 164, 174–75
relativism, 135, 168, 178n24
Rescorla, Michael, 36n8, 39n45
Rorty, Richard, 111
rule-following paradox, 45, 48, 66, 88, 94n50

Scanlon, T. M., 6–7, 136–37, 137n3, 145–46, 149, 152, 156n9, 174–76, 178n25, 179, 184, 186–87, 189, 195, 198n7, 198n10, 198nn15–18
Schueler, G. F., 139–40
secondary qualities, 1, 6, 132, 165–69, 178n16, 181–82, 198n6
semantic context, 3, 54–56, 105–106, 110–11, 115
semantic theory vs. meta-semantic theory, 55–56, 105
Sinclair, Robert, 40n63
Smith, Michael, 137n2, 140–42, 150–53, 156n4, 156nn6–7, 160–63, 177n1, 177n6

social externalism, *see* externalism
solitaire, 16–24, 27, 29–31, 34–35, 40n62, 48, 90, 91n1, 94n41, 94n50, 130–31
solitary language, 82, 94n41
Sosa, Ernest, 103, 114n10, 114n13
Sreenivasan, Gopal, 126–27
Stoutland, Frederick, 36n17, 178n23
Street, Sharon, 156n14, 196–97, 198nn19–20
Stroud, Barry, 2, 5, 53–59, 63n10, 64n22, 94n41, 94n49, 100–107, 113n2, 113nn5–6, 114n8, 114n10, 114n12, 128, 138n20
supervenience, 14, 174, 182
Swampman, 39n56, 70–71
systemic aims, 6, 148–55, 159–62

Talmage, Catherine, 38n32
Tarski, Alfred, 13
third-person point of view, 27–28, 36n17
Thornton, Tim, 63n13
transcendental argument, 91n1, 114n12
triangulation
—linguisitic, 20–23, 28, 30–33, 35, 39n47, 76, 84, 129–33
—primitive, 16–20, 24–25, 30, 33–34, 37n26, 39n47, 76
triangulators, 16–19, 23–24, 34–35, 40n62, 56, 67, 73, 76, 84
truth
—concept of, 11, 33, 159; *see also* objectivity
—theory of, 56, 68

truth conditions, 13–14, 24, 56, 68, 72, 90, 105
Twin Earth, 69–70, 77–79

Velleman, David, 147–48, 152–54, 157n16
Verheggen, Claudine, 36n13, 37nn22–23, 37n26, 37n28, 38n37, 38n39, 39n58, 63n12, 63n14, 64nn26–27, 93n31, 94n41, 94n43, 94n50, 113n5, 114n11
verificationism, 37n18
virtue theory, 189–90

Whiting, Daniel, 62n6
Wikforss, Åsa, 60–61, 62nn2–3, 64n28
Williams, Bernard, 120, 163, 177n9, 177n11, 198n19
Williams, Meredith, 44, 66, 85, 87, 88, 93n31, 94nn40–41, 94nn43–44, 93n48
Williams, Michael, 99, 113n2
Williamson, Timothy, 37n18
Wilson, George, 63n12
Wittgenstein, Ludwig, 18–19, 22, 37n23, 38n37, 44–48, 50, 52, 62n7, 63n9, 63n13, 66, 73, 76, 85, 87–88, 91n8, 103, 130
Wright, Crispin, 43, 173–74

Yalowitz, Steven, 40n61

Zalabardo, José, 63n12, 64n20